2001 EDITION

Economic portrait
of the European Union 2001

Data up to 2000

EUROPEAN
COMMISSION

eurostat

THEME 2
Economy
and finance

.... Immediate access to **harmonized statistical data**

Eurostat Data Shops:

A personalised data retrieval service

In order to provide the greatest possible number of people with access to high-quality statistical information, Eurostat has developed an extensive network of Data Shops (¹).

Data Shops provide a wide range of **tailor-made services**:

★ immediate information searches undertaken by a team of experts in European statistics;

★ rapid and personalised response that takes account of the specified search requirements and intended use;

★ a choice of data carrier depending on the type of information required.

Information can be requested by phone, mail, fax or e-mail.

(¹) See list of Eurostat Data Shops at the end of the publication.

Internet:

Essentials on Community statistical news

★ Euro indicators: more than 100 indicators on the euro-zone; harmonized, comparable, and free of charge;

★ About Eurostat: what it does and how it works;

★ Products and databases: a detailed description of what Eurostat has to offer;

★ Indicators on the European Union: convergence criteria; euro yield curve and further main indicators on the European Union at your disposal;

★ Press releases: direct access to all Eurostat press releases.

For further information, visit us on the Internet at: **www.europa.eu.int/comm/eurostat/**

A great deal of additional information on the European Union is available on the Internet.
It can be accessed through the Europa server (http://europa.eu.int).

Cataloguing data can be found at the end of this publication.

Luxembourg: Office for Official Publications of the European Communities, 2001

ISSN 1680-1687
ISBN 92-894-1207-0

PREFACE

The purpose of this annual review — which has now become a traditional part of Eurostat's publications programme — is to bring together for analysis in a single work a wide range of mainly macroeconomic data on the European Union and its Member States.

Although this review refers to specific national circumstances, the idea is to use the main economic variables to present a profile of the Fifteen and of the euro-zone. Where possible, the comparison is extended to the various economic areas of the world as well as to the Union's main economic partners. Again this year, special importance is attached to the macroeconomic data of the candidate countries.

While the bulk of the information is taken as always from the national accounts, this edition makes greater use than before of data from other sectors of Eurostat activity, such as business statistics. We are convinced that the extra information that this gives readers will more than make up for any risk of inconsistency that might result from this juxtaposition of information sources that are fairly far apart.

Compared with the economic analyses and forecasts prepared by other services of the European Commission, this report provides only a descriptive analysis of the facts. While the emphasis is primarily on the latest available data, retrospective series also figure prominently.

In an age when up-to-the-minute information is crucial to understanding socioeconomic events, it may seem inappropriate to publish and comment on relatively old data. However, these data have certain advantages:

— most of them have been compiled according to the harmonised and comparable concepts and methods of the European system of accounts (ESA 95);

— most of them come from the national statistical institutes of the Member States;

— a knowledge of recent trends helps in getting information about the present.

By presenting and analysing in a single report the main macroeconomic data of the Union and the Member States, this publication will make the information more accessible to users and will contribute significantly to an understanding of the economic phenomena of our time.

Yves FRANCHET

Director General

Eurostat

Under the responsibility of Marco De March, Eurostat Unit B.2 "Economic accounts and international markets: production and analysis" benefited for the production of the present summary report from the expertise of Units B.3, B.4, B.5, C.4, D.2, D.3, E.1, E.2 and E.4. Unit C.1 and the Translation Service of the Commission also provided their essential logistic support.

Overall coordination
Claude Hublart (Unit B.2)

Economic coordination
Ingo Kuhnert (Unit B.2)

Writing team
Roberto Barcellan, Wayne Codd, Marco De March, Claude Hublart, Ingo Kuhnert, Gabriella Manganelli and Silke Stapel (Economic accounts), August Goetzfried, Joachim Hubertus, Aurora Ortega Sanchez, Jenny Runesson, Gunter Schaefer and Alessandra Vestri (Entreprises), Tim Allen (External trade), Paolo Passerini and Nikolaos Chryssanthou (Balance of payments), Axel Behrens and Volker Stabernak (Regions), Aarno Laihonen (Population), Alois Van Bastelaer (Labour market), Giuliano Amerini and Flavio Bianconi (Social protection), Sheldon Warton-Woods, Olivier Delobbe and Gesina Dierickx (Interest rates, euro and exchange rates), Martin Mayer (Prices).

Layout and desktop publishing
Cindy Brockly and Madeleine Larue

Manuscript completed in August 2001

For further information or any suggestions, please contact:

Eurostat — Unit B.2
5, rue Alphonse Weicker
L-2721 Luxembourg
Tel. (352) 43 01-33207
Fax (352) 43 01-33879
marco.demarch@cec.eu.int

All data requests should be addressed to
one of the Eurostat Data Shops listed on the last but one page.

CONTENTS

Introduction   7

1. Economy of the Union

    1.1. Gross domestic product   11

    1.2. GDP per head   16

    1.3. Expenditure of GDP   19

    1.4. Structure of GDP   23

    1.5. Production of GDP: the economy by branch   27

    1.6. Distribution of GDP, disposable income, saving and net lending/borrowing   39

    1.7. The economic situation in the regions   48

2. The Union in the international framework

    2.1. The EU in the world   51

    2.2. GDP of the candidate countries   54

    2.3. External trade   63

    2.4. International trade in services   71

    2.5. Foreign direct investment   74

3. Enterprises in the Union

    3.1. Structural development   87

    3.2. Short-term developments   95

    3.3. High-tech industries   102

4. Household consumption expenditure

    4.1. Overview   109

    4.2. Analysis by purpose   112

5. General government in the Union

    5.1. Major aggregates of general government   119

    5.2. General government revenue and expenditure   120

    5.3. Public debt and deficit   125

6. Population, labour market and social protection in the Union

    6.1. Population   127

    6.2. Employment   131

    6.3. Unemployment   134

    6.4. Social protection and pensions   137

7. Money, interest rates and prices in the Union

7.1. Exchange rates, the euro and EMU   147

7.2. Interest rates   150

7.3. Consumer prices   152

7.4. Purchasing power parities   157

Symbols and abbreviations   **160**

Introduction

In terms of economic performance, 2000 was a much better year than maybe was expected for the European Union, whose gross domestic product (GDP) registered a sizeable acceleration at + 3.3 %, best result of the decade, against + 2.5 % the year before.

Most of the world's economies also experienced a positive evolution with a 2000 growth above the average of the last five years. After four years of vigorous growth, the US economy continued to expand fast, its GDP rising by + 5 %. Notable exception to the overall trend was Japan with only + 1.5 %.

Contrary to 1999, growth among the four major European economies was very even in 2000, France and the United Kingdom enjoying the highest rates (+ 3.1 % each), closely followed by Germany (+ 3.0 %) and Italy (+ 2.9 %). In fact, all Member States except Sweden recorded growth rates higher or at least equal to those of 1999.

Measuring economic performance simply on the basis of GDP growth is "however" a rather short-sighted approach given the complexity of the European economy. To enable a deeper analysis, this publication thus gives a large series of macroeconomic indicators which are required to understand the economy of the Union and its Member States, presenting data, wherever appropriate or feasible, in a wider geographic context, including in particular the United States, Japan and the candidate countries.

At the end of 2000, several indicators attest to the relatively healthy state of the European economy. For the Fifteen as a whole, investment remains dynamic (+ 4.4 %) and employment has risen by 1.8 %, bringing unemployment down to 8.2 %. In addition, the general improvement in public finances continues. The average general government deficits for the Union as a whole and for the euro-zone are positive for the first time since the adoption of the Maastricht Treaty (respectively + 1.2 % and + 0.3 %, against – 0.6 % and – 1.2 % one year before). Only inflation which averaged 1 % in 1999 and tended to 2 % in 2000 could possibly be a subject of concern.

All data presented as averages for the Union as a whole may sometimes disguise significant differences between Member States. Even if we exclude Luxembourg from the following examples due to its rather atypical nature, GDP growth still ranges from 11.5 % in Ireland, one of the highest rates in the world, to 2.9 % in Italy and Denmark. GDP per head varies from 27 100 PPS in Denmark to 15 300 PPS in Greece while the unemployment rate still exceeds 10 % in Spain, Greece and Italy as against just 3.0 % in the Netherlands. Moreover, three countries — Italy, Belgium and Greece — still have a public debt which exceeds 100 % of GDP, while all others are comprised between 62.8 % and 5.3 %, with an European average of 64.2 %. Obviously, the European economy is still divided between convergence and diversity, integration and individuality.

This publication intends to give the reader, mainly in the form of simple and easily understandable tables and graphs, the basic information necessary for a better understanding of the European economy. Confronted with the figures, certainties can quickly waver, intuitions be confirmed or invalidated, judgments be revised. More than ever, an understanding of the fine nuances coupled with appropriate caution are absolutely necessary.

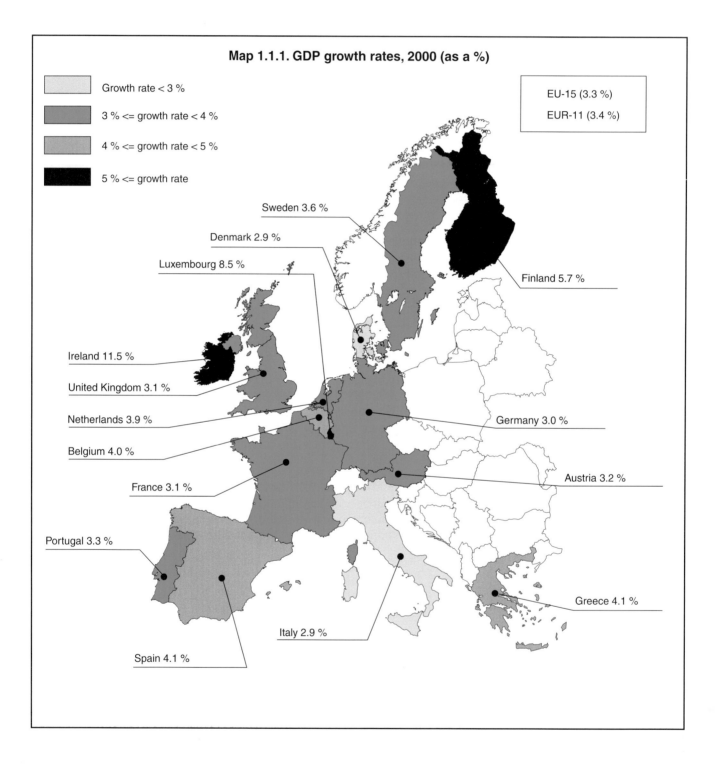

Map 1.1.1. GDP growth rates, 2000 (as a %)

Growth rate < 3 %

3 % <= growth rate < 4 %

4 % <= growth rate < 5 %

5 % <= growth rate

EU-15 (3.3 %)

EUR-11 (3.4 %)

Sweden 3.6 %

Denmark 2.9 %

Luxembourg 8.5 %

Finland 5.7 %

Ireland 11.5 %

United Kingdom 3.1 %

Netherlands 3.9 %

Germany 3.0 %

Belgium 4.0 %

France 3.1 %

Austria 3.2 %

Portugal 3.3 %

Greece 4.1 %

Italy 2.9 %

Spain 4.1 %

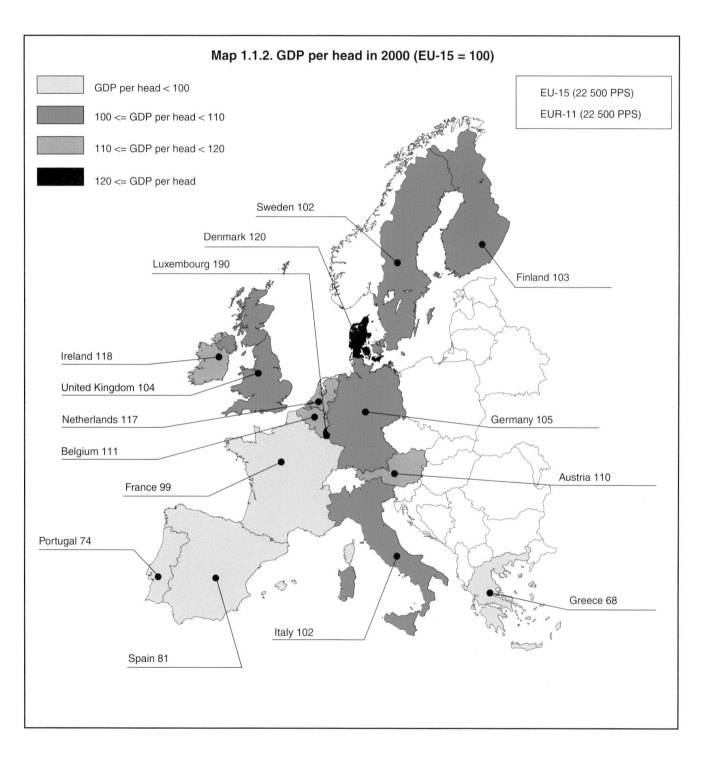

Map 1.1.2. GDP per head in 2000 (EU-15 = 100)

GDP per head < 100

100 <= GDP per head < 110

110 <= GDP per head < 120

120 <= GDP per head

EU-15 (22 500 PPS)

EUR-11 (22 500 PPS)

Sweden 102

Denmark 120

Luxembourg 190

Finland 103

Ireland 118

United Kingdom 104

Netherlands 117

Germany 105

Belgium 111

France 99

Austria 110

Portugal 74

Greece 68

Italy 102

Spain 81

1. Economy of the Union

1.1. Gross domestic product

In 2000, the gross domestic product of the European Union was EUR 8 510 billion ([1]); GDP in the euro-zone was EUR 6 432 billion, which is about 24 % less than the EU total. If we compare the result for the European Union with the figures for its main trading partners, we see that the GDP of the United States (EUR 10 709 billion) exceeds that of the EU by almost 26 %, whereas Japan's (EUR 5 145 billion) is about 60 % that of EU-15.

Germany alone (EUR 2 032.9 billion) accounts for somewhat less than one quarter of the EU's GDP; it is followed by the United Kingdom (EUR 1 534.0 billion in 2000, about 18 % of EU-15 GDP), which itself is followed by France (EUR 1 404.8 billion, or 16.5 % of the total). In 2000, Italy's GDP was EUR 1 165.7 billion, or 13.7 % of the total for EU-15. These four countries together account for 72.1 % of the Union's gross domestic product. If we add Spain, whose EUR 606.3 billion GDP contributes 7.1 % of the EU total, and the Netherlands, which, at EUR 400.6 billion, accounts for 4.7 %, we see that just six countries account for roughly 84 % of the European Union's GDP, the other nine Member States making up the remaining 16 %.

Figure 1.1.1. Gross domestic product at current prices, 2000 (billion EUR)

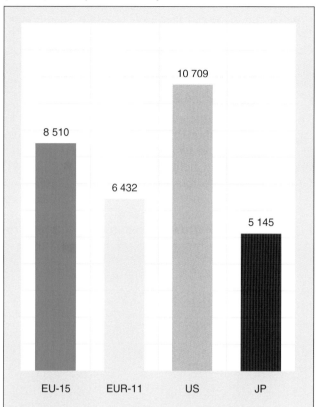

Source: Eurostat.

Figure 1.1.2. Gross domestic product at current prices, 2000

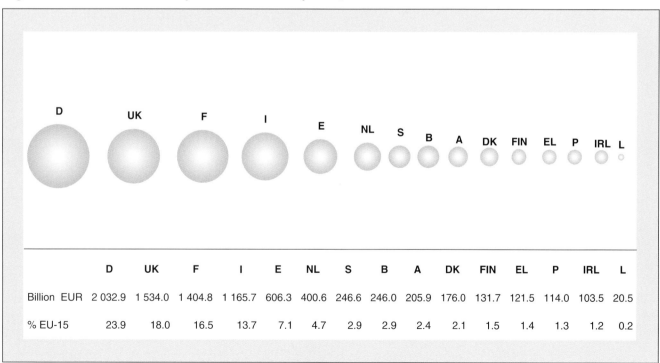

	D	UK	F	I	E	NL	S	B	A	DK	FIN	EL	P	IRL	L
Billion EUR	2 032.9	1 534.0	1 404.8	1 165.7	606.3	400.6	246.6	246.0	205.9	176.0	131.7	121.5	114.0	103.5	20.5
% EU-15	23.9	18.0	16.5	13.7	7.1	4.7	2.9	2.9	2.4	2.1	1.5	1.4	1.3	1.2	0.2

Source: Eurostat.

([1]) GDP at current prices.

GDP growth rates ([2])

In 2000, the European Union's gross domestic product rose by 3.3 %, which means a sizeable acceleration compared to the previous year (2.5 % in 1999). Compared with its main trading partners, the EU's economy still grew slower than that of the United States (+ 4.1 %) but much faster than Japan's (+ 1.5 %) (see Section 2.1).

The growth rate in the euro-zone in 2000 was at 3.4 % slightly stronger than that in the Union as a whole (+ 3.3 %), while the two had been identical the year before (+ 2.5 % in both the euro-zone and EU-15). Growth among the four biggest Member States was

very even in 2000, with France and the United Kingdom recording the highest rate of growth (3.1 % each), followed by Germany (+ 3.0 %) and, close behind, Italy (+ 2.9 %). Still, all four of them showed growth rates below the EU-15 average. In 1999, the growth rates of the "Big four" were significantly less close, even if their order was roughly the same, as France (+ 2.9 %) achieved the highest growth rate, followed by the United Kingdom (+ 2.3 %). Germany, France, the United Kingdom and Italy all saw increases in their GDP growth rates in 2000; in Germany and Italy, these increases were quite sizeable, while in France, the growth rate rose only by 0.2 % from 2.9 % in 1999 to 3.1 % in 2000.

Figure 1.1.3. GDP growth rates in the EU, the euro-zone and the "Big Four" EU countries (as a %)

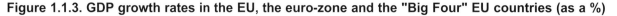

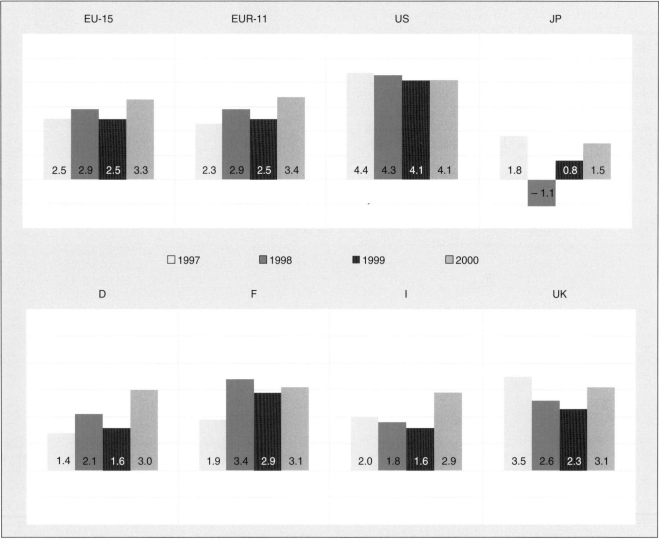

Source: Eurostat.

([2]) The GDP data used throughout this publication are those available on 25 June 2000. Nevertheless, after the revision of their figures by some countries during July, it has been decided, for this section only, to publish the data as available on 9 August 2000.

As in the year before, Ireland and Luxembourg were again remarkable for growth rates well above those in the other Member States in 2000: Ireland's GDP expanded by 11.5 %, while Luxembourg's grew at 8.5 %. Almost three percentage points behind these two, but still markedly ahead of the other Member States, came Finland (+ 5.7 %). All EU Member States except Sweden recorded growth rates higher or at least equal to those of 1999: the biggest increases were recorded in Finland (by + 1.7 points to + 5.7 % in

2000), Germany (by + 1.4 points to + 3.0 %) and Italy (by + 1.3 points to 2.9 %). In the Netherlands and Portugal, the growth rates remained unchanged, and in Sweden, it was 0.5 points lower, at now 3.6 %.

Contributions to GDP growth

In both the euro-zone and EU-15, the contribution of household consumption to GDP growth in 2000 was much smaller than in 1999, but still turned out to be the biggest of all GDP components at 47.6 % of total growth in EU-15 and, markedly lower, at 43.4 % in the euro-zone. The contribution of investments, although lower than in 1999 as well, came second, amounting to 28 % of total growth both in the EU as a whole and in the euro-zone. Public consumption (10.9 % for EU-15 and 11.5 % for the euro-zone) contributed fairly stable to economic growth. The biggest difference in comparison with the year before was the sizeable positive contribution of external trade, which had contributed negatively in 1999. The contribution pattern was thus significantly different from the two preceding years, while resembling the pattern observed in 1997.

The 3.1 % GDP growth recorded in the United Kingdom in 2000 was the net result of a major boost provided by household consumption (+ 80.4 % contribution to GDP growth) and a detrimental effect from the negative external balance (– 26.1 %). In Italy and France, too, the main factor behind GDP growth in 2000 was household consumption, albeit to a lesser extent than in the United Kingdom. It accounted for 60.4 % of growth in Italy and 44.7 % in France. Investments came second in both countries (41.6 % in Italy and 38.4 % in France); external trade also stimulated economic growth in Italy, but not so in France. In Germany, a different pattern was observed: the external balance was the single largest contributor to the 3.0 % increase in GDP growth (+ 34.0 % of GDP growth), followed by private consumption, which accounted for 30.2 % of the economic growth, and investments (+ 18.4 %).

Even if its impact was frequently lower than in 1999, household consumption remained the main factor in GDP growth in 2000 in most Member States, the exceptions being Germany, Luxembourg and Finland, where the biggest boost came from the external balance, and Denmark, where investment was the main factor. Denmark also stood out for being the only Member State where, in 2000, household consumption had a negative impact on GDP growth.

Table 1.1.1. GDP growth rates (as a %)

	1999	2000	
EU-15	2.5	3.3	
EUR-11	2.5	3.4	
B	2.7	4.0	
DK	2.1	2.9	
D	1.6	3.0	
EL	3.4	4.1	
E	4.0	4.1	
F	2.9	3.1	
IRL	10.8	11.5	
I	1.6	2.9	
L	7.6	8.5	
NL	3.9	3.9	
A	2.8	3.2	
P	3.3	3.3	
FIN	4.0	5.7	
S	4.1	3.6	
UK	2.3	3.1	

Source: Eurostat.

Figure 1.1.4. Components' contribution to GDP growth (as a % of total GDP growth)

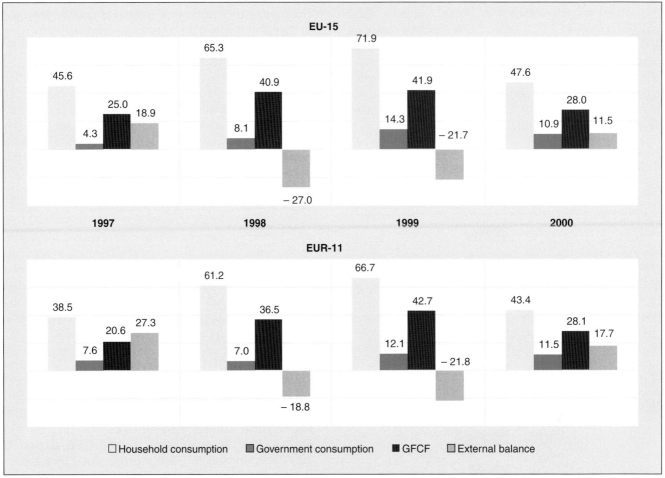

NB: To make the reading easier, the contributions of change in stocks have not been included.
Source: Eurostat.

Table 1.1.2. Components' contribution to GDP growth in 2000 (as a % of total GDP growth)

	Household consumption	Government consumption	Gross fixed capital formation	External balance	Stock		GDP growth rate
EU-15	47.6	10.9	28.0	11.5	2.0	→	3.3
EUR-11	43.4	11.5	28.1	17.7	− 0.8	→	3.4
B	40.3	10.5	23.9	19.0	6.3	→	4.0
DK	− 3.6	5.5	80.1	7.0	11.0	→	2.9
D	30.2	9.0	18.4	34.0	8.4	→	3.0
EL	55.8	2.9	53.4	− 33.9	21.8	→	4.1
E	58.4	11.3	35.2	− 2.3	− 2.5	→	4.1
F	44.7	16.3	38.4	− 3.8	4.5	→	3.1
IRL	43.9	6.6	13.8	31.9	3.8	→	11.5
I	60.4	9.2	41.6	22.0	− 33.3	→	2.9
L	18.3	10.1	1.4	68.8	1.5	→	8.5
NL	50.4	17.9	23.1	12.5	− 3.9	→	3.9
A	47.3	14.0	20.9	10.2	7.6	→	3.2
P	49.2	20.7	42.3	− 3.7	− 8.6	→	3.3
FIN	26.7	2.5	17.7	47.9	5.2	→	5.7
S	55.9	− 11.9	21.7	25.2	9.2	→	3.6
UK	80.4	14.1	17.1	− 26.1	14.5	→	3.1

NB: Negative contributions do not indicate a slowdown in the component growth.
Source: Eurostat.

Figure 1.1.5. Component's contribution to GDP growth in 2000 (as a % of total GDP growth)

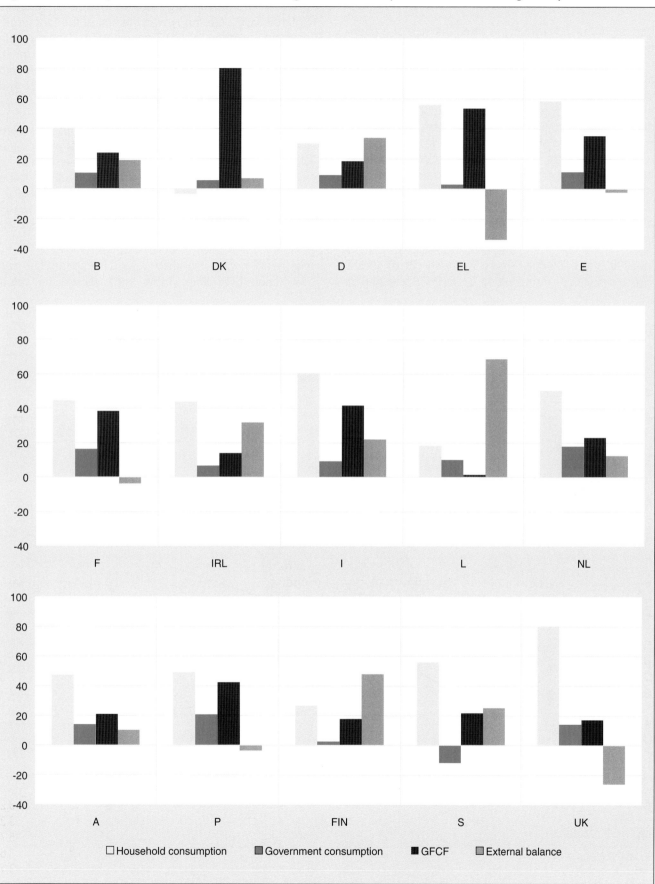

NB: To make the reading easier, the contributions of change in stocks have not been included.
Source: Eurostat.

1.2. GDP per head

If gross domestic product indicates the size of a country's economy in absolute terms, calculating per capita GDP, that is GDP in relation to the population, provides an indication, albeit somewhat simplistic ([3]), of a country's wealth. To make comparison easier and precisely because we are referring to the concept of wealth, the data presented in this chapter have been calculated in purchasing power standards (PPS). The advantage of using PPS is that they eliminate distortions arising from the different price levels in the EU countries: they use conversion factors calculated as a weighted average of the price ratios of a basket of goods and services that are homogeneous, comparable and representative in each Member State.

In 2000, the per capita figure for each citizen in the European Union amounted to 22 500 PPS, equal to the figure for the euro-zone. The highest figures occurred in Luxembourg (42 900 PPS) and Denmark (27 100 PPS). Germany was the first of the four larger countries in terms of GDP per head, ranking seventh out of the Fifteen with 23 600 PPS, with the United Kingdom following close behind in eighth place with 23 300 PPS, while Italy was 11th (22 900 PPS) and France (22 300 PPS) came 12th.

Figure 1.2.1 shows per capita GDP for all the EU countries. The web figure has the advantage of providing a visual overview of the distribution of the figures: if every country had the same figure, then the final shape would be a circle. The figures for 1995 are also shown, but it must be remembered that the PPS figures are at current prices and have been calculated primarily for comparison in terms of space and not time.

However, in order to show how per capita GDP has developed over time, Table 1.2.1 shows the value

Figure 1.2.1. Gross domestic product per head, (in PPS)

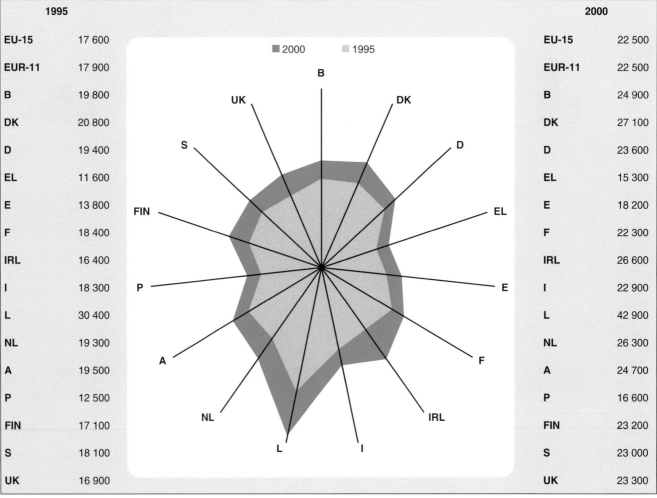

1995			2000	
EU-15	17 600		**EU-15**	22 500
EUR-11	17 900		**EUR-11**	22 500
B	19 800		**B**	24 900
DK	20 800		**DK**	27 100
D	19 400		**D**	23 600
EL	11 600		**EL**	15 300
E	13 800		**E**	18 200
F	18 400		**F**	22 300
IRL	16 400		**IRL**	26 600
I	18 300		**I**	22 900
L	30 400		**L**	42 900
NL	19 300		**NL**	26 300
A	19 500		**A**	24 700
P	12 500		**P**	16 600
FIN	17 100		**FIN**	23 200
S	18 100		**S**	23 000
UK	16 900		**UK**	23 300

Source: Eurostat.

([3]) Per capita GDP provides no indication of the distribution of wealth.

Table 1.2.1. Gross domestic product per head, 2000

	PPS	Value growth index 1995 = 100	
EU-15	22 500	127.8	
EUR-11	22 500	125.7	
B	24 900	125.8	
DK	27 100	130.3	
D	23 600	121.6	
EL	15 300	131.9	
E	18 200	131.9	
F	22 300	121.2	
IRL	26 600	162.2	
I	22 900	125.1	
L	42 900	141.1	
NL	26 300	136.3	
A	24 700	126.7	
P	16 600	132.8	
FIN	23 200	135.7	
S	23 000	127.1	
UK	23 300	137.9	

Source: Eurostat.

growth index (1995 = 100). It is apparent from this that per capita GDP in the EU in 2000 was 27.8 % higher than in the reference year; the corresponding figure for the euro-zone was some two percentage points lower, at + 25.7 %. Among the four largest countries, the United Kingdom stands out with the biggest change (+ 37.9 %), while lower figures were recorded for Italy (+ 25.1 %), Germany (+ 21.6 %) and France (+ 21.2 %). Indeed, it was these three countries that recorded the smallest changes in per capita GDP among all the Member States. The biggest change by far among the Fifteen was recorded in Ireland, where per capita GDP was 62.2 % higher than in 1995, followed by Luxembourg (+ 41.1 %).

To make it easier to compare the Member States, Figure 1.2.2 shows the GDP per capita figures in rela-

tion to the EU average (EU-15 = 100). It is thus easier to observe and measure the big gap between the EU average and the figure for Luxembourg, which has moved even further ahead and is now 90 % above the EU average. The second highest figure is for Denmark, but here the difference is only 20 %. The biggest differences for figures below the EU average are in Greece (32 % below average), Portugal (– 26 %) and Spain (– 19 %). Figure 1.2.2 also shows the situation in 1995, and it can be seen that the positions at the extremes remain unchanged, even if the three lowest ranking countries have moved somewhat closer to the EU average. The most obvious change was for Ireland, which recorded a figure for per capita GDP that was lower than the EU average at the beginning of the period under review (1995 to 2000), while in 2000 it was 18 % above average, placing Ireland third among all EU Member States. The same type of change, though less pronounced, took place in the United Kingdom and Finland, which were both — slightly — above the EU average in 2000.

Figure 1.2.3 shows a set of data intended to show the level of similarities, or differences, between the Member State figures, and how these evolved during the last five years. Firstly, the top figure shows the highest figures (Luxembourg again first, followed by Denmark), the lowest figure (always Greece) and the EU average. The line that links these points shows the range, or the distance between the highest and lowest figures and their position in relation to the average (in this case EU-15). In 2000, the range between the highest and lowest per capita GDP recorded in the Union was 27 600 PPS; expressed differently, per capita GDP in Luxembourg was 2.8 times the figure for Greece. If we exclude Luxembourg, the gap between the figures for Denmark (second highest) and Greece was 11 800 PPS, meaning that the per capita GDP of the Danes was almost 1.8 times that of the Greeks.

To give an overall indication of the range of values for all the EU countries, the relative standard deviation has been calculated, that is, a measure for the average "distance" of the figures from their mean [4], expressed as a percentage of the mean. Thus, in 2000, per capita GDP figures for the 15 Member States had a standard deviation of 25.2 % around the average, a figure somewhat higher than in 1996 but which has only recently begun to rise. If again Luxembourg, as a sort of "outlier", is excluded from the calculation, however, the relative standard deviation shows a considerable drop to 15.5 % and the figure for 2000 turns out to be unchanged compared to the situation in 1996.

---

[4] In this case, the simple arithmetic average and not the EU value, which is a weighted average.

Figure 1.2.2. GDP per head in PPS (EU-15 = 100)

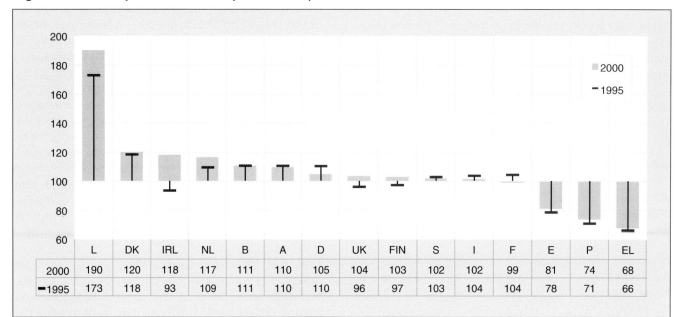

	L	DK	IRL	NL	B	A	D	UK	FIN	S	I	F	E	P	EL
2000	190	120	118	117	111	110	105	104	103	102	102	99	81	74	68
▬1995	173	118	93	109	111	110	110	96	97	103	104	104	78	71	66

Source: Eurostat.

Figure 1.2.3. Variation of GDP per head

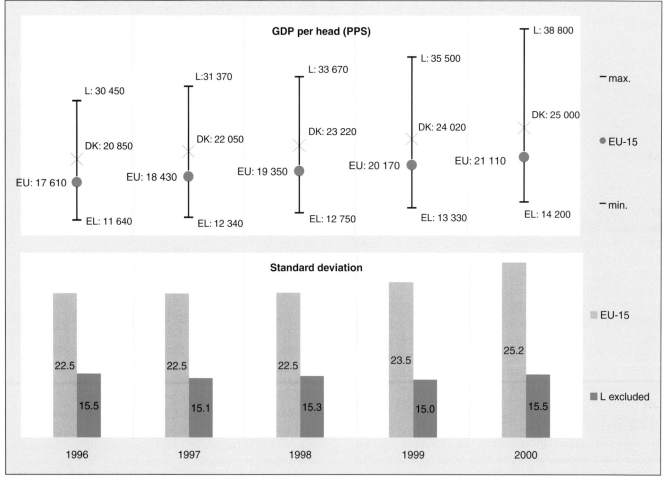

NB: As all maximum figures have been recorded for Luxembourg, we also added the second largest figures. During the period considered these were those of Denmark.
Source: Eurostat.

1.3. Expenditure of GDP

Table 1.3.1 shows the absolute values (^{5}) of the main expenditure components of GDP: household final consumption expenditure, government final consumption expenditure and gross fixed capital formation. Other components of GDP are imports and exports (^{6}) and changes in stocks, but these are left out of consideration in this chapter, for the sake of simplicity.

In 2000, household final consumption in the European Union amounted to EUR 4 956 billion, a level well above those recorded for investments (EUR 1 753 billion) and government final consumption (EUR 1 689 billion). It should be noted, though, that household consumption as used here also includes the consumption expenditure of non-profit institutions serving households such as churches, trade unions, political parties, sports clubs, etc. An interesting situation persists between two of the larger European economies, France and the United Kingdom, which are of roughly comparable size: France has the higher figures for government consumption (EUR 327 billion compared to EUR 287 billion in the United Kingdom) and investments (EUR 277 billion compared to EUR 272 billion), whereas household consumption in the United Kingdom is significantly greater than in France (EUR 1 004 billion in the United Kingdom and EUR 769 billion in France).

Table 1.3.1. Main components of GDP, 2000 (billion EUR, current prices)

	Household consumption	Government consumption	GFCF
EU-15	4 955.9	1 688.6	1 753.0
EUR-11	3 658.0	1 274.9	1 371.5
B	132.4	52.3	52.5
DK	84.2	43.5	38.3
D	1 180.6	383.6	434.9
EL	85.6	18.5	29.4
E	359.9	103.5	154.8
F	769.1	327.1	276.5
IRL	49.8	13.7	24.8
I	704.6	209.5	228.9
L	8.4	3.5	4.2
NL	199.3	91.1	89.2
A	116.7	40.2	48.7
P	72.2	23.4	31.6
FIN	65.0	27.1	25.1
S	124.4	64.9	42.1
UK	1 003.6	286.8	271.7

Source: Eurostat.

Consumption per head

To permit comparisons between countries, the per capita values for household consumption and government consumption (^{7}) have been calculated and expressed in terms of the EU value (EU-15 = 100) (see Table 1.3.2 and Figure 1.3.1). As with GDP, Luxembourg stands out from the other Member States by having, per capita, a much higher household consumption (34 % higher than the EU as a whole) as well as government consumption (+ 64 %). This is in contrast with Denmark, the Member State with the second-highest per capita GDP, where government consumption is also well above the EU average (+ 51 %), but household consumption is lower than the average of the other Member States (– 2 %).

Table 1.3.2. Consumption per head, 2000

	Household consumption		Government consumption	
	PPS	EU-15 = 100	PPS	EU-15 = 100
EU-15	13 120	100	4 470	100
EUR-11	12 820	98	4 470	100
B	13 370	102	5 320	119
DK	12 920	98	6 730	151
D	13 700	104	4 490	100
EL	10 740	82	2 330	52
E	10 810	82	3 140	70
F	12 160	93	5 210	117
IRL	12 850	98	3 570	80
I	13 810	105	4 140	93
L	17 510	134	7 350	164
NL	13 040	99	6 010	134
A	13 970	107	4 850	109
P	10 480	80	3 420	77
FIN	11 400	87	4 800	107
S	11 560	88	6 080	136
UK	15 250	116	4 390	98

Source: Eurostat.

As regards household consumption, the United Kingdom, alongside Luxembourg, stands out as having a per capita figure well above the average (+ 16 %) for all Member States. The United Kingdom and Italy are the only countries where household consumption is above but government consumption is below the EU average. The lowest figures for per capita household consumption are those for Portugal (20 % below the EU average), Spain and Greece (18 % below the average for both of them).

(^{5}) The absolute values are measured at current prices, rates of growth are calculated at constant prices, and per capita PPS values are based on current prices.

(^{6}) A more detailed analysis of external trade is given in Chapter 2.3, using data obtained from Comext. The data reproduced in this chapter, however, were obtained from the national accounts, and are not adjusted for intra-Community trade.

(^{7}) Per capita gross fixed capital formation has not been calculated because the investors do not actually correspond to the population.

The countries with the lowest figures for government consumption are the same, albeit in a different order: Greece has the lowest figure (48 % below the EU average), while Spain is 30 % below the average and Portugal 23 % below. Next comes Ireland, where per capita government consumption is 20 % below the average despite the relatively high GDP per capita. In addition to Luxembourg and Denmark, which, it has already been seen, have the highest figures, Sweden and the Netherlands recorded values which were much higher (36 % and 34 % respectively) than the EU average. Finally, Denmark, France, the Netherlands, Finland and Sweden are the five Member States that have above-average government consumption, but below-average household consumption.

As with per capita GDP, the scatter around the average may be compared across GDP components and time by using the relative standard deviation. Without giving a full set of figures, we state that the scatter between the per capita values for household consumption in the Member States in 2000 is well below that for government consumption: in the case of household consumption, the relative standard deviation in 2000 was 14 %, whereas the figures for government consumption displayed a scatter of almost 28 % with respect to the average. If we examine this indicator for the period from 1996 to 2000, we see that, whereas the scatter for household consumption continued on a downward trend, i.e. differences between Member States tended to diminish, the relative deviation for government consumption was broadly unchanged. It should be remembered that the relative standard deviation for per capita GDP was 25.2 % in 2000.

Growth rates of main GDP components

Turning now to rates of growth in 2000, investments (gross fixed capital formation) in the European Union had the fastest growth of the main components, increasing by 4.4 % compared with the previous year. Household consumption grew by 2.7 % and government consumption by 1.9 %. Over the last five years (1996 to 2000), after two years of relatively low growth (1996 and 1997), investments and household consumption both grew very robustly in 1998 (+ 5.8 % in the case of investments and + 3.3 % for household consumption); both showed a slight decline in the growth rate for 1999, but confirmed their recent strength. In 2000, this development continued, with growth rates for investments and household consumption declining further, yet still well above their 1996–97 levels. In the case of government consumption, however, growth in 2000 slightly accelerated, continuing the previous years' rise. The 1.9 % growth rate recorded in 2000 was the highest of the last five years. The trends in the euro-zone ran in parallel, the only differences being that the increase in investments was more modest in 1998 (+ 5.1 %), and that the acceleration of government consumption continued at unabated speed in 2000 (see Figure 1.3.2 and Table 1.3.3).

Figure 1.3.1. Household consumption (HC) and government consumption (GC) per capita, 2000 (in PPS — EU-15 = 100)

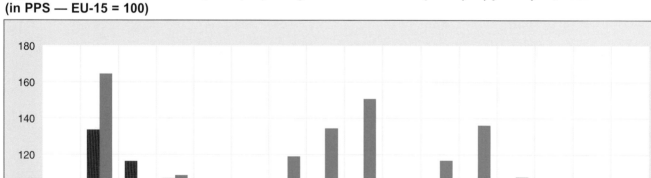

NB: Member States are shown by HC data in a descending order.
Source: Eurostat.

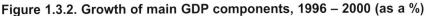

Figure 1.3.2. Growth of main GDP components, 1996 – 2000 (as a %)

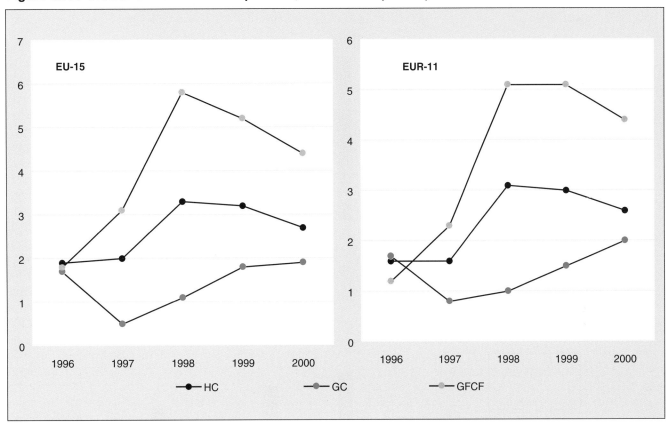

Source: Eurostat.

Table 1.3.3. Growth of main GDP components, 2000 (as a %)

	Household consumption	Government consumption	Household consumption
EU-15	2.7	1.9	4.4
EUR-11	2.6	2.0	4.4
B	3.1	2.0	4.5
DK	− 0.2	0.6	11.1
D	1.6	1.4	2.4
EL	3.2	0.8	9.4
E	4.0	2.6	5.9
F	2.5	2.2	6.1
IRL	9.4	5.7	10.4
I	2.9	1.6	6.1
L	3.5	4.9	0.5
NL	3.9	3.1	4.0
A	2.7	2.3	2.9
P	2.5	3.8	5.1
FIN	3.0	0.4	4.8
S	4.0	− 1.7	4.5
UK	3.7	2.7	2.6

Source: Eurostat.

Household consumption grew the fastest in Ireland (+ 9.4 %) and in Spain and Sweden (by + 4.0 % in both countries). The worst growth rate was recorded in Denmark (− 0.2 %), where household consumption was in fact declining. The second lowest figure was observed in Germany (+ 1.6 %).

Ireland also stands out for having the fastest-growing government consumption (+ 5.7 % in 2000), but the runner-up — Luxembourg in this case with 4.9 % — was not as far behind as for household consumption. Government consumption grew only minimally in Finland (+ 0.4 %), Denmark (+ 0.6 %) and Greece (+ 0.8 %), but the lowest growth rate in 2000 was found to be at − 1.7 % in Sweden.

All in all, investments continued to grow faster than the other components of domestic demand, especially in Denmark (+ 11.1%), Ireland (+ 10.4 %) and Greece (+ 9.4 %), with France, Italy and Spain also recording significant growth rates of about 6 %. In 2000, no Member State did show negative growth, the lowest figures being those of Luxembourg (+ 0.5 %) and, somewhat higher, Germany (+ 2.4 %) and the United Kingdom (+ 2.6 %).

Figure 1.3.3. Growth of main GDP components, 2000 (as a %)

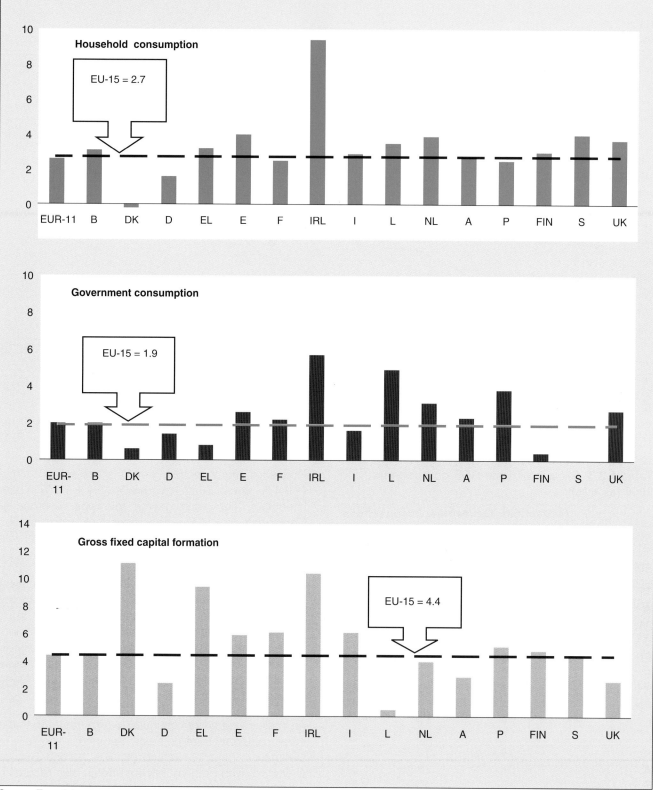

Source: Eurostat.

1.4. Structure of GDP

The main component ([8]) of gross domestic product (GDP) in the European Union is household final consumption expenditure, which in 2000 accounted for 58.2 % of GDP, followed by gross fixed capital formation and government final consumption expenditure with shares of roughly the same size: 20.6 % and 19.8 %, respectively. Together, these three components accounted for practically all the Union's GDP (98.6 %).

The structure in the euro-zone was basically the same as for the Union as a whole, although the percentage for investment was slightly higher at 21.3 %, since the United Kingdom and Sweden had particularly low figures (see Table 1.4.1).

The structure of GDP in the United Kingdom was particularly dominated by household consumption, which, with a figure of 65.5 %, was among the highest amongst all Member States of the Union. The shares for government consumption and investment were about the same size: 18.7 % and 17.7 % respectively. The structure of GDP in Germany and Italy are quite similar, for both, household consumption was again the major component, though with slightly lower shares than in the United Kingdom (58.1 % and 60.4 % respectively). The breakdown between government consumption and investment was fairly even, with investment making up slightly bigger shares. In France,

Figure 1.4.1. Structure of gross domestic product in the EU, 2000 (as a % of GDP)

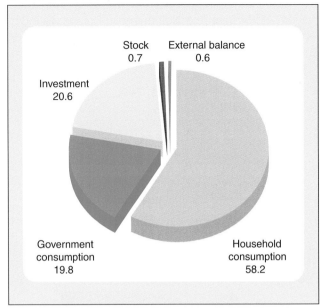

Source: Eurostat.

however, while household consumption accounted for the largest share of GDP (54.8 %), government consumption (23.3 %) was ahead of investment (19.7 %).

Household final consumption expenditure was the biggest component of GDP in every Member State, with figures ranging from 70.5 % in Greece to 41.0 %

Table 1.4.1. Structure of gross domestic product, 2000 (as a % of GDP)

	Household consump- tion	Government consump- tion	GFCF	Stock change	External balance		Imports	Exports
EU-15	58.2	19.8	20.6	0.7	0.6	→	34.9	35.6
EUR-11	56.9	19.8	21.3	0.8	1.1	→	36.0	37.2
B	53.8	21.2	21.3	0.2	3.4	→	84.7	88.1
DK	47.8	24.7	21.8	0.3	5.4	→	37.0	42.4
D	58.1	18.9	21.4	1.3	0.4	→	33.0	33.4
EL	70.5	15.2	24.2	− 0.8	− 9.1	→	30.4	21.3
E	59.4	17.1	25.5	0.3	− 2.3	→	32.2	29.9
F	54.8	23.3	19.7	0.9	1.4	→	27.2	28.7
IRL	48.3	13.3	24.0	− 0.1	14.5	→	78.9	93.4
I	60.4	18.0	19.6	0.8	1.1	→	27.2	28.4
L	41.0	17.0	20.7	0.5	20.8	→	98.8	119.6
NL	49.8	22.7	22.3	0.0	5.2	→	61.9	67.1
A	56.7	19.5	23.7	1.2	− 1.1	→	50.0	48.9
P	63.3	20.5	27.7	0.4	− 11.9	→	43.3	31.4
FIN	49.2	20.6	19.0	1.1	10.1	→	32.4	42.5
S	50.4	26.3	17.1	0.8	5.3	→	42.1	47.4
UK	65.5	18.7	17.7	0.0	− 1.9	→	29.1	27.2

Source: Eurostat.

([8]) The figures for the components of GDP have been calculated in euro at current prices.

in Luxembourg. With respect to the other two main components, investment ranked second in nine of the 15 Member States, while in the remaining six (Denmark, France, the Netherlands, Finland, Sweden and the United Kingdom), government consumption expenditure figured more prominently.

Figure 1.4.2. GDP structure, 2000 (as a % of GDP)

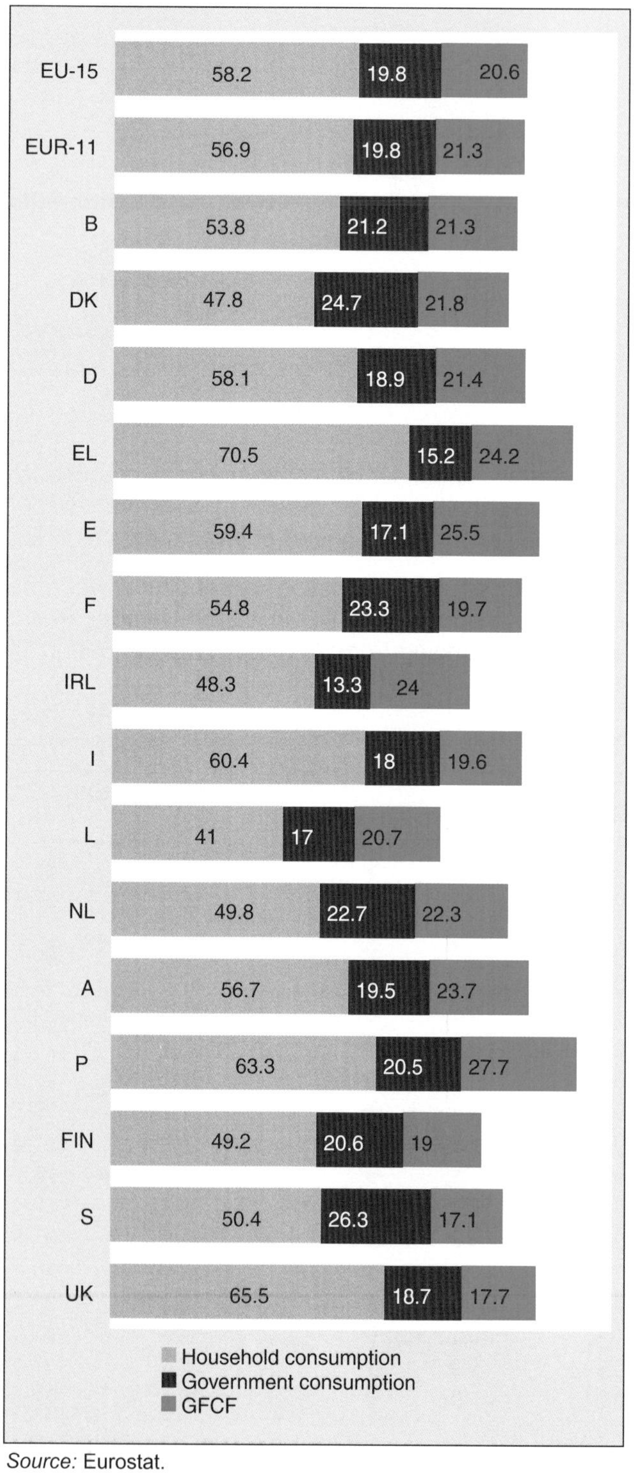

	Household consumption	Government consumption	GFCF
EU-15	58.2	19.8	20.6
EUR-11	56.9	19.8	21.3
B	53.8	21.2	21.3
DK	47.8	24.7	21.8
D	58.1	18.9	21.4
EL	70.5	15.2	24.2
E	59.4	17.1	25.5
F	54.8	23.3	19.7
IRL	48.3	13.3	24
I	60.4	18	19.6
L	41	17	20.7
NL	49.8	22.7	22.3
A	56.7	19.5	23.7
P	63.3	20.5	27.7
FIN	49.2	20.6	19
S	50.4	26.3	17.1
UK	65.5	18.7	17.7

■ Household consumption
■ Government consumption
■ GFCF

Source: Eurostat.

Changes in the expenditure structure during 1996 to 2000

A look at the breakdown of GDP into its components in the last five years shows that GDP structure in the European Union did not change dramatically, though some fluctuations could be observed. Household consumption (+ 0.5 percentage points) and investment (+ 1.0 points) went up, while government consumption (– 0.9 points) and especially the external balance (– 1.3 points) declined. As for trade [9] in particular, the figures for imports and exports both recorded upward changes: up by 6.8 percentage points for imports and by 5.5 points for exports, giving rise to the 1.3 points drop in the share of the external balance (see Figure 1.4.3).

The structure of GDP was slightly more stable in the euro-zone over the five-year period under review. There were increases in the shares of household consumption expenditure (+ 0.1 points) and investment (+ 1.0 points) on the one hand and lower shares of government consumption expenditure (– 0.8 points) and the external balance (– 1.2 points) on the other hand. Import and export shares figures were both marked by significant increases: + 8.3 points for imports and + 7.2 for exports. The fact that the drop in the share of the external balance was more pronounced in EU-15 is attributable mainly to slightly above-average downward variations in the United Kingdom and Sweden.

Among the four biggest economies of the European Union, Italy stood out for having the largest variations in GDP structure: the 2.1 points rise in the share of household consumption was not only the biggest rise among the four, but even among all 15 Member States. Equally, the slight drop of 0.1 point in the share of government consumption was smaller than in most other Member States. On the other hand, Italy also encountered the largest decline in the share of the external balance: – 3.8 points. France and Germany both saw about average changes in the share of government consumption and below-average declines of the relative importance of the external balance. Yet they differ in the development of the other two main GDP components: while household consumption increased its share in Germany, it declined in France. To the contrary, the share of investments rose in France and sank in Germany. In this respect, Germany was the only Member State to register a drop in the shares of investments. Furthermore, the shares of both exports and imports rose significantly faster in Germany than in the other big economies. The United Kingdom registered a quite marked increase in the relative size of household consumption, to which the difference between the EU-15 and the euro-zone figures for this

---

[9] Trade balance figures in this section refer to national accounts and therefore do not include intra-Community trade. They might differ from figures shown in Chapter 2.3.

component are largely attributable. Another peculiarity is that, while the share of the external balance was declining for several countries, the United Kingdom is the only Member State for which this was not due to a stronger rise in the share of imports than of imports, but to a stronger decline in the share of exports than of imports. It should be noted, though, that these observations on shares of GDP do not mean that imports and exports were declining themselves.

Apart from Italy, Germany and the United Kingdom — which have already been mentioned — the share of household consumption expenditure showed a slight increase only in Sweden (+ 0.1 percentage points). All other Member States recorded reductions, some of them quite substantial, as in Ireland (– 5.7 points) and Luxembourg (– 7.6 points). In the case of Ireland, this reduction in household consumption was offset primarily by a 5.2 point increase in the percentage share of

Figure 1.4.3. GDP structure in the EU, 1996 – 2000 (as a % of GDP)

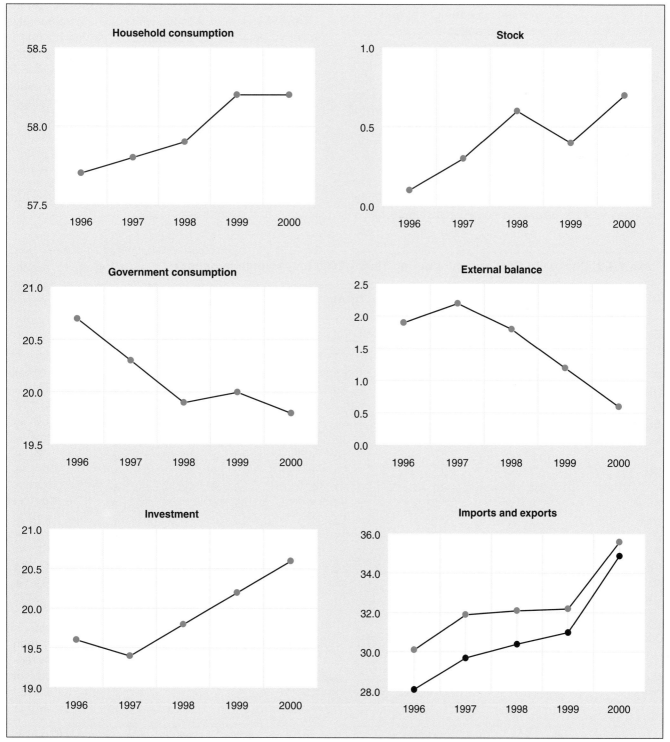

Source: Eurostat.

investment. In Luxembourg, on the other hand, the reduction in private consumption was countered by the contribution of the external balance, which went up by 7.8 points. Among the other Member States, Greece and Portugal were the only countries were the declining share of household consumption coincided with an increase in the share of government consumption. Elsewhere, it was either investment (as in the Netherlands) or investment and the external balance (as in Finland and Denmark) whose shares on GDP increased.

The share of government consumption, as has already been put forward, increased only in Greece and Portugal. In the rest of the Member States the trend was negative. The biggest reductions were observed in Finland (− 2.6 points) and Ireland (− 2.5 points). Gross fixed capital formation, i.e. investment, has increased its share over the last five years in 14 out of 15 Member States, the exception being Germany. The biggest increases where those in Ireland (+ 5.2 points) and Greece and Portugal (+ 4.7 points each).

The variations in the external balance call for some explanation: if the balance is negative, a change with a

"minus" sign does not indicate a lower percentage but an increase in the share. For example, the − 0.6 percentage points change for Germany meant passing from a 1.0 % share of the positive external balance in 1996 to a 0.4 % share in 2000, while the − 1.3 points change for the United Kingdom are the result of the trade deficit passing from − 0.6 % of GDP in 1996 to − 1.9 % of GDP in 2000. For the purpose at hand, this means an increase in the significance of the external balance as a component of GDP for the United Kingdom, even if the effect is negative (deficit). This applies in the case of Greece, Spain, Portugal and the United Kingdom. In Austria, which also has a negative external balance, its share on GDP did not change in the last five years. Among the Member States with a positive external balance, its share increased in Denmark, Ireland, Luxembourg and Finland. In particular, the large variation for Portugal (− 5.3 percentage points) indicates a worsening of the trade deficit, while the 7.8 points change for Luxembourg indicates a growing trade surplus. Yet both mean a bigger significance of trade as a component of GDP. For further analysis, Table 1.4.2 shows variations in GDP percentage, not only for the external balance, but also for imports and exports separately.

Table 1.4.2. Change in GDP structure during 1996 – 2000 (in percentage points)

	Household consumption		Government consumption		GFCF		External balance		Imports		Exports	
EU-15	0.5	↗	− 0.9	↓	1.0	↑	− 1.3	↓	6.8	⬆	5.5	⬆
EUR-11	0.1	↗	− 0.8	↓	1.0	↑	− 1.2	↓	8.3	⬆	7.2	⬆
B	− 0.6	↓	− 0.6	↙	1.2	↑	− 0.6	↓	17.7	⬆	17.0	⬆
DK	− 2.5	⬇	− 1.2	↓	3.2	⬆	0.5	↗	6.2	⬆	6.6	⬆
D	0.7	↑	− 1.0	↓	− 0.4	↙	− 0.6	↓	8.7	⬆	8.1	⬆
EL	− 3.2	⬇	0.7	↑	4.7	⬆	− 1.1	↓	4.9	⬆	3.8	⬆
E	− 0.2	↙	− 0.8	↓	3.9	⬆	− 2.8	⬇	8.8	⬆	6.0	⬆
F	− 1.0	↓	− 0.9	↓	1.2	↑	− 0.3	↙	5.8	⬆	5.6	⬆
IRL	− 5.7	⬇	− 2.5	↓	5.2	⬆	2.9	⬆	12.8	⬆	15.7	⬆
I	2.1	↑	− 0.1	↗	1.3	↑	− 3.8	⬇	6.3	⬆	2.6	⬆
L	− 7.6	⬇	− 1.2	↙	0.4	↗	7.8	⬆	5.8	⬆	13.5	⬆
NL	− 0.1	↙	− 0.4	↙	1.2	↑	− 0.5	↙	9.7	⬆	9.2	⬆
A	− 0.5	↙	− 0.8	↓	0.4	↗	0.0	↗	9.3	⬆	9.3	⬆
P	− 0.6	↓	1.6	↑	4.7	⬆	− 5.3	⬇	7.0	⬆	1.7	↑
FIN	− 3.5	⬇	− 2.6	⬇	2.0	↑	2.5	↑	2.4	⬆	5.0	⬆
S	0.1	↗	− 0.8	↓	1.4	↑	− 1.4	↓	9.7	⬆	8.3	⬆
UK	1.2	↑	− 0.7	↓	1.1	↑	− 1.3	↓	− 0.6	↙	− 1.9	↓

NB:

Stable:	0x0.5 : − 0.5x<0 :	↗ ↙	Small change:	0.5<x1.5 : − 1.5x<− 0.5 :	↑ ↓
Medium: change :	1.5<x2.5 : − 2.5=x<1.5 :	↑ ⬇	Strong change:	x>2.5 : x<− 2.5 :	⬆ ⬇

Source: Eurostat.

1.5. Production of GDP: the economy by branch

GVA growth by branch of production

The analysis of GDP so far has been limited to the expenditure side. In this chapter, we set out to investigate in which parts of the economy gross value added (GVA) — the core of GDP — was created. We use a breakdown of six branches here in order to keep the presentation readable.

The most vigorous growth in gross value added (GVA) in the European Union in 2000 occurred in financial

---

Branches of production

- Agriculture, hunting, forestry and fishing.

- Mining and quarrying; manufacturing; electricity, gas and water supply.

- Construction.

- Wholesale and retail trade, repair of motor vehicles, motorcycles and personal and household goods; hotels and restaurants; transport, storage and communication.

- Financial intermediation, real estate, renting and business activities.

- Public administration and defence; compulsory social security; education; health and social work; other community, social and personal service activities; private households with employed persons.

---

services and business activities (+ 4.9 % compared with the previous year) followed by manufacturing (+ 4.0 %) and trade, transport and communication (+ 3.9 %). Somewhat behind came the public services (+ 1.6 %) and construction (+ 1.4 %), with agriculture (+ 0.1 %) in last place (see Figure 1.5.1). A look at the results in relation to the average for the reference period (1996-2000) shows that most branches grew faster than the average of the last five years, and some, especially manufacturing, even markedly so. The only branch that recorded below average growth in 2000 was agriculture. GVA in this branch nearly stagnated, while during the reference period, it had been growing by an average 1.7 % each year (see Figure 1.5.2).

The euro-zone figures generally matched those of the Union. Three of the four larger EU economies, namely Germany, Italy and the United Kingdom recorded the highest growth rates in 2000 in financial services and business activities: 5.2 % for Germany, 4.6 % for Italy and 4.3 % for the United Kingdom. The second place was held by trade, transport and communication for the case of the United Kingdom (+ 3.8 %) and Italy (+ 3.6 %), while in Germany, manufacturing ranked second with a 5.0 % growth rate. In France, trade, transport and communication (+ 3.3 %) showed the highest growth, but financial services and business activities were only slightly behind (+ 3.2 %). Agriculture showed the weakest results of all branches in Italy (– 2.1 %), the United Kingdom (– 1.4 %) and France (0.0 %), while Germany was exceptional not only by a positive growth rate in agriculture (+ 2.0 %), but also by being the only Member State with a negative growth in construction (– 3.8 %).

Figure 1.5.1. GVA growth rates by branch of production, 2000 (as a %)

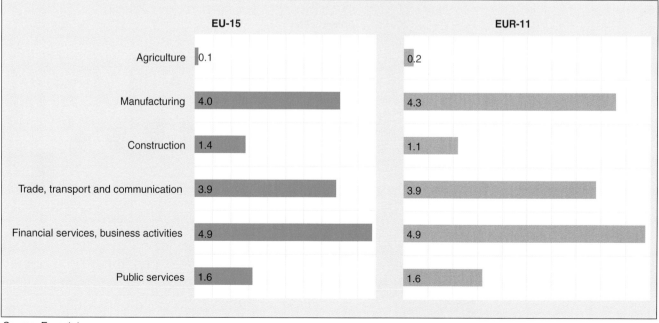

Source: Eurostat.

Figure 1.5.2. GVA growth rates, 2000 and average 1996/2000 (as a %)

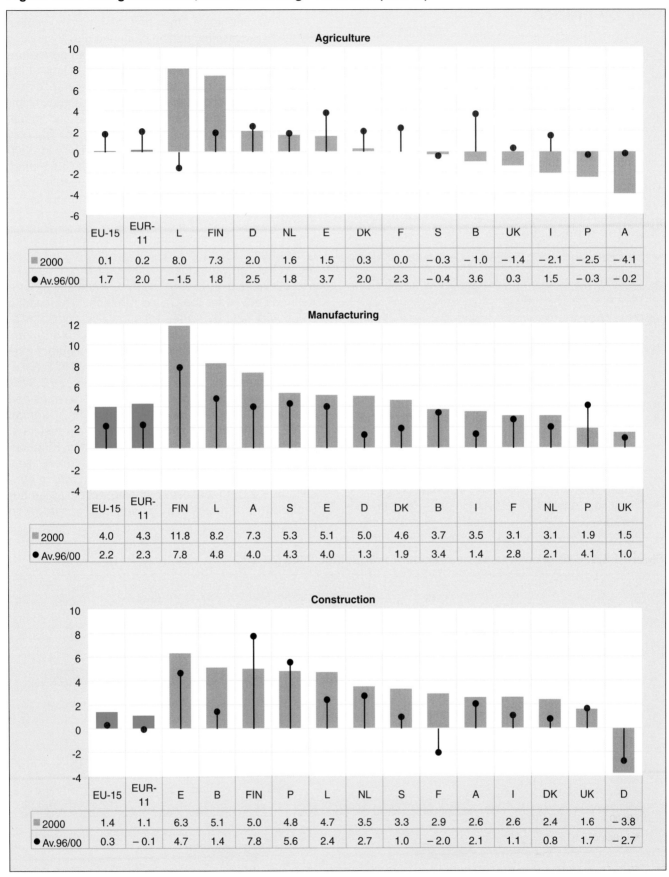

Agriculture

	EU-15	EUR-11	L	FIN	D	NL	E	DK	F	S	B	UK	I	P	A
■ 2000	0.1	0.2	8.0	7.3	2.0	1.6	1.5	0.3	0.0	− 0.3	− 1.0	− 1.4	− 2.1	− 2.5	− 4.1
● Av.96/00	1.7	2.0	− 1.5	1.8	2.5	1.8	3.7	2.0	2.3	− 0.4	3.6	0.3	1.5	− 0.3	− 0.2

Manufacturing

	EU-15	EUR-11	FIN	L	A	S	E	D	DK	B	I	F	NL	P	UK
■ 2000	4.0	4.3	11.8	8.2	7.3	5.3	5.1	5.0	4.6	3.7	3.5	3.1	3.1	1.9	1.5
● Av.96/00	2.2	2.3	7.8	4.8	4.0	4.3	4.0	1.3	1.9	3.4	1.4	2.8	2.1	4.1	1.0

Construction

	EU-15	EUR-11	E	B	FIN	P	L	NL	S	F	A	I	DK	UK	D
■ 2000	1.4	1.1	6.3	5.1	5.0	4.8	4.7	3.5	3.3	2.9	2.6	2.6	2.4	1.6	− 3.8
● Av.96/00	0.3	− 0.1	4.7	1.4	7.8	5.6	2.4	2.7	1.0	− 2.0	2.1	1.1	0.8	1.7	− 2.7

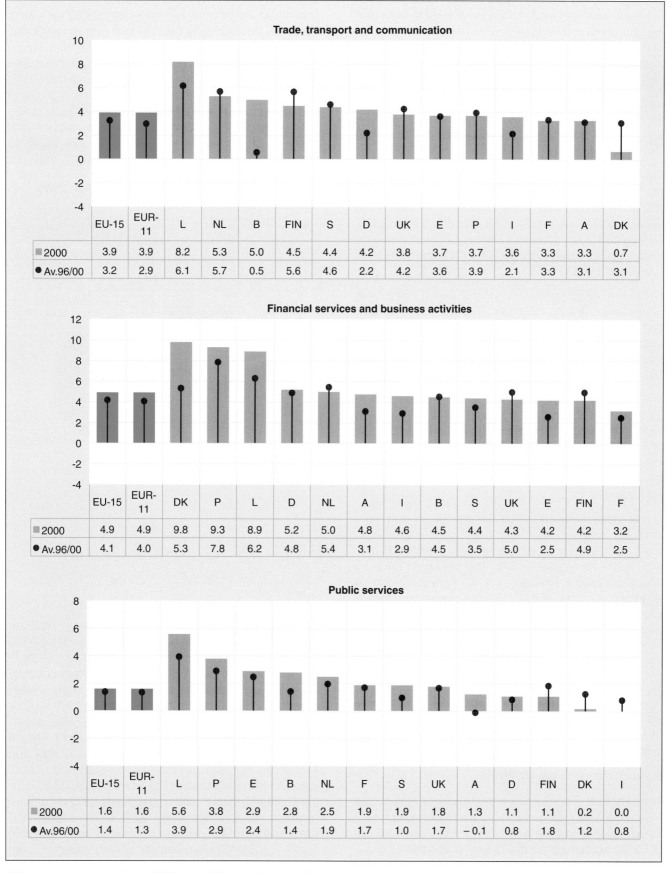

Trade, transport and communication

	EU-15	EUR-11	L	NL	B	FIN	S	D	UK	E	P	I	F	A	DK
■ 2000	3.9	3.9	8.2	5.3	5.0	4.5	4.4	4.2	3.8	3.7	3.7	3.6	3.3	3.3	0.7
● Av.96/00	3.2	2.9	6.1	5.7	0.5	5.6	4.6	2.2	4.2	3.6	3.9	2.1	3.3	3.1	3.1

Financial services and business activities

	EU-15	EUR-11	DK	P	L	D	NL	A	I	B	S	UK	E	FIN	F
■ 2000	4.9	4.9	9.8	9.3	8.9	5.2	5.0	4.8	4.6	4.5	4.4	4.3	4.2	4.2	3.2
● Av.96/00	4.1	4.0	5.3	7.8	6.2	4.8	5.4	3.1	2.9	4.5	3.5	5.0	2.5	4.9	2.5

Public services

	EU-15	EUR-11	L	P	E	B	NL	F	S	UK	A	D	FIN	DK	I
■ 2000	1.6	1.6	5.6	3.8	2.9	2.8	2.5	1.9	1.9	1.8	1.3	1.1	1.1	0.2	0.0
● Av.96/00	1.4	1.3	3.9	2.9	2.4	1.4	1.9	1.7	1.0	1.7	− 0.1	0.8	1.8	1.2	0.8

NB: No constant price data for 2000 are available for Greece and Ireland.

Source: Eurostat.

For those Member States for which data are available ([10]), the majority showed relatively high GVA growth in financial services and business activities, with the highest levels being recorded in Denmark (+ 9.8 %) and Portugal (+ 9.3 %), and even the lowest result still amounted to a 3.2 % growth in France.

The results achieved for GVA in manufacturing were also generally strong, but with a higher level of disparity among Member States, ranging from 11.8 % in Finland and 8.2 % in Luxembourg to 1.5 % in the United Kingdom.

Trade, transport and communication was the third branch to record generally high growth levels, the exception to the rule being Denmark, where only a 0.7 % growth was recorded for the whole year 2000. Among the other Member States, the best performance was in Luxembourg (+ 8.2 %), the lowest in France (+ 3.3 %).

Growth in public services usually shows a lower level of variation among Member States, and this also applies to 2000. High growth rates were recorded in Luxembourg (+ 5.6 %) and Portugal (+ 3.8 %), while the other end of the scale was marked by Denmark (+ 0.2 %) and Italy (0.0 %).

The trend in construction seemed to be upwards in general, with Spain (+ 6.3 %) and Belgium (+ 5.1 %) topping the league. The relatively modest EU-15 result of 1.4 % is mainly attributable to the − 3.8 % recorded in Germany, since the next weakest result was that of the United Kingdom, which, at + 1.6 %, was still above average.

Gross value added in 2000 for agriculture saw very modest results in most Member States and was, in fact, the only branch where several Member States experienced negative growth, the strongest declines being observed in Austria (− 4.1 %), Portugal (− 2.5 %) and Italy (− 2.1 %). The fact that the overall growth rate was still slightly above zero is mainly due to two countries, namely Luxembourg (+ 8.0 %) and Finland (+ 7.3 %), which had agricultural growth rates far above average.

Figure 1.5.2 shows the growth rates per branch. Average growth rates for the period 1996 to 2000 have also been included. Given the quantity of data, it has been presented graphically to allow comparisons both in time and between countries.

Structure of GVA in 2000

The structure of production in the European Union (see Figure 1.5.3) is based mainly on the three service sector headings. Financial services and business activities (27.2 %) accounted for the largest proportion of gross value added (GVA) produced by the 15 Member States

([10]) Constant price data for 2000 are lacking for Greece and Ireland.

in 2000, followed by public services (21.4 %) and trade, transport and communications (21.0 %). Combined, these three branches accounted for almost 70 % of total GVA in the Union's economy. Of the remaining part, the lion's share is accounted for by manufacturing (22.9 % of total GVA). In fact, if the GVA produced by manufacturing and services is disregarded, the remaining contributions made by agriculture and construction are only of secondary importance: 2.2 % and 5.3 % respectively. In the euro-zone, the structure of production was essentially the same as that in the Union as a whole.

Figure 1.5.3. Structure of GVA in the EU, 2000 (as a % of total economy)

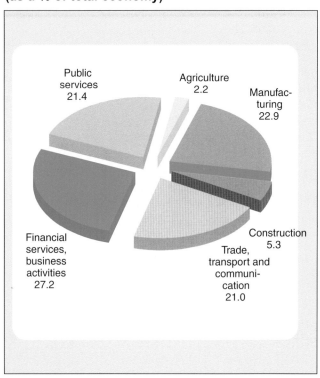

Source: Eurostat.

As in the EU as a whole, in all four larger Member States financial services and business activities played a major role as a source of GVA. In Germany, GVA in this branch contributed 30.4 % to the total economy, while in France the figure was 29.6 %, in the United Kingdom 27.6 % and in Italy 26.1 %. As for the other branches, Germany derived a particularly high contribution from manufacturing (25.2 %), as did France from public services (23.5 %). The figures for Italy and the United Kingdom reveal relatively balanced structures, with manufacturing (23.5 % for Italy, 22.6 % for the United Kingdom) and trade, transport and communication (23.8 % for Italy, 22.3 % for the United Kingdom) of roughly equal importance. In Italy, public services (18.9 %) were somewhat less important than in the other three big economies.

A closer look at the structures in individual Member States ([11]) (see Table 1.5.1) shows that in most cases production in the EU countries is concentrated in one of the service branches. There is one group of countries, namely Belgium, Luxembourg and the Netherlands in addition to Germany, France, Italy and the United Kingdom as mentioned before, where financial services and business activities make the biggest contribution to GVA, with Luxembourg standing out for having a 41.1 % share of total GVA concentrated in this branch. Public services play the main role in Portugal (25.7 %), Sweden (25.3 %) and Denmark (25.0 %), while trade, transport and communication is the branch that is the biggest contributor in Greece (27.9 %), Spain (27.5 %) and Austria (23.7 %). Finally, Ireland and Finland are exceptions, in that the biggest proportion of GVA comes from manufacturing (30.0 % and 27.7 %, respectively).

Figure 1.5.4 shows the structure of GVA by branch, together with the structure of employment. GVA and employment are two fundamental indicators for analysing the branches of the economy, and the web diagrams allow the relations between these two factors to be seen at a glance.

Structure of employment by branch

The number of people employed in each branch is another important factor in defining the importance of the branch in the economy. A look at the structure of employment in the European Union in 2000 shows that public services provided the most jobs (29.3 % of total employment), followed by trade, transport and communication (25.4 %), while only 13.9 % of the workforce was employed in financial services and business activities. The latter branch produced more than a quarter of the value added produced in the EU, while employing a much smaller proportion of the workforce.

Among the Member States for which data are available ([12]), there are some broad similarities in the structure of employment. Throughout the EU, public services and trade, transport and communication are the branches that provide most jobs. Public services account for the largest share in most countries, while trade, transport and communication is the largest provider of employment in Ireland, Luxembourg, Spain, Greece and Austria.

Sweden is the Member State which has the biggest share of employment in public services (38.9 %). Next comes Belgium (36.2 %), followed by Denmark (35.7 %). There were relatively fewer jobs in this branch in Luxembourg (22.0 % of total employment) and Greece and Austria (23.0 % for both). As mentioned earlier, trade, transport and communication accounted for the largest share of employment in

Table 1.5.1. Structure of GVA in 2000 (as a % of total economy)

	Agriculture	Manufacturing	Construction	Trade transport communication	Financial services, business activities	Public services
EU-15	2.2	22.9	5.3	21.0	27.2	21.4
EUR-11	2.3	23.0	5.4	20.6	27.4	21.3
B	1.5	20.8	5.0	20.4	28.7	23.6
DK	2.6	21.0	4.5	23.0	23.8	25.0
D	1.2	25.2	4.9	17.2	30.4	21.1
EL	8.1	14.1	8.3	27.9	22.0	19.6
E	3.5	20.9	8.5	27.5	19.1	20.4
F	2.8	20.9	4.5	18.6	29.6	23.5
IRL	3.8	30.0	6.0	18.7	24.5	17.1
I	2.8	23.5	4.9	23.8	26.1	18.9
L	0.6	12.6	5.4	23.0	41.1	17.3
NL	2.8	20.7	5.7	21.8	26.6	22.5
A	2.0	23.6	8.3	23.7	22.4	20.0
P	3.6	21.5	7.5	24.1	17.6	25.7
FIN	3.5	27.7	5.7	22.1	20.9	20.2
S	1.9	24.5	4.1	19.9	24.3	25.3
UK	1.0	22.6	5.1	22.3	27.6	21.4

NB: 1998 data for Greece, 1999 data for Ireland, Eurostat estimate for Sweden.
Source: Eurostat.

([11]) The structure has been calculated at current prices.

([12]) For Greece, Ireland and Portugal the structure illustrated refers to 1998 and for Luxembourg to 1999. There are no national accounts data available on employment by branch for the United Kingdom.

Figure 1.5.4. Structure of GVA and employment by main branch, 2000 (as a % of total economy)

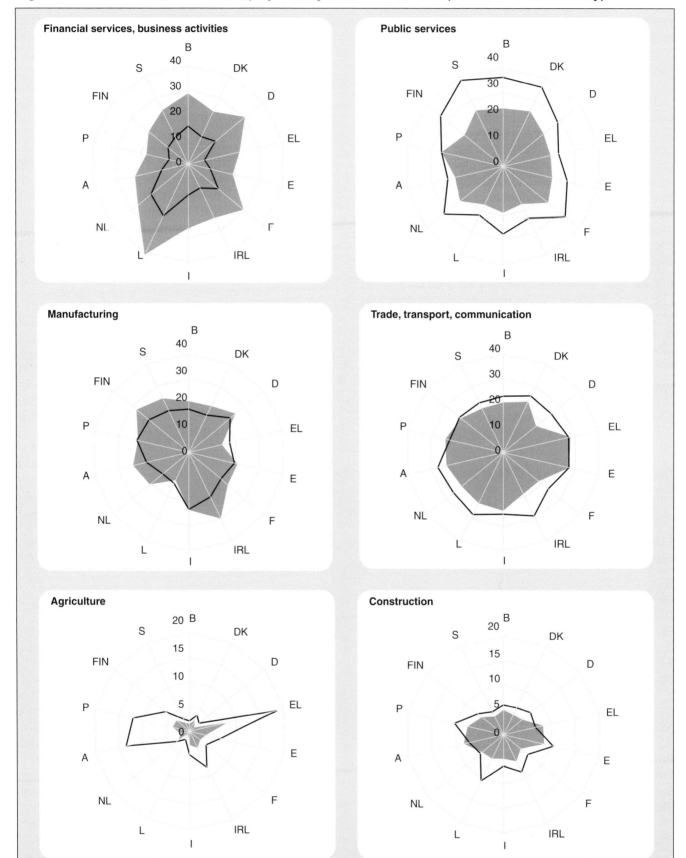

NB: Scales vary between branches to allow comparisons among countries, although this makes it difficult to compare branches. No data are available on employment in the United Kingdom. 1998 employment data for Greece, Ireland and Portugal, 1999 for Luxembourg, 1998 GVA data for Greece, 1999 for Ireland.
Source: Eurostat.

Ireland (28.7 %), Luxembourg (28.2 %) and, close together, Spain (27.4 %), Greece (27.3 %) and Austria (27.2 %). In the case of employment in financial services, Luxembourg (23.5 %) and the Netherlands (19.8 %) stood out with figures markedly higher than those recorded in other EU countries. Italy (23.3 %) and Germany (22.2 %) were remarkable for the importance that employment in manufacturing has in their economies. High percentages for employment in construction are recorded for Luxembourg (10.5 %), Spain (10.4 %) and Portugal (10.2 %). Echoing the situation observed for GVA, Greece (18.5 %) also recorded the largest share of employment in agriculture among Member States. Austria (13.4 %) and Portugal (12.0 %) were also ahead of the other Member States in this respect.

Productivity

To give an overview of the relationship between production and employment in each branch, labour productivity has been calculated as a simple ratio between gross value added and total employment.

Labour productivity, or rather a general productivity indicator of output per unit of labour, allows the branches to be considered in terms of labour and employment and, obviously, also allows the comparison of data from different-sized productive systems. This indicator is, of course, very simplified. Firstly, the ratio should rather be based on hours actually worked ([13]) and not simply on the number of those employed. Secondly, no account is taken of the efficient use of resources and

Figure 1.5.5. Structure of employment in the EU, 2000 (as a % of total economy)

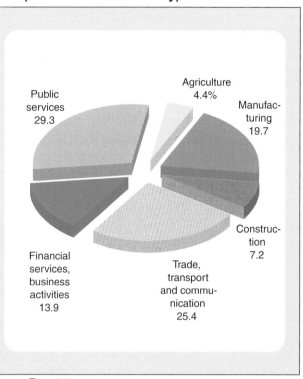

Source: Eurostat.

technical progress. Given the rather simple definition of the labour productivity indicator used here, it should be borne in mind that an increase in productivity may be due to an increase in gross value added or a reduction in employment or both.

Table 1.5.2. Structure of employment in 2000 (as a % of total economy)

	Agriculture	Manufacturing	Construction	Trade transport communication	Financial services, business activities	Public services
EU-15	4.4	19.7	7.2	25.4	13.9	29.3
EUR-11	4.7	20.2	7.3	25.1	13.8	28.9
B	2.1	17.5	6.0	22.9	15.3	36.2
DK	3.6	16.8	6.1	25.5	12.2	35.7
D	2.5	22.2	7.1	25.1	14.6	28.4
EL	18.5	17.5	6.7	27.3	7.0	23.0
E	6.6	19.5	10.4	27.4	9.4	26.7
F	4.4	17.1	6.4	23.6	16.1	32.4
IRL	8.1	20.2	8.4	28.7	11.0	23.5
I	4.8	23.3	6.4	25.2	12.8	27.6
L	1.9	14.0	10.5	28.2	23.5	22.0
NL	3.4	13.9	6.1	26.0	19.8	30.9
A	13.4	17.9	7.2	27.2	11.3	23.0
P	12.0	21.9	10.2	22.3	8.0	25.7
FIN	6.3	21.0	6.7	22.7	10.6	32.5
S	2.7	18.9	5.1	22.4	12.0	38.9
UK	:	:	:	:	:	:

NB: 1998 data for Greece, Ireland and Portugal, 1999 data for Luxembourg.
Source: Eurostat.

([13]) In quantifying the labour effectively employed in a productive process, hours worked would avoid distortions resulting from the inequality between the number of people employed and the number of jobs.

The highest productivity level in the European Union ([14]) in 2000 was achieved in financial services and business activities, where each worker produced EUR 93 100 of value added. Next came manufacturing with EUR 55 400, followed by trade, transport and communications (EUR 39 500) and, quite close together, construction (EUR 35 200) and public services (EUR 34 700). Productivity in agriculture, however, was significantly lower than in the other branches: EUR 23 500 in 2000 (see Figure 1.5.6).

The figures for the euro-zone were more or less in line with those of the EU, albeit a little higher for financial services and business activities (EUR 94 100) and somewhat lower for trade, transport and communication (EUR 38 800) and manufacturing (EUR 53 800).

Data are available for only three of the four larger Member States, since there are no national accounts data on employment by branch in the United Kingdom. Productivity figures in the branches are essentially similar, with the highest figures being recorded for financial services and business activities in Germany (EUR 102 800), France (EUR 101 700) and Italy (EUR 95 400). Manufacturing came next for all three countries: EUR 67 300 in France, EUR 55 700 in Germany and EUR 47 200 in Italy. Italy (EUR 27 200) and particularly France (EUR 35 500) stand out with relatively high figures for productivity in agriculture, while for Germany, productivity in trade, transport and communication is relatively low at EUR 33 700.

A clearer comparison of the Member States can be seen in Table 1.5.3, where the productivity figures for the six branches of the economy are shown in relation to the average for the Union as a whole (EU-15 = 100).

A closer look at these figures shows that the highest productivity in agriculture was achieved in Denmark (EUR 41 300) and Belgium (EUR 41 100), where the figures were about 75 % above the EU average. The top figures in manufacturing were those of Ireland, Denmark and Luxembourg (EUR 71 700, EUR 71 400 and EUR 71 200, respectively) at almost 30 % above the EU average, with Belgium (EUR 69 100), Sweden (EUR 68 800) and Finland (68 500) not far behind. In addition to Greece, Spain and Portugal, where productivity was lower than the EU average in almost every branch, Italy was also below the EU-15 average for manufacturing, with a figure of EUR 47 200 in 2000. The Member States with the highest productivity in construction were Austria (EUR 55 700 per person employed) and Belgium (EUR 48 500), these figures exceeding the EU average by 58 % and 38 %, respectively.

In trade, transport and communication, Luxembourg (EUR 64 500) ranked highest, with Belgium (EUR 52 100) and Finland (EUR 50 500) somewhat behind. Productivity in financial services and business activities was particularly high in Luxembourg, too, at EUR 138 800 which means 48 % above the EU average.

Figure 1.5.6. Productivity by branch in 2000 (EUR, current prices)

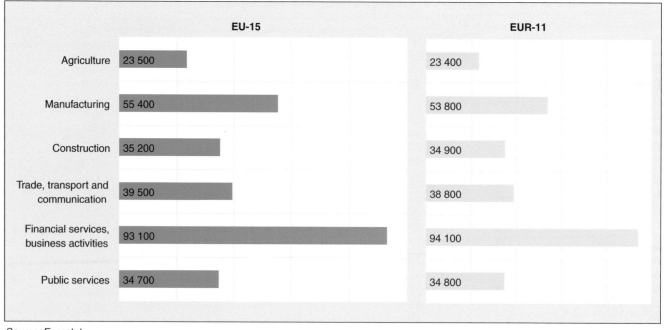

Source: Eurostat.

([14]) Productivity levels have been calculated at current prices; in the calculation of the growth index, GVA is at constant prices.

Table 1.5.3. Productivity by branch in 2000 (EUR, current prices)

	Agriculture		Manufacturing		Construction		Trade transport and communication		Financial services, business activities		Public services		Total	
	EUR	EU = 100	EUR	EU = 100	EUR	EU = 100	EUR	EU = 100	EUR	EU = 100	EUR	EU = 100	EUR	EU = 100
EU-15	23 500	100	55 400	100	35 200	100	39 500	100	93 100	100	34 700	100	47 700	100
EUR-11	23 400	100	53 800	97	34 900	99	38 800	98	94 100	101	34 800	100	47 300	99
B	41 100	175	69 100	125	48 500	138	52 100	132	109 100	117	38 000	110	58 300	122
DK	41 300	176	71 400	129	42 100	120	51 400	130	111 300	120	40 000	115	57 100	120
D	22 800	97	55 700	101	33 700	96	33 700	85	102 800	110	36 400	105	49 200	103
EL	11 900	51	22 500	41	36 700	104	28 500	72	84 600	91	23 400	67	27 900	58
E	19 300	82	38 700	70	29 700	84	36 400	92	73 700	79	27 700	80	36 200	76
F	35 500	151	67 300	121	39 400	112	43 600	110	101 700	109	40 100	116	55 300	116
IRL	25 200	107	71 700	129	34 200	97	31 400	79	102 800	110	34 800	100	48 400	101
I	27 200	116	47 200	85	35 500	101	44 300	112	95 400	102	32 100	93	46 800	98
L	25 900	110	71 200	129	40 400	115	64 500	163	138 000	148	62 100	179	78 900	165
NL	37 100	158	66 800	121	42 300	120	37 700	95	60 400	65	32 700	94	44 900	94
A	7 000	30	63 100	114	55 700	158	41 500	105	95 000	102	41 500	120	47 800	100
P	6 800	29	21 300	38	14 800	42	22 700	57	44 700	48	21 000	61	21 200	44
FIN	28 900	123	68 500	124	43 900	125	50 500	128	102 400	110	32 300	93	52 100	109
S	35 200	150	68 800	124	43 200	123	47 600	121	107 600	116	33 600	97	52 800	111
UK	:	:	:	:	:	:	:	:	:	:	:	:	55 100	116

NB: 1998 data for Greece, Ireland and Portugal, 1999 data for Luxembourg.
Source: Eurostat.

Relatively strong values were also recorded in Denmark (EUR 111 300), Belgium (EUR 109 100) and Sweden (EUR 107 600). Lastly, Luxembourg with EUR 62 100 was the only country where productivity in public services differed greatly from the overall value. The figures for public services in the other Member States were much closer together than in any of the other branches.

Figure 1.5.7. Productivity in 2000, total economy (EU-15 = 100)

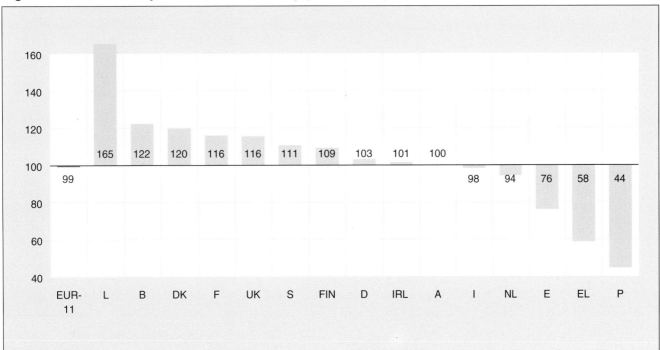

NB: Data for Greece, Ireland, Luxembourg, Portugal and Sweden are Eurostat estimates.
Source: Eurostat.

Figure 1.5.8. Growth index of productivity, 2000 (1995 = 100)

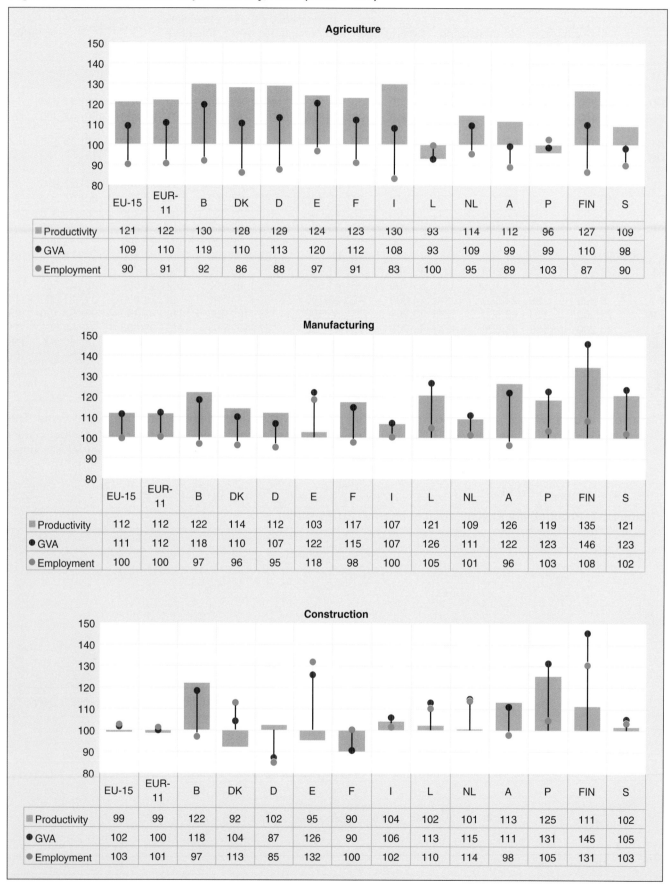

Agriculture

	EU-15	EUR-11	B	DK	D	E	F	I	L	NL	A	P	FIN	S
Productivity	121	122	130	128	129	124	123	130	93	114	112	96	127	109
GVA	109	110	119	110	113	120	112	108	93	109	99	99	110	98
Employment	90	91	92	86	88	97	91	83	100	95	89	103	87	90

Manufacturing

	EU-15	EUR-11	B	DK	D	E	F	I	L	NL	A	P	FIN	S
Productivity	112	112	122	114	112	103	117	107	121	109	126	119	135	121
GVA	111	112	118	110	107	122	115	107	126	111	122	123	146	123
Employment	100	100	97	96	95	118	98	100	105	101	96	103	108	102

Construction

	EU-15	EUR-11	B	DK	D	E	F	I	L	NL	A	P	FIN	S
Productivity	99	99	122	92	102	95	90	104	102	101	113	125	111	102
GVA	102	100	118	104	87	126	90	106	113	115	111	131	145	105
Employment	103	101	97	113	85	132	100	102	110	114	98	105	131	103

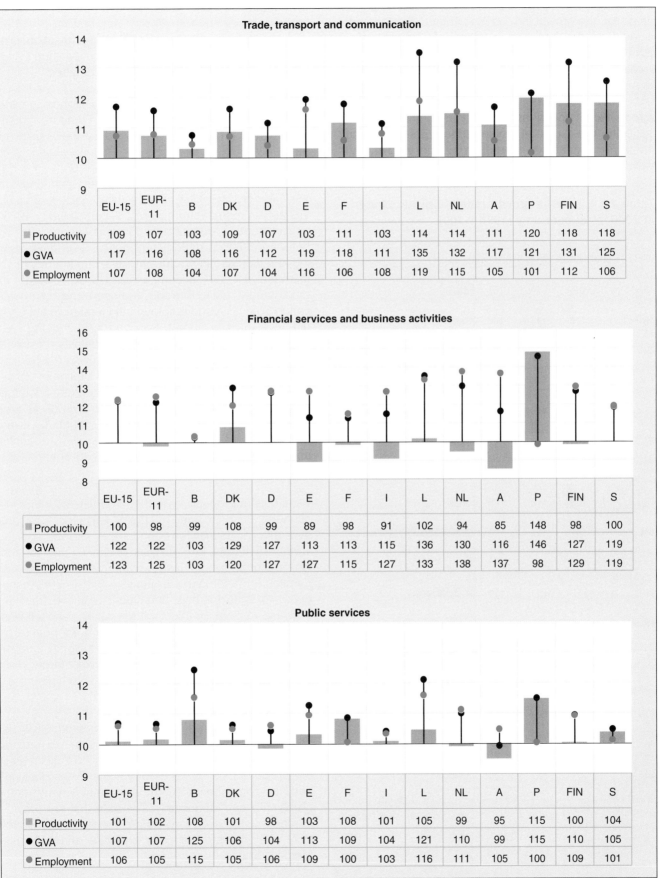

Trade, transport and communication

	EU-15	EUR-11	B	DK	D	E	F	I	L	NL	A	P	FIN	S
Productivity	109	107	103	109	107	103	111	103	114	114	111	120	118	118
GVA	117	116	108	116	112	119	118	111	135	132	117	121	131	125
Employment	107	108	104	107	104	116	106	108	119	115	105	101	112	106

Financial services and business activities

	EU-15	EUR-11	B	DK	D	E	F	I	L	NL	A	P	FIN	S
Productivity	100	98	99	108	99	89	98	91	102	94	85	148	98	100
GVA	122	122	103	129	127	113	113	115	136	130	116	146	127	119
Employment	123	125	103	120	127	127	115	127	133	138	137	98	129	119

Public services

	EU-15	EUR-11	B	DK	D	E	F	I	L	NL	A	P	FIN	S
Productivity	101	102	108	101	98	103	108	101	105	99	95	115	100	104
GVA	107	107	125	106	104	113	109	104	121	110	99	115	110	105
Employment	106	105	115	105	106	109	100	103	116	111	105	100	109	101

NB: Productivity growth was not calculated for the United Kingdom due to lack of data on employment per branch, in Ireland due to lack of data on GVA at constant prices per branch and in Greece, where both were lacking for 2000 and the base for doing estimations by branch was considered too small. Data for Luxembourg and Portugal are Eurostat estimates in part.
Source: Eurostat.

We now take a look at the development of productivity over time. Contrary to the productivity figures presented so far, the growth indices (see Table 1.5.4) are calculated on the basis of constant price gross value added in order to compensate for changes in the price levels. When these figures are considered, it must be remembered that productivity, however simple, is nevertheless a ratio that is the result of two components (gross value added and employment) that work in opposite directions: if value added goes up and employment goes down, productivity is increased, and vice versa. On the other hand, if both components go

up — or down — the increase or reduction in productivity that this causes will depend on the difference in the variations. In the unlikely event that value added and employment show exactly the same variation, productivity would remain the same — even though the two components had increased or decreased.

In the European Union in 2000, the highest growth rate in terms of volume (1995 = 100) was in agriculture, where productivity increased by 21 % in comparison with the reference year. This increase in productivity was a result of growth in GVA (+ 9 %), together with a significant decrease in employment in this branch (– 10 %). Productivity also increased sizeably in manufacturing (+ 12 % compared to 1995) and in trade, transport and communication (+ 9 %), but with different underlying causes. In manufacturing, the increase in productivity was due entirely to an increase in GVA accompanied by no change in employment; while in trade, transport and communication both GVA and employment increased, but GVA did so at greater speed, resulting in increasing productivity. In the other branches, productivity remained essentially unchanged in comparison with the benchmark year: in financial services and business activities, GVA and employment both experienced large and matching variations (respectively + 22 % and + 23 %), with the result that productivity was unchanged. Basically the same applies to public services and construction, although the variations were on a smaller scale.

Table 1.5.4. Volume growth index of productivity in 2000, total economy (1995 = 100)

	Employment	GVA	Productivity	
EU-15	106	114	107	
EUR-11	106	113	107	
B	106	113	107	
DK	105	119	113	
D	103	111	108	
EL	103	116	113	
E	115	118	102	
F	103	112	109	
IRL	131	157	120	
I	105	109	104	
L	118	130	110	
NL	115	120	105	
A	103	113	110	
P	102	124	122	
FIN	111	129	117	
S	104	116	112	
UK	107	115	108	

NB: Employment growth data for Greece, Ireland, Luxembourg and Portugal are Eurostat estimates, as are GVA growth data for Greece and Ireland.
Source: Eurostat.

Variations in productivity in the larger EU countries — although for only three of them, since no data are available for the United Kingdom — showed a wide variety of trends. An analysis of the figures for the whole economy in 2000 shows that productivity rose in parallel in France and Germany (+ 9 % in 2000 compared to 1995 for both countries), resulting from an increase in GVA (+ 12 % and + 11 %, respectively) much larger than in employment (+ 3 % for both). For Italy, the increase in GVA (+ 9 %) was slightly smaller and that in employment (+ 5 %) somewhat larger, with the result that productivity in 2000 was 4 % higher than in the reference year.

As observed, analysing variations in productivity is somewhat complex because it involves two factors and therefore two variations. Figure 1.5.8 illustrates the growth indices in terms of volume for productivity and its components (GVA and employment) both graphically and numerically. The data that are provided can thus be used to compare variations in productivity over the six branches and over the available Member States.

1.6. Distribution of GDP, disposable income, saving and net lending/borrowing

Distribution of GDP — income side

Sections 1.3 and 1.4 looked at GDP as the sum of the end uses of goods and services, i.e. from the demand (or expenditure) side, while Section 1.5 was devoted to the analysis of the production (or output) side, expressing total GVA by adding up the value added over the branch of the economy that created it. Yet another definition, and another way of calculating GDP, is to look at the income produced and how that income is divided among the various recipients. To use the terminology of ESA 95, this is the primary distribution of income, i.e. distribution among the factors of production and general government. For the factors of production, labour is remunerated by compensation of employees and capital by operating surplus and mixed income (in the case of households). General government, however, receives income in the form of taxes.

GDP as the sum of primary incomes that are generated is thus broken down in ESA 95 as follows:

1. compensation of employees;

2. operating surplus or mixed income;

3. net taxes (taxes less subsidies) on production and imports.

It should be noted that income aggregates are compiled in current prices only, since it is conceptually more difficult to define a "volume" component. All value growth indices are based on evaluations in euro.

In 2000, compensation of employees in the European Union accounted for about half (50.9 %) of all generated income, with operating surplus and taxes accounting for 36.5 % and 12.6 % respectively. The structure of the income distribution has not changed much over the last years: compared with 1996, compensation of employees accounted for a slightly smaller share of GDP in 2000, with a figure that was − 0.3 percentage points down on the earlier year. Operating surplus was also down (− 0.8 points), while taxes increased their share

Figure 1.6.1. Gross domestic product in EU-15: income side

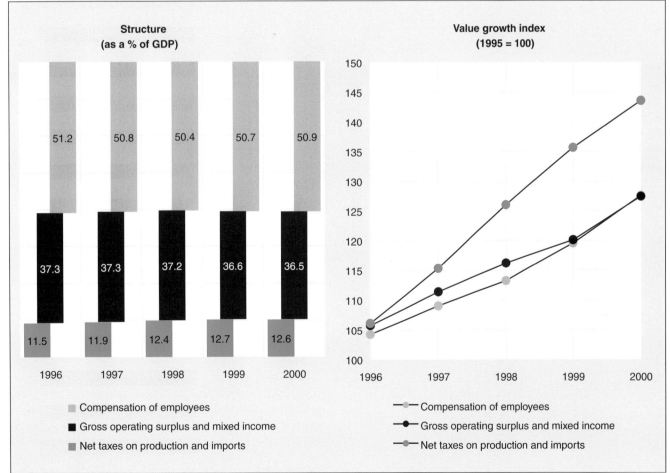

NB: Growth index is in value terms, since data are available only at current prices.
Source: Eurostat.

by 1.1 points. When the changes are considered in absolute terms (value growth index), this time with 1995 as the benchmark year (1995 = 100), incomes in 2000 showed a similar rise for both compensation of employees (+ 27.6 %) and for gross operating surplus and mixed income (+ 27.4 %). Taxes, on the other hand, showed a rise of 43.5 % (see Figure 1.6.1).

With regard to the structure of GDP in the euro-zone, the reduction in the percentage share of compensation

of employees from 1996 to 2000 was more noticeable (– 1.2 points) since this component went up sizeably in the United Kingdom and Sweden. The share of gross operating surplus and mixed income was virtually unchanged over the last five years (+ 0.1 points), while the rise in taxes on production and imports (+ 1.1) matched the EU-15 figure (see Figure 1.6.2). A look at the value growth index (1995 = 100) presented in Table 1.6.2 shows that the figures for the three components were consistently lower in the euro-zone than

Table 1.6.1. Structure of GDP — income side, 2000 (as a % of GDP)

	Compensation of employees	Gross operating surplus and mixed income	Net taxes on production and imports	Compensation … Gross operating … Net taxes …
EU-15	50.9	36.5	12.6	
EUR-11	49.7	38.0	12.3	
B	51.2	36.4	12.4	
DK	52.4	33.3	14.3	
D	53.4	35.9	10.7	
EL	33.6	53.9	12.5	
E	50.4	39.5	10.2	
F	52.2	33.6	14.2	
IRL	39.9	48.7	11.4	
I	40.5	45.4	14.0	
L	49.3	36.8	14.0	
NL	51.2	37.5	11.3	
A	51.8	35.3	12.9	
P	42.8	44.4	12.7	
FIN	47.0	41.2	11.8	
S	58.3	28.5	13.1	
UK	55.7	30.5	13.9	

NB: Eurostat estimation for Greece, Ireland and Portugal.
Source: Eurostat.

in the Community as a whole: + 17.3 % against + 27.6 % for compensation of employees, + 22.7 % against + 27.4 % for gross operating surplus and mixed income and + 34.0 % against + 43.5 % for net taxes. Here, again, a major factor in these differences was the performance of the United Kingdom, where growth figures for every variable were among the highest in the Union.

Regarding the four biggest economies of the European Union, compensation of employees showed a decreasing importance as a component of GDP in Germany and Italy, while remaining virtually unchanged in France and increasing its percentage share in the United Kingdom. For gross operating surplus, Germany was the only one of the four bigger economies that increased this component's share of GDP significantly, whereas this share went down in Italy and particularly so in the United Kingdom. Lastly, taxes increased their percentage share in all four countries except France, with Italy showing a particularly strong increase. For France, the composition of GDP changed only marginally since 1996.

As for the absolute variation (value growth index 1995 = 100) of income components in the big Member States, the United Kingdom stood out in 2000 for the size of its increases for all components of income: + 83.7 % for compensation of employees, + 64.9 % for gross operating surplus and mixed income and + 89.1 % for net taxes on production and imports. The increases were noticeable in Italy as well, especially for taxes, which showed an increase of + 79.2 % compared with 1995. In Germany and France the variations were more contained.

A more detailed look at the structure of GDP shows that compensation of employees was the major component in most Member States in 2000, with the highest figures occurring in Sweden (58.3 %) and the United Kingdom (55.7 %). In Greece, Ireland, Italy and Portugal, however, it was gross operating surplus that was the single largest contributor to GDP. Greece clearly stood out in having the lowest percentage share for compensation of employees (33.6 %) of all Member States and the highest for gross operating surplus and mixed income (53.9 %) (see Table 1.6.1).

When comparing the situation in 2000 with that of 1996 in Figure 1.6.2, there seems to be a tendency towards declining shares of compensation of employees as a component of GDP for most of the Member States of the euro-zone and Denmark, while these shares in Greece, Sweden and the United Kingdom went up, the latter two now having the highest shares in the Union.

In the case of gross operating surplus and mixed income, the development was not uniform: Its share fell markedly in Greece, Spain, Sweden and the United Kingdom, while the opposite was true for Ireland, Portugal and Finland. The share in GDP of taxes on production and imports went up in most Member States, the exceptions being Portugal and France, where the downward changes were rather small, though. The biggest increases in the percentage share of taxes on GDP were recorded in Italy, Luxembourg and Sweden (see Figure 1.6.2).

A look at the absolute variation (value growth index 1995 = 100) shows that the Member States which recorded the biggest variations for every component were the United Kingdom and Ireland. Compensation of employees showed only quite modest increases in Germany (+ 4.3 %) and Austria (+ 9.6 %). Gross operating surplus and mixed income more than doubled in Ireland (+ 127.3 %) over the period under review, while at the other extreme Sweden recorded a + 9.9 % rise.

The component that produced the biggest increases was taxes on products and imports: apart from Ireland (+ 117.4 %) and the United Kingdom (+ 89.1 %), there were significant increases also in a number of other Member States, notably Italy (+ 79.2 %), Sweden (+ 69.9 %), Spain (+ 59.0 %) and Greece (+ 58.7 %) (see Table 1.6.2).

Disposable income: breakdown between consumption and saving

Still on the income side, when net income abroad (i.e. the balance between transfers to and from other countries) is deducted from GDP, the result is a figure for national income. When current transfers ([15]) are excluded from national income, what is left is national disposable income, or the resources that a country has at its disposal. These resources are divided between consumption and saving.

([15]) Current taxes on income, capital, etc., social contributions, social benefits and other current transfers.

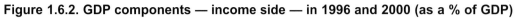

Figure 1.6.2. GDP components — income side — in 1996 and 2000 (as a % of GDP)

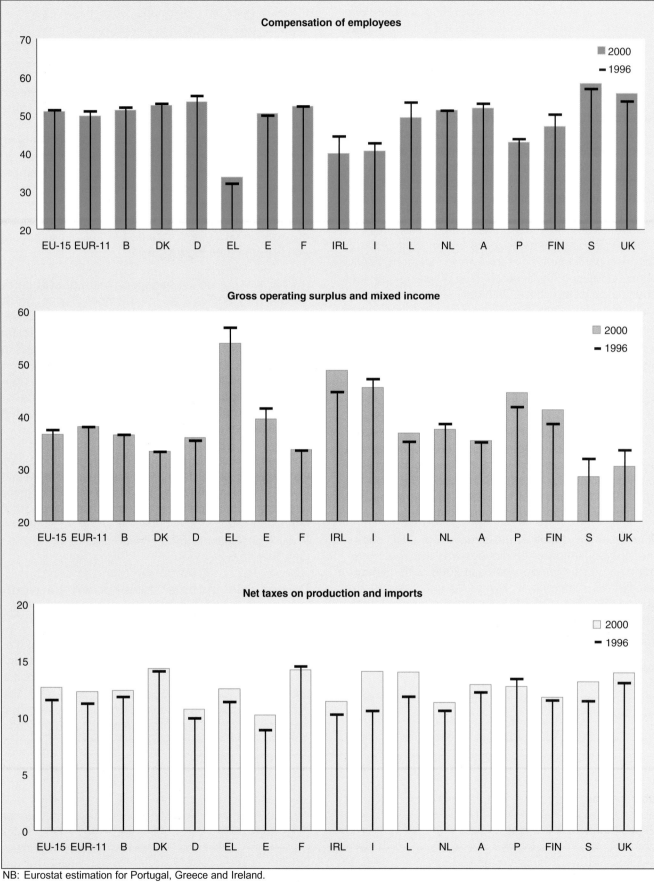

NB: Eurostat estimation for Portugal, Greece and Ireland.
Source: Eurostat.

Table 1.6.2. Value growth index of GDP components — income side, 2000 (1995 = 100)

	Compensation of employees	Gross operating surplus and mixed income	Net taxes on production and imports	Compensation … Gross operating … Net taxes …
EU-15	127.6	127.4	143.5	
EUR-11	117.3	122.7	134.0	
B	114.7	115.9	127.6	
DK	126.7	126.9	134.0	
D	104.3	111.5	117.4	
EL	141.0	127.5	158.7	
E	136.9	129.3	159.0	
F	118.5	117.1	119.9	
IRL	180.0	227.3	217.4	
I	132.4	135.5	179.2	
L	136.7	153.5	171.8	
NL	126.2	122.6	140.0	
A	109.6	120.0	121.2	
P	134.4	146.1	131.0	
FIN	125.6	140.4	141.3	
S	143.1	109.9	169.9	
UK	183.7	164.9	189.1	

NB: Eurostat estimation for Greece, Ireland and Portugal.
Source: Eurostat.

The disposable income of the European Union in 2000 amounted to EUR 8 433 billion, with EUR 6 642 billion going into both private and public consumption and EUR 1 792 billion earmarked for saving. In percentage terms, consumption accounted for 78.8 % of disposable income, and saving for the remaining 21.2 %. In absolute growth terms, disposable income in 2000 was 29.4 % higher than in the reference year (1995). The corresponding figure for consumption was 29.3 %, with saving showing a slightly higher increase of 29.9 % (see Figure 1.6.3).

In the euro-zone the division between consumption and saving is marked by a higher proportion devoted to saving; at 22.4 %, it is more than one percentage point higher than for the Union as a whole. The main reason for this is the situation in the United Kingdom, which stands out from all the other Member States with the lowest percentage of disposable income earmarked for saving (16.1 % in 2000). There is a much greater propensity for saving in Italy (20.8 %), Germany (21.7 %) and France (22.0 %) (see Table 1.6.3). When these figures are compared with the benchmark figures

Figure 1.6.3. Gross disposable income: redistribution

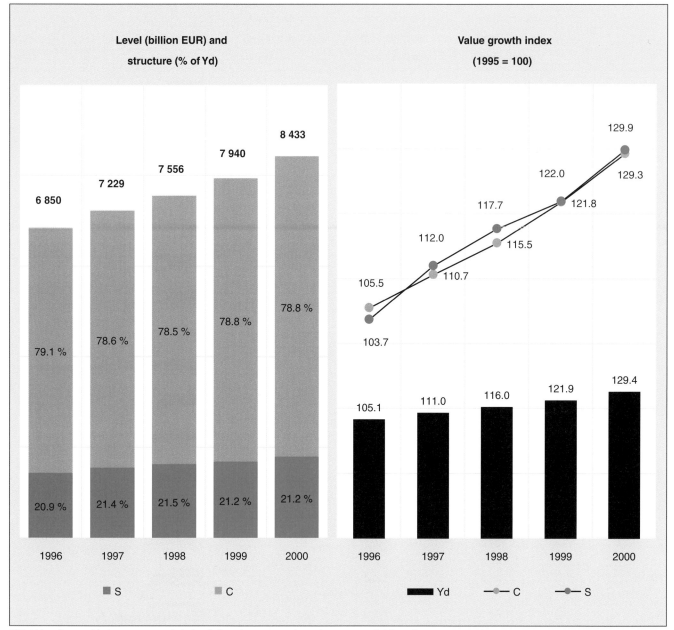

NB: Yd = disposable income; growth index is in value terms, since data are available only at current prices.
Source: Eurostat.

for 1996, it shows that there were no important changes in the United Kingdom and Germany. In Italy, however, there was a shift of 1.5 percentage points from saving towards consumption, while in France, on the other hand, saving as a percentage of disposable income went up by 2.6 points (see Table 1.6.4). As for the absolute variation in value terms compared to 1995, saving in France increased by 33.2 %, com-

pared with 16.2 % for consumption, whereas the increases in Germany were fairly contained (+ 5.6 % for saving and + 8.5 % for consumption). The variations in Italy were much larger in scale, with consumption (+ 42.3 %) ahead of saving (+ 32.6 %). Even bigger increases occurred in the United Kingdom, where saving increased by 75.2 % and consumption by 79.3 % between 1995 and 2000 (see Table 1.6.5).

Table 1.6.3. Disposable income and redistribution, 2000

	Disposable income (billion EUR)	Redistribution C	Redistribution S
EU-15	8 433	78.8%	21.2%
EUR-11	6 356	77.6%	22.4%
B	245	75.2%	24.8%
DK	169	75.4%	24.6%
D	1 998	78.3%	21.7%
EL	130	79.2%	20.8%
E	600	77.3%	22.7%
F	1 405	78.0%	22.0%
IRL	88	72.1%	27.9%
I	1 154	79.2%	20.8%
L	18	65.9%	34.1%
NL	402	72.3%	27.7%
A	201	77.4%	22.6%
P	115	82.8%	17.2%
FIN	129	71.8%	28.2%
S	241	78.5%	21.5%
UK	1 537	83.9%	16.1%

NB: Eurostat estimation for Greece, Ireland and Austria.
Source: Eurostat.

Among the Member States, those that are most inclined to save rather than consume are Luxembourg (34.1 % of disposable income), Finland (28.2 %), Ireland (27.9 %) and the Netherlands (27.7 %). At the other extreme, consumption is highest — and saving lowest, of course — in the United Kingdom (83.9 %) and Portugal (82.8 %) (see Table 1.6.3).

Table 1.6.4. Change in redistribution of disposable income between 1996 and 2000 (as % points)

	C	change as % points		S
EU-15	↗	–	0.4	+	↗
EUR-11	↗	–	0.7	+	↗
B	↗	–	0.4	+	↗
DK	↓	–	3.4	+	↑
D	↗	–	0.1	+	↗
EL	↓	–	4.3	+	↑
E	↗	–	0.6	+	↗
F	↓	–	2.6	+	↑
IRL	↓	–	4.0	+	↑
I	↑	+	1.5	–	↓
L	↑	+	1.7	–	↓
NL	↗	–	0.9	+	↗
A	↗	–	0.9	+	↗
P	↑	+	2.1	–	↓
FIN	↓	–	6.8	+	↑
S	↓	–	1.5	+	↑
UK	↗	+	0.6	–	↗

Reading note:

↗ ↗   slight variation: below 1 percentage point

↑ ↓   moderate variation: 1-3 percentage points

↑ ↓   strong variation: over 3 percentage points

NB: Eurostat estimation for Greece, Ireland and Austria.
Source: Eurostat.

When the composition of disposable income for 1996 and 2000 is compared, the biggest changes appear in Finland, Greece, Ireland and Denmark, for all of which saving significantly increased its share in disposable income. Over the same period, a declining propensity to save, though not of comparable size, was observed in Portugal, Luxembourg and Italy (see Table 1.6.4).

As for the absolute variation (value growth index 1995 = 100), saving in Ireland more than doubled over the period under review (+ 137.0 %). There were also considerable increases in the United Kingdom (+ 75.2 %), Finland (+ 69.9 %) and Greece (+ 66.9 %). The United Kingdom (+ 79.3 %) and Ireland (+ 76.5 %) were also the countries with the largest increases in the value of consumption in comparison to the reference year 1995 (see Table 1.6.5).

Table 1.6.5. Value growth index of disposable income components, 2000 (1995 = 100)

	■ Saving	■ Consumption	
EU-15	129.9	129.3	
EUR-11	123.1	120.5	
B	115.5	115.9	
DK	148.1	121.5	
D	105.6	108.5	
EL	166.9	129.5	
E	136.6	133.2	
F	133.2	116.2	
IRL	237.0	176.5	
I	132.6	142.3	
L	112.6	129.9	
NL	128.3	125.2	
A	115.9	113.2	
P	116.2	140.0	
FIN	169.9	125.4	
S	139.1	134.8	
UK	175.2	179.3	

NB: Eurostat estimation for Greece, Ireland and Austria.
Source: Eurostat.

Net lending/borrowing

In the final analysis, a country's resources that are not consumed are either saved or invested or transferred to or from the country. The balance between saving, investment (capital formation) and net capital transactions with other countries therefore provides a summary of the country's lending/borrowing in relation to the rest of the world.

In 2000, the European Union's lending position amounted to about EUR 11.5 billion. This position remained steadily in the black in the period under review, with the figure peaking in 1997, when EUR 122.5 billion was lent to the rest of the world. The figures for the euro zone were a little below the EU-15 figures until 1999, when the EUR-11 figure of EUR 45.3 billion slightly exceeded the figure for the Union as a whole (EUR 43.0 billion). This gap widened in 2000, when the euro-zone lent EUR 24.6 billion to the rest of the world, well ahead of the EU-15 figure of EUR 11.5 billion. The main reason for this difference was the increased borrowing position of the United Kingdom, where in 2000 the net borrowing figure reached EUR 23.3 billion. France and Italy produced net lending figures throughout the period under review (1996–99), though diminishing in size. Germany, on the other hand, consistently generated borrowing positions, amounting to EUR 11.1 billion in 2000 (see Table 1.6.6).

Table 1.6.6. Net lending and borrowing (billion EUR, current prices)

	1996	1997	1998	1999	2000
EU-15	76.7	122.5	82.7	43.0	11.5
EUR-11	69.4	102.5	75.1	45.3	24.6
B	9.8	10.1	8.5	8.0	8.0
DK	2.1	0.7	− 1.4	4.6	2.7
D	− 7.5	− 1.8	− 3.1	− 16.0	− 11.1
EL	− 1.0	− 0.6	0.2	:	:
E	5.8	7.9	2.6	− 6.4	− 13.4
F	11.0	31.5	30.5	29.7	20.5
IRL	2.0	2.4	1.6	0.7	:
I	31.2	31.5	21.9	13.4	3.6
L	:	:	:	:	:
NL	15.8	19.2	13.6	19.9	20.8
A	− 4.2	− 4.2	− 4.4	− 5.4	− 5.2
P	− 1.2	− 2.9	− 4.9	− 7.3	− 10.3
FIN	3.9	6.2	6.1	7.7	10.4
S	6.1	8.2	8.1	6.0	7.6
UK	0.2	10.7	0.6	− 13.8	− 23.3

NB: Eurostat estimation for Ireland. For Luxembourg, no ESA 95 data are available. The ESA 79 net lending/borrowing had been EUR 3.5 billion in 1997.
Source: Eurostat.

Apart from the United Kingdom and Germany — which have just been mentioned — Spain, Austria and Portugal were the other Member States known to be in a position of net borrowing in 2000, while besides France, the Netherlands, Finland, Belgium and Sweden were important net lenders.

Figure 1.6.4. Net lending/borrowing

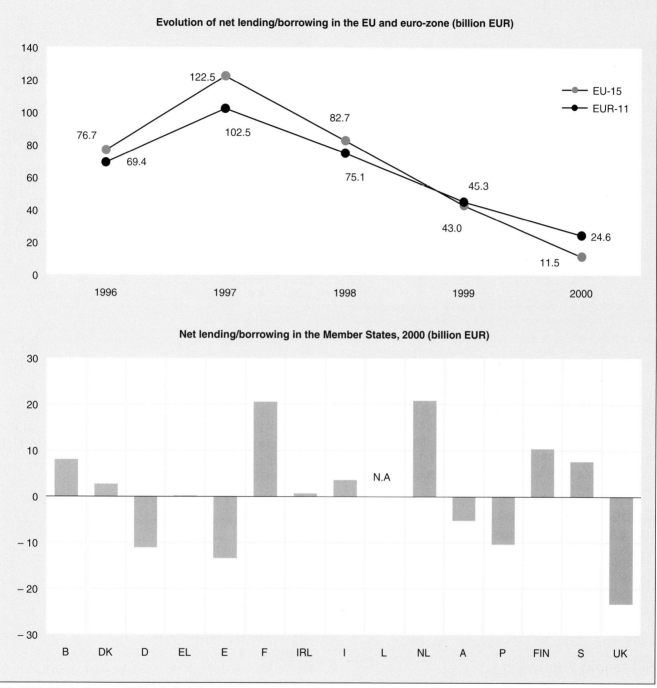

NB: 1998 data for Greece, 1999 data for Ireland.
Source: Eurostat.

1.7. The economic situation in the regions

Per capita GDP of EU regions in 1998

Per capita gross domestic product at market prices, one of the key indicators for the structural and regional policies of the EU, showed a larger span in 1998 than in 1997. It varied in 1998 between 8 452 PPS in the Greek region of Ipeiros and 49 202 in Inner London. The figures thus ranged from 43 % to 243 % of the overall EU average (PPS 20 213).

Table 1.7.1 shows that in 1998 these two regions differed markedly from the other regions with high and low per capita GDP values. The figure for Hamburg, the region with the second highest value, was 57 percentage points below the figure for Inner London. The other regions with relatively high values also lie more or less in the centre of the EU. The situation is quite different for the regions with the lowest per capita GDP figures. They are either in the Mediterranean area — five of them in Greece, one each in Portugal and Spain — or belong to the French Overseas Departments (three regions).

It is striking that all the regions with high per capita GDP values in PPS are relatively small. A key underlying factor here is net commuter inflow, which takes regional production activity beyond the level possible with working residents alone. Table 1.7.1 also shows the per capita GDP values (as a percentage of the EU average) for 1997.

Comparison between the 1995 and 1998 per capita GDP values

A comparison of the situation in 1995 and 1998 highlights distinct shifts between the regions of the European Union. In 91 out of the 211 regions for which basically comparable data are available, per capita GDP as a percentage of the EU average fell between 1995 and 1998. In 34 regions the figure hardly changed (range between 1.0 and − 1.0 percentage points). In 86 regions, however, it rose.

The sharpest relative rise in the reference period occurred in the Finnish region of Åland, where per capita GDP rose over this period by more than 32 percentage points from 90 % to 122 % of the EU average. Table 1.7.2 shows further regions that recorded particularly sharp increases or decreases in per capita GDP in PPS. It is notable that the largest number of particularly strong rises was recorded in the United Kingdom (5 regions). The other members of the top 10 are located in Finland (2 regions), Ireland (2 regions) and in the Netherlands (1 region). As regards the regions with the strongest falls, there are six French, two Italian, one German and 1 Swedish region in this group. However,

Table 1.7.1. The regions of the EU with the highest/lowest per capita GDP in PPS, EU-15 = 100

Regions	1997	1998
Inner London	233	243
Hamburg	197	186
Luxembourg (Grand Duchy)	174	174
Région Bruxelles-Capitale	169	169
Wien	164	163
Oberbayern	165	161
Darmstadt	165	154
Île de France	153	152
Bremen	145	144
Utrecht	126	142
EU-15 = 100	**100**	**100**
Ionia Nisia	60	56
Anatoliki Makedonia, Thraki	60	55
Guyane	n/a	53
Peloponissos	57	53
Dytiki Ellada	56	53
Guadeloupe	n/a	52
Acores	51	52
Extremadura	55	50
Réunion	n/a	50
Ipeiros	43	42

Source: Eurostat.

Table 1.7.2. The regions of the EU with the highest increase and decrease in percentage points of the per capita GDP in PPS relative to EU-15 per capita GDP in PPS 1995 – 98

Regions	Relative increase/ decrease
Åland	32.2
Hampshire and Isle of Wight	17.5
Southern and eastern	16.8
Uusimaa	14.4
Inner London	13.3
Berkshire, Buckinghamshire and Oxfordshire	13.1
Surrey, East and West Sussex	12.6
Utrecht	11.7
Bedfordshire and Hertfordshire	9.6
Border, Midland and Western	9.0
EU-15	**0.0**
Centre (F)	− 5.6
Provence-Alpes-Côte d'Azur	− 5.6
Friuli-Venezia Giulia	− 5.7
Alsace	− 5.9
Lorraine	− 5.9
Haute-Normandie	− 6.2
Västsverige	− 7.9
Île de France	− 8.7
Berlin	− 9.8
Valle d'Aosta	− 10.3

Source: Eurostat.

the relative changes reflect not only developments within the production activities but also changes in the size and structure of the population and in the purchasing power parities.

Regional unemployment in 2000

The unemployment rate in the European Union, i.e. the ratio of unemployed persons to the total economically active population, stood at 8.4 % in April 2000. Taking only the NUTS 2 regions into consideration, the unemployment rate varied between 1.7 % in the Finnish region of Åland and 33.1 % in the French region of Réunion. Related in each case to 100 members of the economically active population, Réunion thus had around 19 times more jobless people than the region of Åland.

Of the 211 regions under consideration, as many as 50 achieved an unemployment rate in April 2000 of at most 4.2 % — lower than half the EU average. These 50 NUTS-2 regions were spread over 11 Member States, with Greece, Spain and France being the only countries where no NUTS-2 region had an unemployment rate of less than or equal to 4.2 %. This was also the case for Denmark. At the other end of the scale were 17 regions in Italy, Spain, France and Germany where the unemployment rate stood at more than 16.8 % and

was thus at least double as high again as the overall European Union average.

Change in the unemployment rate from 1995 to 2000

From April 1995 to April 2000, the unemployment rate at EU level fell by 2.3 percentage points. Some 160 of the 196 regions that could be studied because data are available registered a decrease — of up to 11.2 percentage points in the case of Cataluña (E). As many as 31 regions recorded a distinct increase, reaching 5.6 percentage points in the Greek region of Notio Aigaio. A total of five regions remained unchanged.

Table 1.7.4 shows that of the 10 regions featuring the sharpest fall in the unemployment rate between April 1995 and April 2000, no fewer than nine are in Spain. The remaining one is in Ireland. Moreover, all the regions studied in Belgium, Spain, Ireland, the Netherlands, Portugal, Finland and Sweden recorded a fall in the rate of unemployment over the period under review.

As regards the regions with the largest increases in unemployment rates between 1995 and 2000, there are seven regions in Greece, two in Italy and one in Germany.

Table 1.7.3. The regions of the EU with the highest/lowest unemployment rates in April 2000 (as a %)

Regions	Unemployment rate
Åland	1.7
Centro (P)	1.8
Berkshire, Buckinghamshire and Oxfordshire	1.9
Utrecht	2.1
Noord-Brabant	2.2
Madeira	2.3
Luxembourg (Grand Duchy)	2.4
Oberösterreich	2.6
Surrey, East and West Sussex	2.6
Gelderland	2.6
Guyane	22.0
Campania	23.6
Sicilia	24.2
Extremadura	24.8
Andalucia	25.3
Ceuta y Melilla	25.5
Guadeloupe	26.1
Martinique	27.7
Calabria	27.7
Réunion	33.1

Source: Eurostat.

Table 1.7.4. The regions in the EU with the highest increase and decrease of unemployment rates from 1995 to 2000, (in percentage points)

Regions	Decrease/Increase
Cataluña	– 11.2
País Vasco	– 10.9
Comunidad Valenciana	– 10.7
Murcia	– 10.6
Canarias	– 9.5
Baleares	– 9.2
Madrid	– 9.1
Aragón	– 9.0
Southern and eastern	– 8.8
Andalucía	– 8.5
EU-15	– 2.3
Sicilia	2.2
Berlin	2.5
Voreio Aigaio	2.5
Kriti	2.5
Peloponnisos	3.3
Ipeiros	3.3
Sterea Ellada	4.4
Thessalia	4.7
Calabria	5.0
Notio Aigaio	5.6

Source: Eurostat.

2. The Union in the international framework

2.1. The EU in the world

In 2000, most of the world's economies experienced growth above the average of the last five years (see Table 2.1.1). The US economy continued to expand fast after having grown vigorously also during the four preceding years: GDP rose by an annual rate of 5.0 %. Domestic demand expanded strongly: + 8.8 % for investment, + 5.3 % for private consumption and + 2.0 % for government consumption. In view of its large share of GDP, private consumption was the principal driving force behind GDP growth, accounting for about 71 % of the total 5.0 % rate (see Table 2.1.2).

Canada also maintained robust growth, with a 2000 annual rate of 4.7 %. Investment recorded a very strong increase with a 11.2 % rate, and again contributed to more than half of GDP growth (see Table 2.1.2). Private consumption increased by 4.0 % and government consumption by 2.4 %.

The Japanese economy fared somewhat better than in the previous year. Still, 2000 GDP growth, was at 1.5 % behind that of most other major economies. As in the previous year, government consumption was the most buoyant component with an annual growth rate of 3.6 %. Private consumption grew only slightly at an annual rate of 0.5 %, and investment showed a modest 0.6 % rise, which nevertheless meant an important improvement compared to the negative growth recorded in the two preceding years.

Among the G7 countries, differences in economic growth have somewhat diminished. Still, the overall picture remains the same as in the years before: the United States and Canada accounted for the strongest growth, Japan is slowly recovering, and the European Union ([1]) is recording healthy growth between these two extremes.

In Asia, the NICs ([2]) only slightly accelerated compared to the 1999 growth rate, which had already been above average. The group of the four most developed Asian countries achieved GDP growth of + 8.2 %. Among these the strongest acceleration and the highest overall growth was recorded in Hong Kong, where real GDP grew by 10.5 %, up 7.4 percentage points from 1999. For Singapore, too, the economy accelerated strongly by 4.0 percentage points to 9.9 %. In South Korea, GDP slowed down, but still grew by 8.8 %. In Taiwan, the growth rate increased only moderately to

Table 2.1.1. Real GDP growth rates (as a %)

	1999	2000	Average 1996/2000
EU-15	2.5	3.3	2.6
EUR-11	2.5	3.4	2.5
US	4.2	5.0	4.3
Canada	4.5	4.7	3.7
JP	0.8	1.5	1.3
Australia	4.7	3.8	4.4
Russia	3.2	7.5	0.6
Latin America	0.2	4.1	3.1
Argentina	− 3.4	− 0.5	2.6
Brazil	0.8	4.2	2.2
Chile	− 1.1	5.4	4.6
Mexico	3.8	6.9	5.5
NICs Asia	7.9	8.2	5.1
Hong Kong	3.1	10.5	3.4
Taiwan	5.4	6.0	5.8
South Korea	10.9	8.8	4.8
Singapore	5.9	9.9	6.3
Malaysia	5.8	8.5	4.6
Philippines	3.3	3.9	3.5
Thailand	4.2	4.3	0.2
China	7.1	8.0	8.3
India	6.6	6.4	6.2
Middle East	0.8	5.4	4.0
Israel	2.3	6.0	3.8
Africa	2.3	3.0	3.4
South Africa	1.9	3.2	2.5

Source: IMF, Eurostat.

now + 6.0 %. With the exception of Singapore, investment was the fastest growing component of domestic demand, with private consumption also making major contributions to GDP growth. Singapore was noticeable for a relatively high importance of government consumption. Among the other south-east Asian countries, Malaysia was also seen to speed up economic growth to 8.5 %, compared to 5.8 % in 1999. Results in Thailand (+ 4.3 %) and the Philippines (+ 3.9 %) were not as strong, but still higher than in 1999. Among these three, the Philippines stand out for a negative growth contribution of investment, which, once again, figured prominently in Malaysia.

With a growth of 8.0 % in 2000, China stepped up the pace of economic expansion, which had been fast all

---

([1]) The EU countries which are also G7 countries are Germany, France, Italy and the United Kingdom.

([2]) "NIC" stands for "newly industrialised countries". In Asia, Hong Kong, Taiwan, South Korea and Singapore are referred to as "NICs Asia".

the preceding years, though with growth rates declining gradually. Government consumption proved to be the fastest growing component of domestic demand, still private consumption contributed stronger to economic growth. For India, a small decrease in the annual growth rate was observed, which turned out to be 6.4 % in 2000. Private consumption and investment grew at almost identical speed, resulting in the former being the largest contributor to overall growth. Government consumption was a far less important growth contributor.

The countries of Latin America fared much better than in 1999: overall GDP growth rose from near stagnation by almost four percentage points to 4.1 % in 2000. Argentina (– 0.5 %) continued to record a fall in output, but much less pronounced than in the previous year. Brazil (+ 4.2 %), Chile (+ 5.4 %) and Mexico (+ 6.9 %) all saw healthy growth above that of 1999. The negative result for Argentina was due mainly to an almost stagnating private consumption coinciding with recessing

investment. For the other countries mentioned, private consumption was the main contributor to economic growth, with investments adding to the boost.

In order to give a more detailed picture of economic results in 2000, in addition to Table 2.1.1, illustrating GDP growth, Table 2.1.2 indicates the growth rates of the main components (^{3}) of GDP, their contribution to overall GDP growth and their share of GDP.

In order to compare different countries and regions, the population and GDP have been selected to give an indication of size, whilst per capita GDP gives a measure of wealth (see Figure 2.1.1).

When compared with other major countries and regions, the population of the EU (6.2 %) as a share of the world's is well above that of the United States (4.6 %) and nearly three times Japan's (2.1 %). In all, it is roughly equivalent to half the total population of Africa and less than a third of China's.

Figure 2.1.1. Size of world's main economies (as a % of world total)

	GDP	Population	GDP per head (world = 100)
EU-15	20.0	6.2	320
EUR-11	16.0	5.0	321
United States	22.0	4.6	478
Japan	7.3	2.1	348
Russian Federation	2.5	2.5	100
Latin America	8.4	8.5	99
NICs Asia	3.4	1.3	262
China	11.6	21.1	55
India	4.6	16.6	28
Africa	3.2	12.2	26

NB: X-axis shows the GDP (in PPS) shares in total for the world while the Y-axis indicates the share in world population. The size of the bubbles is proportional to GDP per capita, in PPS, compared to the world average.
Source: Eurostat, IWF, World Bank.

(^{3}) The external balance was not included, since an extensive description of world trade is given in Section 2.3.

Table 2.1.2. GDP main components, 2000

	Growth rates (as a %)			Contribution to GDP growth (as a % of GDP growth rate)			Structure (as a % of GDP)		
	PC	GC	I	PC	GC	I	PC	GC	I
EU-15	2.7	1.9	4.4	48	11	28	58	20	21
EUR-11	2.6	2.0	4.4	43	12	28	57	20	21
US	5.3	2.0	8.8	71	5	39	68	14	21
Canada	4.0	2.4	11.2	48	9	51	56	18	20
JP	0.5	3.6	0.6	17	37	11	56	17	26
Australia	3.5	4.9	1.4	54	23	9	59	18	23
Russian Federation	− 3.5	0.9	2.4	− 118	4	12	53	14	16
Argentina	0.1	− 0.4	− 8.3	− 10	10	340	70	13	19
Brazil	7.2	1.6	5.4	105	7	25	62	19	19
Chile	4.1	3.5	4.3	52	3	21	65	12	21
Mexico	9.3	5.5	10.4	87	8	31	68	10	21
Hong Kong	5.4	2.1	8.8	30	2	24	60	10	26
Taiwan	5.2	1.6	7.3	52	4	33	:	:	:
South Korea	7.5	2.5	10.6	42	2	34	56	10	28
Singapore	6.2	9.3	7.6	25	10	28	39	10	33
Malaysia	20.2	18.0	92.1	112	33	272	42	11	22
Philippines	3.5	0.2	− 1.6	68	0	− 9	67	13	19
Thailand	4.7	6.9	8.1	60	15	40	56	11	21
China	13.8	34.4	− 0.3	104	53	− 1	47	13	36
India	6.9	4.7	7.0	67	9	23	68	12	22
Israel	5.7	2.7	− 1.2	66	11	− 6	60	29	20
South Africa	3.2	− 2.5	1.4	70	− 15	9	63	19	15

NB: PC: private consumption; GC: government consumption; I: investment that is, gross fixed capital formation.
Source: Eurostat, WEFA, World Bank.

If we consider its economic weight in the world, the EU's share of world GDP (20.0 %) is more than three times its share of the population. Though their share of world population is higher, the GDP generated in the 15 European countries is somewhat lower than that produced in the United States (22.0 %), but it is more than twice Japan's (7.3 %). Compared with some less well-off countries, although in population terms the imbalance is great, the EU's GDP is roughly twice that of China, four times that of India and more than six times the GDP produced on the African continent.

2.2. GDP of the candidate countries

Annual GDP growth

Candidate countries rediscover booming growth

This section sets out the most important national accounts data of the candidate countries for membership of the European Union (CCs). The candidate countries are Bulgaria, Cyprus, the Czech Republic, Estonia, Hungary, Latvia, Lithuania, Malta, Poland, Romania, the Slovak Republic, Slovenia and Turkey.

After stagnant economic growth in 1999, the candidate countries, as a combined group of 13 nations, enjoyed a return to encouraging economic growth of 5 % in 2000, bettering the 3.3 % seen in EU-15, as shown in Table 2.2.1, bettering the 3.3 % seen in EU-15. Turkey blazed the way, with GDP higher than the previous year by 7.2 %, though 1999 had been a disastrous year because of the August earthquake. All CCs benefited from positive growth in 2000, with Latvia and Estonia recording high rates of 6.6 % and 6.4 % respectively. Romania posted the weakest growth of the CCs, with 1.6 %, though this was higher than in the previous year and continued the recovery initiated in 1998.

Poland and Slovenia have displayed the most stable growth rates over the seven-year period with minimum/maximum ranges of 3.8 to 7.0 % and 2.8 to 5.3 % respectively.

Figure 2.2.1. Annual GDP growth rates (as a %)

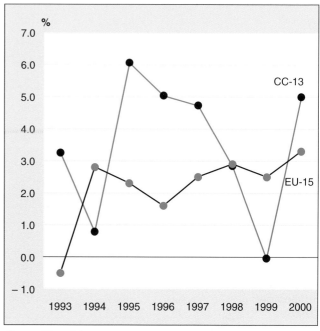

Source: Eurostat.

Table 2.2.1. GDP growth rates, percentage change on previous year

	1993	1994	1995	1996	1997	1998	1999	2000
Bulgaria (BG)	– 1.5	1.8	2.9	– 10.1	– 7.0	3.5	2.4	5.8
Cyprus (CY)	0.7	5.9	6.1	1.9	2.5	5.0	4.5	4.8
Czech Republic (CZ)	0.1	2.2	5.9	4.8	– 1.0	– 2.2	– 0.8	3.1
Estonia (EE)	– 9.0	– 2.0	4.3	3.9	10.6	4.7	– 1.1	6.4
Hungary (HU)	– 0.6	2.9	1.5	1.3	4.6	4.9	4.2	5.2
Latvia (LV)	– 14.9	0.6	– 0.8	3.3	8.6	3.9	1.1	6.6
Lithuania (LT)	– 16.2	– 9.8	3.3	4.7	7.3	5.1	– 3.9	3.3
Malta (MT)	4.5	5.7	6.2	4.0	4.9	3.4	4.0	4.7
Poland (PL)	3.8	5.8	7.0	6.0	6.8	4.8	4.1	4.0
Romania (RO)	1.5	3.9	7.1	3.9	– 6.1	– 4.8	– 2.3	1.6
Slovak Republic (SK)	– 3.7	11.0	6.7	6.2	6.2	4.1	1.9	2.2
Slovenia (SI)	2.8	5.3	4.1	3.5	4.6	3.8	5.2	4.6
Turkey (TR)	8.4	– 5.5	7.2	7.0	7.5	3.1	– 4.7	7.2
Total (CC-13)	**3.2**	**0.8**	**6.1**	**5.0**	**4.7**	**2.8**	**0.0**	**5.0**
EU-15 (1)	**– 0.5**	**2.8**	**2.3**	**1.6**	**2.5**	**2.9**	**2.5**	**3.3**
EU-minimum (1)	– 1.6 EL	2.0 EL	1.6 A	0.8 D	1.3 A	1.8 I	1.6 D	2.9 I
EU-maximum (1)	2.7 IRL	5.8 IRL	9.7 IRL	7.7 IRL	10.7 IRL	8.6 IRL	9.8 IRL	10.6 IRL

(1) Based on ESA 79 up to 1995, ESA 95 from 1996 onwards.
Source: Eurostat.

GDP in euro

Total CC-13 GDP increasing in comparison to the EU-15 area

In simple euro terms, the CC-13, even with the inclusion of relatively large countries such as Poland and Turkey, amounts to a very small economic area compared to the European Union. In 2000, however, it did jump to 7.3 % of the EU, compared to 6.6 % in 1999.

Like the EU Member States, the candidate countries' economies are very diverse in size, ranging from EUR 3.9 billion in Malta to EUR 217.4 billion in Turkey. The Maltese economy, in euro terms, is five times smaller than that of Luxembourg, the smallest EU Member State. Adding together the six smallest CC GDPs still gives a total of only EUR 51.7 billion, barely 0.6 % of the EU-15 total.

CCs register slight improvements in euro GDP per head, compared to the EU

The CCs display equally wide-ranging figures in terms of "GDP per head", from EUR 1 600 in Bulgaria to EUR 14 200 in Cyprus. Most of the CCs are far below those of the EU but this is partly a symptom of higher price levels in the EU. More meaningful comparisons can be made by expressing figures in purchasing power standards (PPS) instead of euro, as shown in the following section.

GDP in real terms

Cyprus and Slovenia maintain a strong position

Figure 2.2.2 summarises the current position of the CCs in 2000 using the three key indicators of "annual

Table 2.2.2. GDP at current prices and exchange rates in billion EUR

	1996	1997	1998	1999	2000
BG	7.8	9.0	11.0	11.6	13.0
CY	7.0	7.5	8.1	8.7	9.5
CZ	45.5	46.8	50.4	49.7	53.7
EE	3.4	4.1	4.7	4.8	5.4
HU	35.6	40.4	41.9	45.1	49.5
LV	4.0	5.0	5.4	6.4	7.7
LT	6.2	8.5	9.6	10.0	12.2
MT	2.6	2.9	3.1	3.4	3.9
PL	113.3	127.1	141.3	145.5	171.0
RO	27.8	31.2	37.2	33.0	40.0
SK	15.6	18.0	19.0	18.5	20.9
SI	14.9	16.1	17.5	18.8	19.5
TR	143.1	167.8	177.8	173.1	217.4
CC-13	426.8	484.2	526.9	528.6	623.8
EU-15	6 911.5	7 280.4	7 621.2	8 003.8	8 510.2
% of EU-15	6.2	6.7	6.9	6.6	7.3
EU-15 min.	14.3	15.4	16.4	18.1	20.5
	L	L	L	L	L

Source: Eurostat.

growth", "GDP per head in PPS" and "economic size" (total GDP in PPS).

The most widely - used indicator of economic prosperity, GDP per head, is displayed on the horizontal axis and shows Cyprus and Slovenia ahead of the CC pack. With growth of almost 5 % in 2000, consolidating

Table 2.2.3. GDP per head at current prices and exchange rates

	EUR					EU-15 = 100				
	1996	1997	1998	1999	2000	1996	1997	1998	1999	2000
BG	900	1 100	1 300	1 400	1 600	5	6	7	7	7
CY	10 800	11 500	12 300	13 000	14 200	59	59	61	61	63
CZ	4 400	4 500	4 900	4 800	5 200	24	23	24	23	23
EE	2 300	2 800	3 200	3 300	3 800	13	14	16	16	17
HU	3 500	4 000	4 100	4 500	4 900	19	20	20	21	22
LV	1 600	2 000	2 200	2 700	3 300	9	10	11	13	15
LT	1 700	2 300	2 600	2 700	3 300	9	12	13	13	15
MT	6 900	7 700	8 100	8 800	9 900	37	40	40	42	44
PL	2 900	3 300	3 700	3 800	4 400	16	17	18	18	20
RO	1 200	1 400	1 700	1 500	1 800	7	7	8	7	8
SK	2 900	3 300	3 500	3 400	3 900	16	17	17	16	17
SI	7 500	8 100	8 800	9 400	9 800	40	42	43	45	44
TR	2 300	2 700	2 800	2 700	3 200	12	14	14	13	14
CC-13	2 500	2 900	3 100	3 100	3 600	14	15	15	15	16

NB: For the calculation of per capita GDP, the data for the total population is taken from the national accounts; it may be different from that obtained via demographic statistics.
Source: Eurostat.

healthy growth rates throughout the 1990s, they are positioned near the advantageous top-right-hand portion of the graph.

Romania and Lithuania find themselves in a less desirable position, with low GDP per head and relatively modest growth. Bulgaria has the lowest GDP per head, at 24 % of the EU-average, but achieved impressive growth of 5.8 % in 2000.

Candidate countries smaller than most Member States, in real terms

When making comparisons between the GDP of different countries, it is better to express figures in an artificial currency unit called PPS (purchasing power standard). This makes allowances for the varying price levels in different countries and makes the comparisons of GDP, both in absolute terms and "per head", more meaningful.

Table 2.2.4 shows that the CC-13 group is not as small compared to EU-15 as it appeared in euro terms (see Table 2.2.2). It amounts to 16.0 % of the EU total in 2000, compared to just 7.3 % when using the euro figures.

With certain exceptions, most of the candidate countries have small economies compared to the EU Member States. Turkey and Poland, on the other hand, appear in sixth and eighth place in a league table of the 28 Member States and candidate countries. All but four of the candidate countries are larger than Luxembourg.

Table 2.2.4. GDP at current prices in billion PPS

	1996	1997	1998	1999	2000
D	1 660.6	1 719.8	1 770.6	1 845.8	1 939.7
UK	1 068.8	1 165.7	1 231.0	1 297.8	1 391.7
F	1 122.0	1 149.8	1 204.0	1 264.8	1 349.2
I	1 096.0	1 138.6	1 208.3	1 257.1	1 320.5
E	576.2	609.2	631.8	673.5	719.7
TR	346.5	385.1	402.8	392.6	433.3
NL	306.7	340.6	367.2	388.1	418.7
PL	253.9	280.3	298.2	317.2	337.9
B	207.9	219.3	228.9	238.9	255.1
S	165.8	175.5	182.2	191.9	203.5
A	166.3	174.1	179.5	188.8	200.3
P	129.7	143.7	147.2	156.4	166.8
EL	129.3	134.2	142.0	150.6	160.8
DK	115.9	123.0	128.4	134.5	144.4
CZ	123.5	126.3	125.3	127.2	135.1
RO	138.0	134.0	129.4	129.4	135.4
FIN	90.4	99.1	105.8	110.7	120.1
HU	87.6	94.6	100.7	108.0	117.0
IRL	63.0	73.6	79.3	88.4	100.8
SK	45.8	50.3	53.1	55.4	58.3
BG	38.4	36.9	38.8	40.6	44.3
SI	24.2	26.2	27.6	29.7	32.0
LT	19.6	21.8	23.2	22.8	24.3
L	13.1	14.3	15.1	16.7	18.9
LV	11.6	13.0	13.7	14.2	15.6
CY	9.5	10.1	10.8	11.6	12.4
EE	9.0	10.3	10.9	11.0	12.1
MT	3.6	3.9	4.0	4.3	4.6
CC-13 ([1])	1 111.3	1 192.8	1 238.4	1 264.1	1 362.2
EU-15	6 911.5	7 280.4	7 621.2	8 003.8	8 510.2
% of EU-15	16.1	16.4	16.2	15.8	16.0

([1]) Not including Malta.
Source: Eurostat, OECD, ÖSTAT.

Figure 2.2.2. Growth, size of GDP and GDP per head (as a % of EU average), in PPS, in 2000

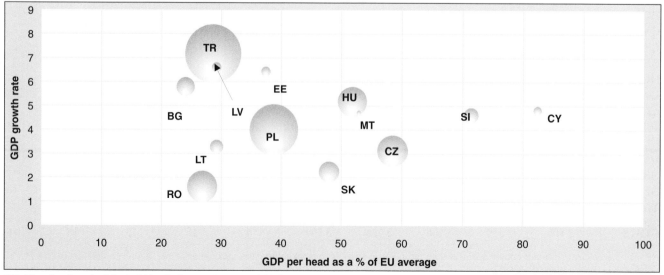

NB: The size (area) of the bubbles indicates the level of GDP in PPS.
Source: Eurostat.

Cyprus and Slovenia closest to EU in real GDP per head

Table 2.2.5 shows Cyprus and Slovenia maintaining their position as leading CCs in terms of GDP per head in PPS (82 % and 71 % of EU-average, respectively), both above the EU minimum, Greece (68 %), and with Cyprus also exceeding Spain and Portugal.

For the first time, Malta is able to supply data in PPS, and take fourth place in the ranking of candidate countries.

Most of the CCs' figures have remained fairly constant compared to the EU-15 average between 1996 and 2000. The greatest changes can be seen in Hungary whose index has increased from 46 % to 52 %, and the Czech Republic who have seen their comparative percentage slashed from 65 % to 58 % of the EU-15 figure. Romania's GDP per head also deteriorated further, from 33 % in 1996 to just 27 % in 2000.

Table 2.2.5. GDP per head at current prices in PPS

	In PPS					EU-15 = 100				
	1996	1997	1998	1999	2000	1996	1997	1998	1999	2000
L	31 400	33 700	35 200	38 300	42 900	170	174	173	181	190
DK	22 100	23 300	24 200	25 300	27 100	119	120	119	119	120
IRL	17 400	20 100	21 400	23 600	26 600	94	104	105	111	118
NL	19 800	21 800	23 400	24 500	26 300	107	112	115	116	117
B	20 500	21 500	22 400	23 400	24 900	111	111	110	110	111
A	20 600	21 600	22 200	23 300	24 700	111	111	109	110	110
D	20 300	21 000	21 600	22 500	23 600	110	108	106	106	105
UK	18 200	19 800	20 800	21 800	23 300	98	102	102	103	104
FIN	17 600	19 300	20 500	21 400	23 200	95	99	101	101	103
S	18 800	19 800	20 600	21 700	23 000	102	102	101	102	102
I	19 100	19 800	21 000	21 800	22 900	103	102	103	103	102
F	18 800	19 200	20 100	21 000	22 300	102	99	99	99	99
CY	14 700	15 400	16 300	17 500	18 500	79	79	80	82	82
E	14 700	15 500	16 000	17 100	18 200	79	80	79	81	81
P	13 100	14 500	14 800	15 700	16 600	71	75	73	74	74
SI	12 200	13 200	13 900	15 000	16 100	66	68	69	71	71
EL	12 300	12 800	13 500	14 300	15 300	66	66	67	67	68
CZ	12 000	12 300	12 200	12 400	13 200	65	63	60	58	58
MT	9 400	10 100	10 500	11 100	11 900	51	52	52	52	53
HU	8 600	9 300	10 000	10 700	11 700	46	48	49	51	52
SK	8 500	9 300	9 800	10 300	10 800	46	48	49	48	48
PL	6 600	7 300	7 700	8 200	8 700	36	37	38	39	39
EE	6 100	7 100	7 500	7 700	8 400	33	36	37	36	37
LT	5 300	5 900	6 300	6 200	6 600	29	30	31	29	29
LV	4 700	5 300	5 600	5 900	6 600	25	27	28	28	29
TR	5 500	6 200	6 300	6 100	6 400	30	32	31	29	29
RO	6 100	5 900	5 800	5 800	6 000	33	31	28	27	27
BG	4 600	4 400	4 700	4 900	5 400	25	23	23	23	24
CC-13	6 600	7 100	7 300	7 400	7 900	36	36	36	35	35
EU-15	18 500	19 400	20 300	21 200	22 500	100	100	100	100	100

NB: For the calculation of per capita GDP, the data for the total population is taken from the national accounts: it may be different from that obtained via demographic statistics.
Source: Eurostat, OECD, ÖSTAT.

GDP main aggregates

Expenditure components

In 2000, the share of GDP accounted for by final consumption of households and NPISH varied amongst the CCs from 51.5 % in Hungary to 73.9 % in Romania, according to Table 2.2.6.

EU-15 figures, however, are even more wide-ranging, from 41.0 % in Luxembourg to 70.5 % in Greece. There is a general tendency for the poorer countries (low GDP per head) to use a higher share of their GDP for this component, in order to satisfy basic needs from limited incomes.

Concerning final consumption of general government, CC figures range from just 12.5 % in Romania to 22.2 % in Estonia. Most of the CCs fall within the EU range, however, which begins with 13.3 % in Ireland and ends with the high Scandinavian rates of 24.7 % and 26.3 % in Denmark and Sweden.

The Slovak Republic also displays the highest value of gross fixed capital formation, as a % of GDP, with 30.0 %, though this is declining after the high peak of 38.0 % in 1998. CC investment rates are generally higher than those in the EU, though comparable with the levels seen in Greece, Ireland, Portugal and Spain.

In 2000, Malta continued to be the heaviest trader, relative to their economic size. In fact, exports grew from 87.0 % of their GDP in 1996 to 103.8 % in 2000. Imports also grew, by 13 percentage points from 100.3 % to 113.5 %. Estonia also saw trade increase rapidly over the four-year period, and slashed their trade deficit (in terms of GDP) from 11.5 % to 4.3 %. No CC recorded a positive trade balance in 2000, though seven countries did manage to reduce their trade deficits between 1996 and 2000.

CCs switch from agricultural production to service activities

Table 2.2.7 and Figure 2.2.4 show GVA broken down into the main branches for 1996 and 2000. Production in the CC-13 as a whole has become slightly less dominated by agriculture (10.1 % in 1996 to 8.2 % in 2000) and more directed towards services. Romania has seen the greatest shift in this direction with agriculture dropping from 20.1 % to 12.6 % of GVA and services rocketing from 38.3 % to 51.5 %. This pattern of change is also evident in Latvia and Lithuania, though the agriculture branch in these countries was already much smaller, and services larger.

Table 2.2.6. Main GDP components (as a % of total GDP)

| | Final consumption | | | | | | | | | | | | | | | | | |
| | of house- holds and NPISH | | | of general government | | | GFCF | | | Exports | | | Imports | | | External trade balance | | |
	96	98	00	96	98	00	96	98	00	96	98	00	96	97	00	96	98	00
BG	76.6	72.9	72.2	11.9	15.1	17.6	13.6	13.2	16.2	62.9	48.0	58.5	59.8	50.9	64.1	3.1	− 2.9	− 5.6
CY	83.0	86.8	84.3 (1)	:	:	:	22.3	20.8	18.7 (2)	46.9	43.5	46.1	53.1	51.1	50.3	− 6.2	− 7.5	− 4.2
CZ	52.2	52.9	53.9	19.9	19.5	19.5	31.9	28.1	27.2	52.5	59.7	73.3	58.9	61.0	77.1	− 6.4	− 1.3	− 3.8
EE	60.7	59.5	58.6	24.1	21.8	22.2	26.7	29.7	23.5	67.1	79.9	96.5	78.6	90.4	100.8	−11.5	−10.5	− 4.3
HU	51.9	50.8	51.5	22.0	21.7	22.0	21.4	23.6	24.6	38.9	50.6	62.5	39.9	52.7	66.7	− 1.1	− 2.1	− 4.1
LV	67.6	64.5	62.5	21.6	21.4	18.9	18.1	27.3	24.6	50.9	51.3	45.8	59.0	64.8	54.3	− 8.1	−13.5	− 8.5
LT	66.4	63.1	64.3	18.9	24.4	21.5	23.0	24.3	18.8	53.4	47.2	45.5	63.2	59.1	51.9	− 9.8	−11.9	− 6.4
MT	63.7	62.1	63.7	21.6	19.7	18.7	28.7	24.5	26.3	87.0	87.7	103.8	100.3	93.2	113.5	−13.2	− 5.6	− 9.7
PL	63.3	63.6	65.0	16.4	15.4	15.4	20.7	25.1	25.3	24.3	28.2	31.2	25.8	33.4	38.1	− 1.6	− 5.2	− 6.9
RO	69.5	76.0	73.9	13.1	14.2	12.5	23.0	18.3	18.5	28.1	23.5	34.1	36.6	31.5	39.9	− 8.4	− 8.1	− 5.8
SK	52.6	53.3	53.4	21.8	21.5	19.0	34.2	38.0	30.0	55.2	61.2	73.5	66.8	72.2	76.0	−11.6	−11.0	− 2.5
SI	61.5	55.7	54.9	20.1	20.3	20.8	22.5	24.6	26.7	55.8	56.6	59.1	56.8	58.2	62.7	− 1.0	− 1.5	− 3.6
TR	69.3	67.5	69.8	11.9	12.4	13.7	25.8	24.0	21.7	22.2	23.8	23.4	28.7	27.2	30.6	− 6.5	− 3.5	− 7.2
CC-13	63.5	63.3	64.6	16.0	16.0	16.1	24.4	24.6	23.5	32.8	35.3	39.3	37.6	39.9	45.4	− 4.8	− 4.6	− 6.1
EU-15	57.7	57.9	58.2	20.7	19.9	19.8	19.6	19.8	20.6	30.1	32.1	35.6	28.1	30.4	34.9	2.0	1.7	0.7

(1) Total final consumption.

(2) Gross capital formation.

Source: Eurostat.

Figure 2.2.3. GDP per head, in thousands of PPS, 2000

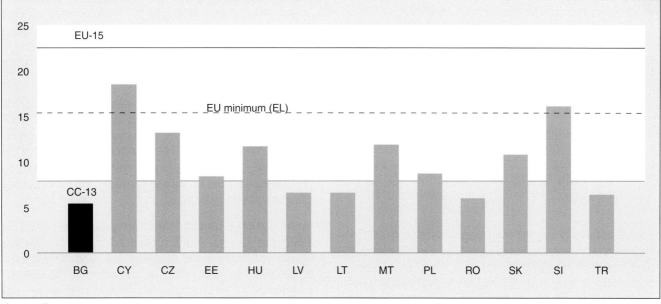

Source: Eurostat.

At the same time there are general slight declines for industry and construction in most of the candidate countries.

In 2000, Bulgaria had the largest agricultural branch (14.5 %), and Malta the smallest, relative to GDP (2.3 %). Cyprus had the biggest services branch (76.3 %), and Turkey the smallest (51.2 %).

Table 2.2.7. Gross value added by branch (as a % of the total)

	Agriculture, fishing		Industry, including energy		Construction		Service activities	
	1996	2000	1996	2000	1996	2000	1996	2000
BG	15.4	14.5	25.9	24.1	4.3	3.7	54.4	57.7
CY	4.8	3.8	14.7	12.8	8.9	7.1	71.6	76.3
CZ	4.8	3.8	36.3	34.8	7.7	7.1	51.1	54.3
EE	7.5	5.3	22.2	21.1	5.8	5.6	64.5	68.0
HU (1)	6.6	4.8	26.3	27.7	4.3	4.7	62.8	62.8
LV	9.0	4.5	26.4	18.5	4.7	6.8	59.9	70.2
LT	12.2	7.6	25.8	26.2	7.1	6.2	54.9	59.9
MT	2.9	2.3	24.8	27.0	3.1	2.3	69.3	68.3
PL	6.4	3.3	30.1	27.8	7.4	8.4	56.1	60.5
RO	20.1	12.6	34.8	30.5	6.8	5.3	38.3	51.5
SK	5.2	4.5	32.2	28.9	7.8	5.2	54.8	61.3
SI	4.4	3.2	32.0	31.4	5.6	6.0	58.0	59.3
TR	14.9	14.0	29.3	29.5	6.1	5.3	49.7	51.2
CC-13	10.1	8.2	30.1	28.8	6.6	6.3	53.2	56.8

(1) 2000 data are not available. 1999 shown instead.
Source: Eurostat.

Figure 2.2.4. GVA by branch (as a % of the total), 2000

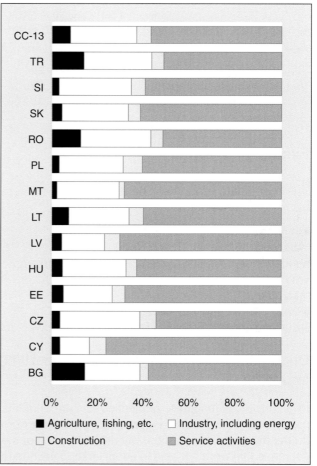

Source: Eurostat.

The candidate countries send data to Eurostat four times each year using the same standardised format as the Member States, though the completeness of the tables varies from country to country. Data for this publication were, in most cases, supplied prior to mid-May 2001, and have been validated by Eurostat.

Data quality

All candidate countries are working towards ESA 95 compliance but this is a long and difficult process. In particular, Turkey currently bases its accounts on SNA 1968 while Malta's data are derived from the national system of 1954, with some elements of SNA 1968.

The CCs have generally made significant progress in improving the coverage and quality of their estimates over the past couple of years. This has been supported by a series of EU-sponsored projects and workshops, which has helped to improve the sources and methods used to compile national accounts and heightened the exhaustiveness and consistency of the different national accounting systems. However, not all the changes have yet been implemented in the accounts for all years and the problem of consistent time series, in particular, remains to be solved in most CCs. Therefore, revisions of both the level and growth rates of GDP should be anticipated in the future.

All data in this publication should therefore still be treated with an appropriate level of caution, as full comparability with EU Member States cannot yet be guaranteed.

Exchange systems

The candidate countries have adopted different exchange rate systems:

- managed floating exchange rate: Romania, Slovakia, Slovenia, Czech Republic;
- independent floating system: Poland and Turkey;
- movable fluctuation margins ("crawling peg"): Hungary;
- fixed parity ("peg"): Cyprus, Latvia, Malta; currency board: Bulgaria, Estonia, Lithuania.

Changes in exchange rates between 1995 and 2000

In general, the monetary authorities of the candidate countries stabilised their currencies against the euro during the period in question, with the exception of the countries that were not able to adopt binding exchange rate systems.

In Bulgaria, after a turbulent phase, the lev stabilised in July 1997 following the introduction of the currency board, when it was linked to the German mark. It was subsequently linked to the euro (as from 1 January 1999). In July 1999, following a further monetary reform, the authorities decided to divide the currency by 1 000 (1 000 old leva are now worth 1 lev).

The Cyprus pound was very stable relative to the ecu/euro throughout the period in question. As from January 1999, it was linked to the euro at the central rate of CYP 0.5853 = EUR 1 with a fluctuation margin of 2.25 %. This fluctuation margin was increased to +/– 15 % as from 1 January 2001, while the central rate remained unchanged.

In the Czech Republic, after falling by almost 10 % in 1997, the koruna (CZK) recovered by 8 % in the following year only to fall again by 3 % against the euro in 1999 and to recover by the same amount in 2000. It continued to rise slightly against the euro over the first five months of 2001.

The Estonian kroon was stable throughout the reference period, thanks to the fixed exchange rate against the German mark adopted by the monetary authorities. As from January 1999, this link with the mark became a de facto link with the euro.

In Hungary, the forint fell by almost 30 % against the ecu between the beginning of 1996 and the end of 1998. In 1999, however, it was stable, fluctuating by only +/– 1 % around the annual average. The downward tendency reappeared in 2000 with a 4 % devaluation against the euro. It picked up again slightly (by around 2.5 % against the euro) in the first five months of 2001.

In Latvia, the exchange rate system adopted by the monetary authorities allowed the country to cope with the turbulence resulting from the financial crises in Asia and Russia. In 1999, the lat rose by almost 14 % against the euro as a result of the trends in the US dollar and the yen relative to the euro and the predominance of these two currencies in the SDR (special drawing rights) - the reference currency for the lat. The lat's upward trend against the euro continued, but eased off in 2000 and the first few months of 2001.

Like the other two Baltic countries, Lithuania enjoyed a high level of monetary stability after the currency board was introduced. Lithuania's currency has been linked to the US dollar, at the rate of LTL 4 = USD 1, since 1994. 1999 and 2000 were strongly influenced by the trend in the euro against the US dollar, which is why the litas rose by 16 % and 8 % respectively against the euro in each of the last two years. This upward trend continued but eased off in the first five months of 2001.

Table 2.2.8. Exchange rates of candidate countries (period average) 1 ECU/EUR ([1]) = ...

			1993	1994	1995	1996	1997	1998	1999	2000	Jan.-May 2001
BG	Lev	BGN	0.032	0.064	0.088	0.225	1.902	1.969	1.956	1.954	1.950
CY	Pound	CYP	0.583	0.584	0.592	0.592	0.583	0.577	0.579	0.574	0.578
CZ	Koruna	CZK	34.17	34.15	34.7	34.46	35.93	36.32	36.89	35.60	34.66
EE	Kroon	EEK	15.49	15.4	14.99	15.28	15.72	15.75	15.65	15.65	15.65
HU	Forint	HUF	107.61	125.03	164.55	193.74	211.65	240.57	252.77	260.05	264.53
LV	Lat	LVL	0.794	0.664	0.690	0.700	0.659	0.660	0.608	0.559	0.566
LT	Litus	LTL	5.087	4.732	5.232	5.079	4.536	4.484	4.263	3.695	3.630
MT	Pound	MTL	0.447	0.449	0.461	0.458	0.437	0.435	0.426	0.404	0.405
PL	Zloty	PLN	2.122	2.702	3.17	3.422	3.715	3.918	4.227	4.008	3.681
RO	Leu	ROL	886	1972	2662	3922	8112	9985	16345	19922	24788
SK	Koruna	SKK	36.03	38.12	38.86	38.92	38.11	39.54	44.12	42.48	43.55
SI	Tolar	SIT	132.49	152.77	154.88	171.78	181.00	185.96	194.47	206.61	215.94
TR	Lira	TRL	12 879	35 535	59 912	103 214	171 848	293 736	447 229	574 816	863 774

([1]) Euro from 1999/ecu until 1998.
Source: Eurostat.

As from 1996, the Maltese pound regularly rose against the euro, except in 1998, with the greatest rise (6 %) in 1999. This was largely the result of the movements of the US dollar and the pound sterling against the euro, since the reference basket is made up of 56.8 % EUR, 21.6 % GBP and 21.6 % USD.

In Poland the zloty fell by more than 20 % between the end of 1995 and the end of 1999. This was because of a devaluation plan adopted by the monetary authorities (0.3 % per month from March 1999 to 11 April 2000 against a basket comprising 55 % euro and 45 % dollar). As from 12 April 2000, the zloty floated freely on the exchange markets. Although it initially dropped substantially against the euro (from April to June 2000), it is interesting to note that it rose by 20 % between 2000 and May 2001.

In Romania, where inflation is still very high, the leu fell from 3 384 to the ecu at the end of 1995 to 24 142 to the euro at the end of 2000. In 2000 alone it fell by 24 % against the euro.

The Slovak koruna was relatively stable up to August 1998, at 38 or 39 to the ecu; it was then linked to a basket comprising the German mark and the US dollar. On 2 October 1998, the Slovak monetary authorities introduced a managed floating system. As from that date, the value of the currency fell sharply to 45.9 to the euro in May 1999. The rate then rose and stabilised at between 41.2 and 43.7 to the euro in 2000. This situation appears to have continued in the first five months of 2001.

The Slovenian tolar fell steadily against the ecu/euro throughout the period under review, from 165.58 to the ecu/euro at the end of 1995 to 213.54 at the end of 2000, representing a devaluation of around 5 % per year. 1998 was the only exception: the currency fell by only 1 % in that year.

In Turkey the lira fell from 47 303 to the ecu/euro at the beginning of 1995 to 624 267 at the end of 2000 — a devaluation of 92.4 %. This trend continued in 2001, with a drop of almost 40 % over the first five months. As from 22 February 2001, Turkey adopted a floating exchange rate system because of the financial crisis in the country.

Public deficit and debt

Reliable and comparable national accounts statistics on government deficit/surplus and debt of the candidate countries are not yet available. However, with the help of technical assistance from the EU, countries will very soon be able to report these data to Eurostat consistent with the European system of accounts (ESA 95).

The deficit/surplus data in Table 2.2.10 are based on the IMF's GFS (government finance statistics) methodology, but with adjustments made to approximate to national accounts methodology. With some exceptions, the public finance position of countries during 1993–99 does not compare unfavourably with that of EU countries, particularly in terms of the debt. However, the large structural changes which have taken place in these economies have resulted, at least for some countries, in sharp swings in the deficit/surplus.

Table 2.2.9. Interest rates as a % (day-to-day money market rates, annual average)

	1993	1994	1995	1996	1997	1998	1999	2000
BG	:	97.5	69.9	286.4	136.8	2.4	2.6	2.9
CY	:	:	:	6.9	4.7	4.8	5.2	6.0
CZ	9.6	7.9	10.6	11.6	19.2	13.6	6.8	5.3
EE	:	5.7	4.9	3.5	6.5	11.7	4.9	4.8
HU	15.4	25.6	31.3	23.8	20.8	18.0	14.8	11.1
LV	51.4	37.2	22.4	13.1	3.7	4.4	4.7	3.0
LT	:	:	:	:	:	6.1	6.3	3.6
MT	:	:	:	:	5.2	5.5	5.0	4.7
PL	17.5	18.7	26.4	21.2	22.7	21.1	14.1	18.1
RO	61.5	92.9	48.6	53.4	86.0	80.9	80.8	44.8
SK	:	13.1	5.7	11.6	24.6	14.5	11.5	8.0
SI	38.6	28.7	12.0	13.8	9.6	7.4	6.8	6.8
TR	62.2	131.0	72.4	76.2	70.3	74.6	73.5	56.7

Source: Eurostat.

Interest rates

The link between interest rates and inflation has been apparent among the candidate countries: rates have tended to be higher in those countries suffering from relatively high inflation, most notably Romania, Turkey, and (until 1998) Bulgaria. As the general trend in inflation in 1993-99 has been downwards, so have interest rates fallen. This trend has been particularly evident in Latvia, Lithuania, Slovenia, Hungary, and more recently Bulgaria (following the establishment of a currency board in July 1997).

In 2000, the downward trend in interest rates continued in most of the countries. The biggest declines (in annual average terms) were in the highest-inflation countries, Turkey and Romania. However, Turkish interest rates moved sharply upwards towards the end of 2000, as weaknesses in the stabilisation programme became apparent, causing a financial crisis. The main exception to the downward trend in rates was Poland, where monetary policy was tightened in order to reduce inflationary pressures and the risk of an overheating economy.

Interest rates tended to ease further in several countries during the first quarter of 2001. Official interest rates, those determined by national central banks, were lowered in the Czech Republic, Hungary, Poland, and the Slovak Republic.

Table 2.2.10. General government deficit (–) or surplus (+) as a % of GDP

	1993	1994	1995	1996	1997	1998	1999
BG	−11.3	−5.2	−5.1	−15.3	−0.3	1.3	0.2
CY (1)	−1.9	−1.3	−0.9	−3.3	−5.2	−5.5	:
CZ	0.4	−1.2	−1.1	−1.7	−2.1	−2.3	−1.6
EE	2.5	3.3	0.0	−1.6	2.6	−0.2	−4.6
HU	−9.3	−9.2	−6.6	−3.2	−5.4	−7.2	−3.7
LV	:	−1.9	−2.9	−1.3	1.8	0.1	−3.6
LT	2.1	−1.7	−1.6	−2.8	−0.7	−3.4	−5.7
MT	−3.4	−4.3	−3.5	−7.7	−6.6	:	:
PL	:	−2.2	−2.0	−2.3	−2.4	−2.1	−2.7
RO	0.5	−2.0	−2.1	−3.5	−4.4	:	:
SK	−6.7	−0.5	1.0	−2.1	−3.9	−4.6	−0.5
SI	0.8	−0.1	0.0	0.3	−1.2	−0.8	−0.6
TR (1)	−6.7	−3.9	−4.1	−8.4	−7.9	−7.9	−12.5

(1) Excludes local government.
Source: Eurostat / IMF.

Table 2.2.11. Central government debt (as a % of GDP)

	1993	1994	1995	1996	1997	1998	1999
BG	:	:	:	:	:	:	52.8
CY	58.5	53.5	51.5	53.9	57.3	59.7	:
CZ	18.5	16.4	14.1	11.8	11.4	11.5	13.3
EE	:	:	:	6.8	6.1	4.3	:
HU	89.5	86.6	85.2	71.9	62.9	61.5	60.2
LV	:	11.2	16.0	14.4	12.0	10.4	13.1
LT	:	:	:	:	15.3	15.6	22.1
MT	31.5	33.0	35.9	52.8	51.3	:	:
PL	:	67.6	54.3	47.9	46.9	42.9	42.9
RO	:	:	:	:	:	:	:
SK	:	:	:	:	:	29.2	30.0
SI	21.1	18.5	18.8	22.7	23.5	23.9	24.6
TR	33.7	44.0	35.8	37.9	43.9	41.4	53.5

Source: IMF.

2.3. External trade

Extra-EU trade

Total extra-EU trade flows

Figure 2.3.1 shows that extra-EU trade increased each year between 1990 and 2000. However, as the figures are measured in nominal terms, it is sometimes difficult to assess the actual size of the increase, especially when there has been high inflation or exchange rate movements.

In 2000, the EU again recorded a much increased deficit

Between 1990 and 2000 the average export growth rate has been 9.1 %, due to the combination of sluggish growth during the early 1990s followed by a sharp upturn in EU sales to non-member countries, starting in 1993. In 2000, extra-EU exports were strong, with a growth rate of 23.1 % over the previous year.

Among the Member States, Germany has always been the main extra-EU exporter, accounting for 27.7 % of the total in 2000. France, the United Kingdom and Italy follow with shares of 14.5 %, 14.2 % and 12.4 % respectively. During the 1990s, the total share of the four leaders has remained almost stable at about 70 %. Ireland, whose export share has more than trebled since 1990, has recorded the most spectacular increase.

The general trend in extra-EU imports has been similar to that for exports. After declining in 1992, EU purchases from non-member countries started rising slightly in 1993 and registered a sharp increase in 1994. In 2000, extra-EU imports grew by 31.6 %, well above the average annual growth rate for the 1990s (8.8 %).

Germany was the main outlet for exports from non-member countries to the Union, with 23.7 % of the total in 2000, followed by the United Kingdom (18.3 %), France (12.4 %), the Netherlands (11.1 %), and Italy (10.9 %). The total share of these five countries together was stable during the 1990s, representing over three quarters of total extra-EU imports.

Figure 2.3.1. Extra-EU trade flows 1990–2000 (billion EUR)

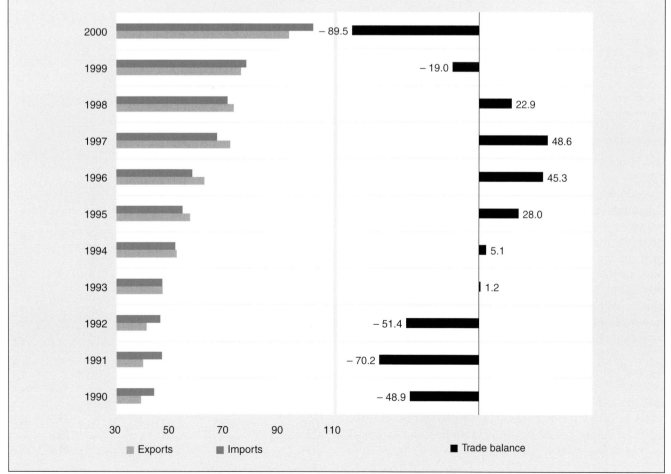

Source: Eurostat, Comext.

Table 2.3.1. Extra-EU trade

	1990	1998	1999	2000	1990	1998	1999	2000
	EU-15 exports (billion EUR)				EU-15 imports (billion EUR)			
	390.6	733.4	760.2	936.1	439.4	710.5	779.2	1 025.6
	Exports as a % of EU-15				Imports as a % of EU-15			
B (1)	5.0	5.3	5.2	5.3	5.8	6.1	5.9	5.5
DK	2.3	2.0	2.1	1.9	1.8	1.7	1.7	1.5
D	28.8	28.8	28.5	27.7	23.2	24.3	24.1	23.7
EL	0.5	0.6	0.6	0.7	1.1	1.3	1.1	1.2
E	3.8	3.9	3.7	3.9	5.7	5.0	5.1	5.4
F	15.5	14.7	15.1	14.5	13.9	12.5	12.6	12.4
IRL	1.0	2.4	3.0	3.3	1.0	2.1	2.2	2.1
I	12.7	12.9	12.1	12.4	12.3	10.4	10.2	10.9
L (1)	:	:	0.1	0.2	:	:	0.2	0.2
NL	5.2	5.5	5.5	5.7	8.8	10.3	11.1	11.1
A	2.7	2.8	3.0	3.0	2.6	2.3	2.4	2.4
P	0.6	0.5	0.5	0.6	1.2	1.1	1.1	1.0
FIN	2.0	2.3	2.2	2.4	1.9	1.4	1.3	1.4
S	4.3	4.3	4.4	4.4	3.5	2.6	2.7	2.8
UK	15.6	14.0	13.9	14.2	17.3	18.8	18.3	18.3

(1) Luxembourg included with Belgium until 1998.
Source: Eurostat, Comext.

Between 1991 and 1997 the extra-EU trade balance had improved each year, and a surplus of ECU 48.6 billion was reached in 1997. In 1998 the surplus fell to ECU 22.9 billion, in 1999 the EU recorded a trade deficit of EUR 19.0 billion, which rose to 89.5 billion in 2000.

While the total extra-EU trade flows are in deficit, the balances of individual Member States are widely divergent. Germany has usually recorded the greatest surplus among the Member States. During recent years, after absorbing the shock of reunification in the early 90s, it has again produced the greatest extra-EU surplus, reaching EUR 16.4 billion in 2000. Sweden ranked in second place (EUR 13.2 billion) and Ireland was third (EUR 9.5 billion).

By contrast, the Netherlands and the United Kingdom registered, as almost always, the highest deficits totalling EUR 61.1 billion and EUR 55.4 billion respectively in 2000. Nevertheless, the Dutch deficit should be seen in the light of its intra-EU surplus and its transit role in EU trade.

Table 2.3.2. Extra-EU trade growth rates (as a %)

	Exports		Imports	
	2000/1999	2000/1990	2000/1999	2000/1990
EU-15	23.1	9.1	31.6	8.8
B (1)	24.9	9.8	23.1	8.3
DK	15.7	7.2	20.3	7.0
D	19.7	8.7	29.4	9.1
EL	38.6	12.9	40.3	9.9
E	28.1	9.3	39.7	8.3
F	18.4	8.4	29.7	7.6
IRL	35.6	22.9	26.5	17.1
I	25.7	8.9	40.2	7.5
L (1)	27.8	:	9.9	:
NL	26.2	10.1	31.7	11.4
A	20.6	10.1	32.1	7.9
P	34.8	8.3	31.1	7.4
FIN	32.2	11.0	36.2	5.5
S	25.4	9.5	36.2	6.3
UK	25.5	8.1	31.8	9.5

(1) Luxembourg included with Belgium until 1998.
Source: Eurostat, Comext.

Extra-EU trade by main partner

Exports

In the period under review, the group of industrialised countries made up of the United States, Japan and EFTA represented the main market for the EU as a whole. The United States is the main individual partner for extra-EU exports with a 24.7 % share in 2000. Japan's share of extra-EU exports has fallen from its 1996 peak to 4.8 %, while the share of exports to EFTA has declined slightly to 10.5 %.

The central and east European countries (CEECs) and the Commonwealth of Independent States (CIS) together received 16.3 % of extra-EU exports in 2000, and have steadily increased their share of EU exports over recent years.

African markets dramatically reduced their share, partly due to the fall in primary goods prices and the loosening of colonial economic ties in this period.

Latin America's share of extra-EU exports went down to 5.8 % in 2000. In fact thanks to the economic recovery, the EU export share to these countries has begun to increase from the beginning of the 1990s.

The export share of the dynamic Asian economies (DAE) reached 8.7 % in 2000, and has begun to recover from the financial crisis in the region.

Table 2.3.3. Extra-EU trade balance

	1990	1998	1999	2000	2000/ 1999
	In billion EUR				Absolute variation
EU-15	– 48.9	22.9	– 19.0	– 89.5	– 70.4
B (1)	– 6.0	– 5.0	– 6.0	– 6.7	– 0.7
DK	1.0	2.3	2.6	2.4	– 0.2
D	10.9	38.5	28.9	16.4	– 12.5
EL	– 3.0	– 4.8	– 4.1	– 5.9	– 1.7
E	– 10.2	– 6.9	– 11.6	– 19.4	– 7.9
F	– 0.5	18.6	16.3	8.2	– 8.1
IRL	– 0.3	2.8	5.9	9.5	3.6
I	– 4.6	20.6	12.6	4.3	– 8.3
L (1)	:	:	– 0.8	– 0.7	0.1
NL	– 18.4	– 32.9	– 44.7	– 61.1	– 16.4
A	– 0.7	4.2	4.5	3.3	– 1.2
P	– 3.0	– 3.5	– 4.3	– 5.5	– 1.2
FIN	– 0.5	7.1	6.3	7.9	1.6
S	1.5	13.0	12.4	13.2	0.9
UK	– 15.2	– 31.0	– 36.9	– 55.4	– 18.5

(1) Luxembourg included with Belgium until 1998.
Source: Eurostat, Comext.

The relatively low share of extra-EU exports to China in comparison to other partners (2.7 % in 2000) should be noted.

Table 2.3.4. Extra-EU trade, by partner

	1990	1998	1999	2000	1990	1998	1999	2000
	EU-15 exports (billion EUR)				EU-15 imports (billion EUR)			
	390.6	733.4	760.2	936.1	439.4	710.5	779.2	1 025.6
	Exports as a % of EU-15				Imports as a % of EU-15			
US	21.2	22.0	24.1	24.7	20.8	21.4	20.6	19.2
JP	6.3	4.3	4.7	4.8	11.7	9.3	9.2	8.3
EFTA	15.3	11.5	11.6	10.5	13.3	11.2	10.8	10.4
CEEC	6.2	13.5	13.4	13.3	5.4	10.1	10.3	10.0
CIS	:	4.0	2.8	3.0	:	3.9	4.1	5.3
Africa	11.9	8.0	7.5	7.0	11.6	7.5	7.3	8.1
Latin America	4.3	6.8	6.0	5.8	6.2	5.0	4.8	4.7
DAE	7.9	8.2	8.2	8.7	8.2	11.0	10.9	10.6
China	1.5	2.4	2.5	2.7	2.6	5.9	6.4	6.8
Near-Middle East	7.9	6.7	6.5	6.3	6.0	3.4	4.1	5.1
Oceania	2.6	2.2	2.3	2.1	1.6	1.5	1.3	1.2
ACP	4.5	4.5	4.1	4.1	4.8	4.4	4.2	4.2
Mediterranean Basin	12.4	11.9	11.6	11.6	10.1	8.1	8.1	8.6
ASEAN	4.4	4.2	4.1	4.3	4.0	7.4	7.1	6.9
OPEC	9.6	6.4	5.8	5.7	10.6	5.7	6.2	8.3
NAFTA	24.9	25.3	27.6	28.4	23.8	23.8	22.9	21.7

Source: Eurostat, Comext and IMF, DOTS.

EU exports to Near and Middle Eastern countries have fallen back to below 7 % in recent years.

Oceania's extra-EU export share has remained at around 2.2 % since 1991.

Imports

The group of industrialised countries constituted by the United States, Japan and EFTA are by far the most important suppliers of the European Union. The United States is also the main individual partner for extra-EU imports, with a share of 19.2 % in 2000. Japan's share has declined, from a peak of 12.2 % in 1992 to 8.3 % in 2000. The share of imports from EFTA has also declined in the last three years, to 10.4 % in 2000.

The CEECs and CIS, which accounted for 9.0 % in 1992, accounted together for 15.3 % of total extra-EU imports in 2000. This trend reflects the economic changes that occurred in these countries during these years. After the crisis that followed the dissolution of Comecon, the CEECs quickly redirected their trade towards the EU markets.

Africa, Latin America and Oceania all saw a decrease in their shares during the period under review.

The DAE and China have become very important suppliers to the European Union in recent times. Their

shares of total EU imports were 10.6 % and 6.8 % in 2000.

Trade balance

The EU's trade balance with the United States has moved into a significant surplus over recent years, reaching EUR 33.6 billion in 2000.

Both in relative terms (as a percentage of trade with each country), and in value, bilateral trade with China recorded the biggest deficit in 2000 (46.8 % or EUR 44.6 billion), whereas Japan ranked in second place for the same year (31.3 % or EUR 40.8 billion).

The European Union has registered remarkable improvements in its trading position with the CEECs. A surplus of ECU 0.5 billion in 1990 shifted to a surplus of EUR 22.5 billion in 2000. Trade with the CIS has moved into deficit over the last two years, due both to the financial crisis in the region and increases in the price of oil.

The EU balance with Latin America and Near and Middle Eastern countries declined in 2000, reaching surpluses of EUR 5.7 billion and EUR 7.0 billion (5.6 % and 6.3 % in relative terms).

The trade position with the DAE continued to worsen in 2000, with the surplus of the middle 90s turning into a EUR 27.3 billion deficit.

Table 2.3.5. Extra-EU trade balance by partner

	1990	1998	1999	2000	1990	1998	1999	2000
	Billion EUR				As a % of total trade (^{1})			
Extra EU-15	− 48.9	22.9	− 19.0	− 89.5	− 5.9	1.6	− 1.2	− 4.6
US	− 8.7	9.5	22.4	33.6	− 5.0	3.0	6.5	7.8
JP	− 26.9	− 34.5	− 36.4	− 40.8	− 35.5	− 35.3	− 34.0	− 31.3
EFTA	1.1	4.8	3.3	− 8.4	0.9	2.9	1.9	− 4.1
CEEC	0.5	27.2	21.7	22.5	1.0	15.9	11.9	9.9
CIS	:	1.1	− 11.0	− 26.9	:	1.9	− 20.8	− 32.8
Africa	− 4.5	5.6	− 0.1	− 17.8	− 4.6	5.0	− 0.1	− 11.9
Latin America	− 10.1	14.2	8.5	5.7	− 23.0	16.6	10.3	5.6
DAE	− 5.2	− 17.8	− 23.0	− 27.3	− 7.8	− 12.9	− 15.7	− 14.4
China	− 5.6	− 24.6	− 30.3	− 44.6	− 32.4	− 41.4	− 43.9	− 46.8
Near-Middle East	4.5	25.2	17.7	7.0	7.9	34.2	21.8	6.3
Oceania	2.9	5.4	7.3	7.4	16.7	20.5	26.8	23.7
ACP	− 3.6	1.5	− 1.0	− 5.0	− 9.3	2.4	− 1.6	− 6.2
Mediterrean Basin	4.3	29.8	25.0	20.5	4.6	20.6	16.5	10.4
ASEAN	− 0.4	− 21.9	− 24.1	− 30.2	− 1.1	− 26.4	− 27.9	− 27.3
OPEC	− 9.1	6.6	− 4.4	− 31.9	− 10.8	7.5	− 4.8	− 22.9
NAFTA	− 7.1	17.0	31.3	42.7	− 3.5	4.8	8.0	8.8

(^{1}) Imports and exports.
Source: Eurostat, Comext and IMF, DOTS.

Table 2.3.6. Extra-EU trade, by product

	1990	1998	1999	2000	1990	1998	1999	2000
	Exports (billion EUR)				Imports (billion EUR)			
Total	390.6	733.4	760.2	936.1	439.4	710.5	779.2	1 025.6
	Exports as a %				Imports as a %			
Raw material	**12.2**	**10.0**	**10.0**	**10.6**	**33.1**	**21.7**	**21.7**	**24.6**
Food, beverages, tobacco	7.4	6.1	5.8	5.4	8.4	7.1	6.5	5.4
Crude material	2.3	2.0	2.0	2.0	7.7	6.0	5.2	4.9
Energy	2.5	1.9	2.2	3.2	17.0	8.7	10.0	14.4
Manufactured goods	**81.7**	**87.8**	**87.4**	**87.0**	**61.0**	**75.2**	**75.5**	**72.1**
Chemicals	11.3	13.1	14.0	13.7	6.5	7.8	7.6	6.9
Machinery, transport	39.9	47.1	46.3	46.5	28.3	37.6	39.2	38.1
Other manufactured goods	30.5	27.6	27.1	26.8	26.2	29.7	28.8	27.1
Not classified elsewhere	**6.1**	**2.2**	**2.6**	**2.4**	**5.9**	**3.1**	**2.8**	**3.3**

Source: Eurostat, Comext.

Extra-EU trade by main product

The European Union is a traditional exporter of manufactured products; in 2000, the share of manufactured products in total extra-EU exports reached 87.0 %.

Among manufactured products, the biggest share of extra-EU exports was accounted for by machinery and transport equipment (46.5 % of total extra-EU exports in 2000). During the period under consideration, the share of chemical products also grew while the group "Other manufactures" remained stable at around 27 %.

The corresponding reduction in the share of raw materials was mainly due to the declining importance of extra-EU exports of agri-food products (5.4 % in 2000). Meanwhile exports of crude materials were fairly stable at around 2 %.

The trend in extra-EU imports clearly shows the growing role of manufactured products. Raw materials accounted for only 24.6 % in 2000. During the last decade, various factors substantially modified the EU import structure and consequently the share of manufactured imports increased reaching 72.1 % in 1999.

Machinery and transport equipment increased its share and it became the most important group of products imported, reaching 38.1 % in 2000. Chemicals and other manufactured products were more stable, with shares of 6.9 % and 27.1 % in 2000. Over the last two years the rising oil price has led to a dramatic increase in the share of energy in EU imports, from 8.7 % in 1998 to 14.4 % in 2000.

The European Union economy, based on manufacturing industry, has a structural deficit in the primary sector. For manufactured products the relative surplus was 4.8 % in 2000.

Table 2.3.7. Extra-EU trade balance, by product

	1998	1999	2000	1998	1999	2000
	Billion EUR			As a % of total trade ([1])		
Total	22.9	− 19.0	− 89.5	1.6	− 1.2	− 4.6
Raw material	**− 81.4**	**− 93.0**	**− 153.2**	**− 35.8**	**− 37.9**	**− 43.6**
Food, beverages, tobacco	− 6.0	− 6.4	− 4.6	− 6.3	− 6.8	− 4.4
Crude material	− 27.8	− 24.9	− 31.4	− 48.8	− 44.8	− 45.9
Energy	− 47.7	− 61.6	− 117.2	− 63.0	− 65.0	− 66.1
Manufactured goods	**110.1**	**76.2**	**75.1**	**9.3**	**6.1**	**4.8**
Chemicals	40.4	47.7	57.2	26.6	28.8	28.8
Machinery, transport	78.3	46.3	45.1	12.8	7.1	5.5
Other manufactured goods	− 8.7	− 17.9	− 27.1	− 2.1	− 4.2	− 5.1
Not classified elsewhere	**− 5.7**	**− 2.2**	**− 11.4**	**− 15.0**	**− 5.5**	**− 20.0**

([1]) Intra and extra.
Source: Eurostat, Comext.

Intra-EU trade

> The Intrastat system was introduced on 1 January 1993 due to the abolition of customs formalities within the EU. Since that date, data have been collected directly from firms. As the Intrastat system for collecting data is different from the system used in previous years, the change in the figures between 1992 and 1993 should be interpreted with caution.

Share of intra-EU trade in total EU trade flows

Intra-EU trade has always represented more than 50 % of the EU's total trade, and at present it is around 60 %. Since 1970, there have been four periods when intra-EU trade declined as a percentage of total EU trade. During the periods 1973–75, 1979–81 and 1998–2000, the relative importance of intra-EU trade fell sharply due to increases in primary goods prices. The total value of extra-EU imports went up, raising total extra-EU trade figures in comparison with intra-EU trade. In 1993, in spite of implementation of the internal market, another decline in the relative importance of intra-EU trade occurred. At this time the collection of intra-EU data was reorganised. A substantial drop in

Figure 2.3.2. Intra-EU trade (as a % of total trade)

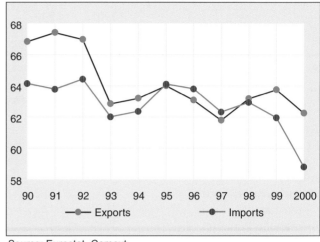

Source: Eurostat, Comext.

intra-EU figures, implying a certain degree of underestimation of flows, corresponded with the introduction of Intrastat. In particular, arrivals are underestimated, and dispatches are considered the most reliable figure of intra-EU trade. However, it is difficult to assess to what extent the shift in 1993 is a statistical phenomenon.

Table 2.3.8. Intra-EU dispatches/arrivals

	1990	1998	1999	2000	1990	1998	1999	2000
	Dispatches (billion EUR)				Arrivals (billion EUR)			
	787.3	1 258.9	1 337.5	1 544.2	786.6	1 207.1	1 269.2	1 464.1
	As a % of total exports (^{1})				As a % of total imports (^{2})			
EU-15	66.8	63.2	63.8	62.3	64.2	62.9	62.0	58.8
B (^{3})	79.9	76.2	76.4	75.0	74.2	71.1	70.4	69.3
DK	68.4	66.4	67.0	67.2	69.4	70.4	69.8	68.5
D	64.0	56.5	57.5	56.5	62.1	59.0	57.8	55.4
EL	68.0	53.8	51.6	43.4	67.7	65.6	66.2	58.7
E	67.6	71.1	71.2	69.4	62.3	70.6	68.7	64.6
F	65.3	62.4	62.4	61.4	68.1	67.6	66.6	64.7
IRL	78.6	69.3	66.0	62.9	73.9	61.6	61.7	61.3
I	62.8	56.9	58.2	54.9	61.9	62.0	61.5	56.3
L (^{3})	:	:	85.4	83.9	:	:	81.7	82.9
NL	81.4	78.9	79.5	78.7	63.7	58.1	55.1	51.3
A	67.2	64.2	62.9	61.7	70.7	73.7	72.3	68.5
P	81.2	82.0	83.2	79.4	72.0	78.1	78.1	74.0
FIN	62.2	56.1	57.7	55.7	60.5	65.7	65.4	61.9
S	62.3	57.9	58.4	55.9	63.4	69.2	67.7	64.1
UK	57.3	58.0	58.6	56.9	56.5	53.4	53.2	49.3

(^{1}) Dispatches and exports.
(^{2}) Arrivals and imports.
(^{3}) Luxembourg included with Belgium until 1998.
Source: Eurostat, Comext.

The volume of intra-EU trade did in fact increase significantly with the enlargement of the EU in 1995, since the trade of Austria, Sweden and Finland is strongly geared to the EU market. Thus, the intra-EU share of total EU trade before the three new Member States joined the EU was 58 % in 1994. One year later, in 1995, when the enlargement took place, the share of intra-EU trade reached around 64 %. The EU time series presented in this publication do not show this shift, because they are calculated as if all 15 Member States had belonged to the EU since the beginning in order to keep the time series stable. Nevertheless, the time series reflects the increasing importance of intra-EU trade within total EU trade. This has become possible because the links among Member States' economies have become stronger over the last few decades.

The share of intra-EU trade varies widely from one Member State to another. As a general rule, for relatively small countries such as Luxembourg, Portugal, Belgium, the Netherlands and Austria, the shares are higher, while Germany and the United Kingdom have lower ratios. Some countries like France are in an intermediate position.

As mentioned above, dispatches are considered the most reliable figure for analysing intra-EU trade. Manufactured goods registered the highest share of total intra-EU trade with 80.5 % in 2000. As in the case of extra-EU trade, the most dynamic product category in the last 10 years has been machinery and transport equipment, which grew from 36.2 % in 1990 to 41.4 % in 2000, while chemical products increased by two percentage points during the same period.

The intra-EU share for raw materials decreased from 17.3 % in 1990 to 16.2 % in 2000. In 2000, intra-EU trade as a percentage of total EU trade in raw materials

and manufactured products was fairly similar (around 59 % and 61 %), although up to 1992 the ratio for manufactured products was always significantly higher. This reflects the fact that extra-EU trade in manufactured goods is becoming more important. Major differences can be found between product categories. In the case of raw materials the intra-EU ratios for food products were conspicuously higher (72 % in 2000) than those for fuel products and crude material (around 43 % and 57 % respectively), which are more oriented to extra-EU trade. As for manufactured products, the intra-EU ratios for chemicals were higher (66 %) than those for machinery and transport equipment and other manufactured goods (both 60 %).

Intra-EU trade balance

Since 1993 and the introduction of the Intrastat system (see note above), the sums of the intra-EU arrivals and dispatches recorded by the Member States do not tally as they should have done theoretically. Before 1993, although divergences existed, they were relatively small, but from 1993 new statistical problems occurred, mainly because of non-response from firms and the threshold system introduced.

As far as the threshold system is concerned, the import (arrival) flow is in principle less concentrated than the export (dispatch) flow and this could partially explain the underestimation of arrivals: with Intrastat, the smaller companies are no longer obliged to make a statistical declaration. Only a few Member States produce 'corrected' figures which take account of the threshold effect.

The statistical discrepancies in intra-EU trade flows make it difficult to assess the development of intra-EU trade balances by Member States. This applies particularly to the transition from 1992 to 1993. However, the following can be concluded.

Table 2.3.9. Intra-EU dispatches, by product (as a %)

	1990	1998	1999	2000
Total (billion EUR)	787.3	1 258.9	1 337.5	1 544.2
Shares (as a %)				
Raw material	17.3	16.1	15.6	16.2
Food, beverages, tobacco	9.9	10.5	9.7	8.9
Crude material	4.0	3.2	3.0	2.9
Energy	3.5	2.4	2.9	4.4
Manufactured goods	78.6	82.6	82.2	80.5
Chemicals	10.7	12.8	12.6	12.8
Machinery, transport	36.2	40.9	42.0	41.4
Other manufactured goods	31.7	28.9	27.6	26.3
Not classified elsewhere	4.1	1.3	2.2	3.3

Source: Eurostat, Comext.

Table 2.3.10. Intra-EU share of total trade ([1]) by product (as a %)

	1990	1998	1999	2000
Total	65.5	63.1	62.9	60.5
Raw material	58.4	64.6	62.8	58.5
Food, beverages, tobacco	70.1	74.4	73.4	72.1
Crude material	59.3	58.8	58.8	57.2
Energy	39.0	43.9	43.9	42.6
Manufactured goods	67.5	63.2	63.0	60.7
Chemicals	69.6	67.9	67.1	66.4
Machinery, transport	66.7	62.1	62.3	59.8
Other manufactured goods	67.7	62.9	62.3	59.5
Not classified elsewhere	62.3	37.3	58.4	66.2

([1]) Intra and extra.
Source: Eurostat, Comext.

Since 1985, the Netherlands have almost always recorded the largest intra-EU surplus. In 2000, it reached EUR 76.5 billion, followed by Germany (EUR 36.2 billion), Belgium (EUR 21.3 billion) and Ireland (EUR 18.5 billion). Nevertheless, the Netherlands is a special case, as an important part of its trade is "in transit" (i.e. coming from outside the EU and going to another Member State). This is consistent with its large extra-EU deficit. As for Germany, the fall in its intra-EU surplus in 1991 after reunification had taken place is evident. The growth in the Irish surplus during the 1990s is particularly impressive.

Figure 2.3.3. Total intra-EU dispatches and arrivals (billion EUR)

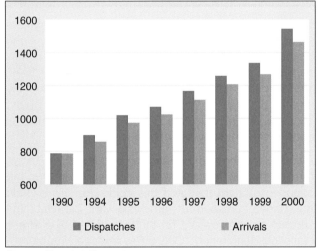

Source: Eurostat, Comext.

Table 2.3.11. Intra-EU trade balance (billion EUR)

	1990	1998	1999	2000
B ([1])	4.2	16.5	19.5	21.3
DK	1.4	− 0.4	1.6	3.1
D	33.9	26.0	36.3	36.2
EL	− 6.3	− 12.5	− 12.3	− 12.7
E	− 10.4	− 15.1	− 17.4	− 19.6
F	− 16.2	− 7.1	− 6.2	− 17.4
IRL	2.6	16.0	17.1	18.5
I	− 4.6	3.8	1.4	− 2.9
L ([1])	:	:	− 2.0	− 2.7
NL	20.7	49.2	56.3	76.5
A	− 5.5	− 9.0	− 9.4	− 8.7
P	− 3.6	− 8.7	− 10.1	− 10.6
FIN	0.2	2.6	3.2	4.7
S	1.2	1.6	2.9	2.1
UK	− 16.9	− 11.2	− 12.5	− 7.6

([1]) Luxembourg included with Belgium until 1998.
Source: Eurostat, Comext.

Spain, France, Greece and Portugal recorded the largest intra-EU deficits, totalling EUR 19.6 billion, EUR 17.4 billion, EUR 12.7 billion and EUR 10.6 billion respectively in 2000.

For some countries at different periods, their global deficits (their extra-EU deficits must be added) have shown a dramatic increase in comparison with the size of their economies (e.g. Italy in the early 1980s and Spain in the early 1990s).

Figure 2.3.4. Intra-EU trade balance (billion EUR)

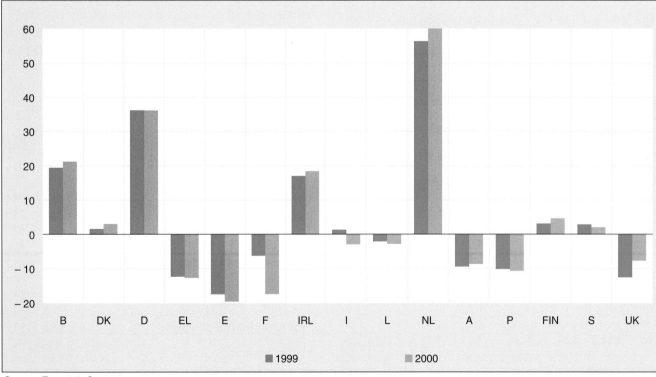

Source: Eurostat, Comext.

2.4. International trade in services

Balance of payments

A country's external trade in services is registered in its balance of payments (BOP).

The balance of payments records all economic transactions undertaken between the residents and non-residents of a country during a given period of time.

The balance of payments of the European Union is compiled as the sum of harmonised balance of payments accounts of the 15 Member States.

The methodological framework is that of the fifth edition of the International Monetary Fund (IMF) balance of payments manual.

In 1999, the EU was the largest trader in services in the world in value terms, representing 24 % (EUR 485.1 billion) of total services transactions (exports and imports), followed by the United States with a 22 % share while Japan registered an 8 % share.

The EU balance of services experienced a decrease of its surplus from ECU 11.7 billion in 1998 to EUR 6.9 billion in 1999 (– 41 %). This was mainly due to the significant rise of the travel deficit that doubled from ECU – 2.1 billion to EUR – 4.3 billion. Moreover, the surplus performed by transportation and other services [4] decreased reaching EUR 2.3 billion and EUR 8.9 billion respectively.

Evolution of the EU trade in services with the rest of the world

Over the last 10 years, the performance of the EU trade in services (excluding intra-EU transactions) was characterised by an overall growth of exports and imports. From 1990 to 1995, imports grew more steadily than exports (except in 1992). This resulted in a progressive reduction of the services surplus from ECU 19.3 billion in 1990 to ECU 11.9 billion in 1995. From 1995 to 1997, trade in services rose rapidly reaching ECU 17.8 billion in 1997. Afterwards, the balance of services deteriorated sharply reaching the amount of EUR 6.9 billion in 1999, a worsening of EUR 10.9 billion compared to 1997. Similarly to what has been described for the current account the rise registered by services' exports (+ 1 % in 1998, + 5 % in 1999) could not offset the performance shown by imports (+ 4 % in 1998, + 7 % in 1999).

Figure 2.4.1. EU trade in services with the rest of the world 1990-99; exports, imports and balance (billion EUR)

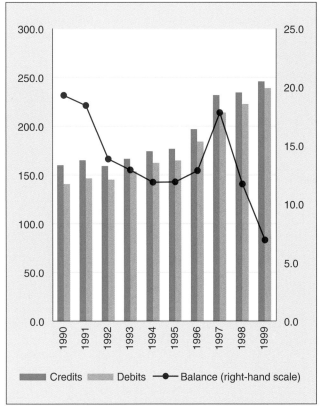

NB: Until 1991 data refer to EU-12 and from 1992 onwards data refer to EU-15. Intra-EU transactions are excluded.
Source: Eurostat.

The breakdown of the EU services

The analysis of the different services components in 1999 showed that the pattern of repartition of each services component remained generally unchanged compared to the previous year. Travel (with a share of 27 %), transportation (24 %) and other business services [5] (24 %) accounted for three quarters of the EU total external transactions in services. Far behind these three sub-components, shares fell to 6 % for royalties and licence fees and 4 % for both financial and construction services. Computer and information services accounted for 3 % (gaining 1 point compared to 1998) whereas each of the remaining components amounted to 2 % of the total. Nevertheless, the EU external surplus in services deteriorated by – 41 % in comparison with 1998. This decline was the result of different factors.

---

[4] The item "other services" covers services other than transportation and travel. It includes communications services, construction services, insurance services, financial services, computer and information services, royalties and licence fees, other business services, personal, cultural and recreational services and government services, n.i.e.

[5] The item "other business services" includes merchandising and other trade-related services; operational leasing; legal, accounting, management consultancy and public relations services; advertising, market research and public opinion polling services; research and development services; architectural, engineering and other technical services; agricultural, mining and onsite processing; other; services between affiliated enterprises, n. i. e.

Figure 2.4.2. Composition of the EU-15 total transactions in services in 1999

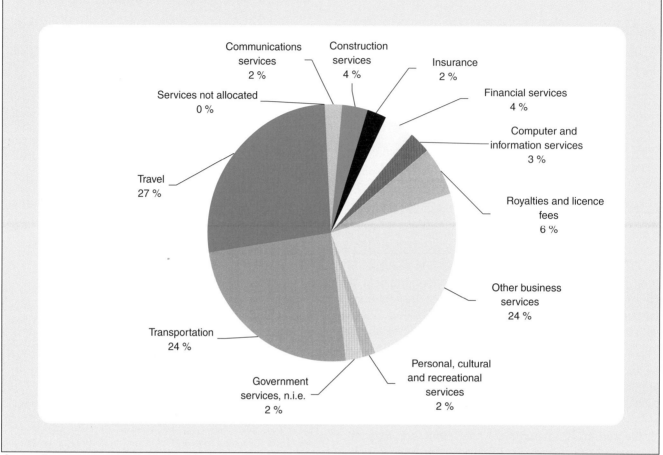

Source: Eurostat.

On the one hand, some items improved their surpluses. This was the case for insurance, financial, computer and information services that experienced significant growths of 80 %, 29 % and 79 % respectively. Moreover, the surplus performed by air transport increased by 43 % expanding from ECU 4.9 billion to EUR 7 billion. On the other hand, the fall of the sea transport deficit to EUR – 4.4 billion and the reversal of the other transportation balance to a deficit of EUR – 0.3 billion led to a reduction of the total transportation surplus by – 32 %, at EUR 2.3 billion. In addition, the contraction of the surpluses experienced by construction (– 34 %), other business services (– 52 %) and government services (– 57 %) as well as the expansion of the deficits in royalties and licence fees (10 %) and personal, cultural and recreational services (29 %) offset the positive balances of the other services' sub-

items. As a consequence, the surplus of other services as a whole deteriorated from ECU 10.6 billion to EUR 8.9 billion (– 16 %). The results performed by transportation and other services, added to the outstanding and decisive increase of the travel deficit to EUR – 4.3 billion, brought the services balance down to EUR 6.9 billion.

The EU partners in trade in services

The EU total trade in services (including intra-EU flows) was characterised by a share of 55 % within the EU, which remained unchanged, compared to 1998. Regarding total trade in services outside the EU the main partner was America with a share of 45 % and of 37 % for the United States alone. Asia (excluding Japan) and EFTA countries ([6]) were in second position

---

([6]) EFTA (European Free Trade Association) includes Iceland, Liechtenstein, Norway and Switzerland.

with an identical share of 14 %, followed by other European countries (⁷) (10 %), Africa (7 %) and Japan (5 %).

Concerning the economic partner zones (⁸) of extra-EU trade in services, the OECD (excluding EU Member countries) and the North American Free Trade Association (NAFTA) were by far the biggest traders with Europe representing 67 % and 40 % respectively of total extra EU transactions. Nevertheless, these results should be considered in the light of the fact that the United States belongs to both partner zones and performed 37 % of the EU external trade in services. EU total external transactions in services with the majority of the partner zones fluctuated by +/– 9 % in comparison to 1998. In addition, partners NAFTA, countries from Mashrek and ACP countries registered significant growths of 13 %, 15 % and 25 % respectively.

Figure 2.4.3. Total extra-EU transactions in services by geographical zone in 1999

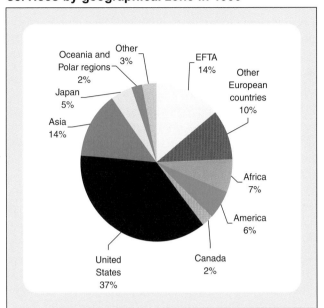

NB: Other European countries: excluding EU and EFTA; America: excluding United States and Canada; Asia: excluding Japan.
Source: Eurostat.

Table 2.4.1. The EU balance of trade in services by partner in 1999 (million EUR)

	Extra EU-15	EFTA	Other European countries	Africa	United States of America	America (¹)	Japan	Asia (²)	Australia, Oceania and other territories	Other
Services	6 916	5 269	– 3 611	– 58	– 4 757	– 95	6 949	2 379	917	– 77
Transportation	2 258	1 420	– 2 453	– 1 261	3 141	374	1 237	– 595	288	108
Travel	– 4 263	4 608	– 3 368	– 2 598	– 470	– 2 440	3 321	– 1 720	– 258	– 1 338
Other services	8 911	– 754	2 213	3 799	– 7 431	1 977	2 395	4 691	888	1 134
Communications services	– 1 043	– 84	– 441	– 177	192	– 282	– 4	– 215	– 38	7
Construction services	3 522	– 198	416	1 256	550	596	– 47	933	– 15	31
Insurance services	4 981	323	256	211	2 636	278	322	803	145	8
Financial services	8 016	368	781	523	2 938	857	914	1 320	297	19
Computer and information services	2 473	1 275	216	186	– 595	364	136	336	95	460
Royalties and license fees	– 8 421	– 432	269	225	– 9 829	234	178	692	174	66
Other business services	2 150	– 1 636	1 156	1 862	– 1 434	326	860	978	240	– 202
Personal, cultural and recreational services	– 3 580	– 311	– 199	– 53	– 2 918	– 142	82	– 28	– 4	– 6
Government services, n.i.e.	817	– 59	– 241	– 232	1 031	– 253	– 48	– 124	– 3	746
Services not allocated	10	– 4	– 3	2	3	-5	– 3	2	– 1	19

(¹) America excluding United States.

(²) Asia excluding Japan.
Source: Eurostat.

(⁷) Other European countries are European countries other than EU and EFTA countries.

(⁸) OECD: Organisation for Economic Cooperation and Development, NAFTA: North American Free Trade Association, OPEC: Organisation of Petroleum Exporting Countries, ACP countries: African, Caribbean and Pacific countries which signed the Lomé Convention, ASEAN: Association of South-East Asian Nations, CIS: Commonwealth of Independent States, Mercosur: countries of the South Cone common market.

2.5. Foreign direct investment

Foreign direct investment (FDI) statistics give information on one of the major aspects of globalisation. FDI is a supplement or an alternative to cross-border trade in goods and services.

Within the balance of payments statistics Eurostat maintains an FDI database that comprises harmonised and thus comparable data with a geographical and activity breakdown of inward and outward FDI flows, positions and earnings for the European Union, its Member States and its major FDI partners.

> **Foreign direct investment** (FDI) is the category of international investment that reflects the objective of obtaining a lasting interest by a resident entity in one economy in an enterprise resident in another economy. The lasting interest implies the existence of a long-term relationship between the direct investor and the enterprise, and a significant degree of influence by the investor on the management of the enterprise. Formally defined, a direct investment enterprise is an unincorporated or incorporated enterprise in which a direct investor owns 10 % or more of the ordinary shares or voting power (for an incorporated enterprise) or the equivalent (for an unincorporated enterprise).
>
> **FDI flows and positions**
>
> Through direct investment flows, an investor builds up a foreign direct investment position that features on his balance sheet. This FDI position (or FDI stock) differs from the accumulated flows because of revaluation (changes in prices or exchange rates) and other adjustments like rescheduling or cancellation of loans, debt forgiveness or debt-equity swaps.

This section first gives a brief overview by presenting the latest FDI flows figures (for 2000 and revised data for 1999) for individual EU Member States and for the EU as a whole. Secondly, we look at the detailed geographical and activity breakdown of the outward, inward and intra-EU FDI, using longer and more complete series that cover flows up to 1999 and end–1998 positions ([9]).

EU FDI: First results for 2000 ([10])

The acceleration of globalisation in recent years has brought a characteristic strong rise in foreign direct investments (FDI) among the world's main economic actors. For the European Union this trend was especially strong during the second half of the nineties. Especially for intra-EU FDI, the efforts to complete the internal market and the recent establishment of the European monetary union have undoubtedly been important forces behind this evolution.

Intra-EU FDI still growing faster than extra-EU FDI

Preceded by several years of a significant rise in EU FDI accounts, 2000 was another strong year for foreign direct investments in the European Union. Helped by favourable economic environment in the world economy, FDI flows to extra-EU partners remained very strong in 2000. Incoming FDI from extra-EU partners grew by about 20 % between 1999 and 2000, bringing the recent years' increase in EU's FDI net outflow to a halt. Most significant, however, was the change in intra-EU FDI which rose by nearly 50 % during that period.

Figures indicate a characteristic boom in FDI among EU Member States (intra-EU) at the start of the European monetary union in 1999 after several years where intra-flows were at the level of out- and inflows with extra-EU partners.

A further look at the trends in EU FDI flows combined with comparable figures from the United States, shows that the US market was the main focus of international direct investors in recent years. FDI flows with Japan remained insignificant in 2000 after 1999 flows were downgraded ([11]).

Table 2.5.1. Cross shares of FDI inflows and outflows between EU-15 and the United States

	EU-15		United States	
	Shares of US in extra-EU outward as a %	Shares of US in extra-EU inward as a %	Shares of EU-15 in outward as a %	Share of EU-15 in inward as a %
1995	53.8	65.3	57.5	61.4
1996	36.4	62.8	52.6	60.2
1997	41.7	52.9	60.5	60
1998	61.6	55.4	61.8	82.1
1999	62.9	73.6	41.6	84.5
2000	48.4	78.2	56.2	70.8

Source: Eurostat.

([9]) See Eurostat EU FDI Yearbook 2000 for a complete presentation of the detailed series, also with respect to its breakdown between industrial activities.

([10]) The preliminary figures presented here cover equity capital and inter-company loans but exclude reinvested earnings.

([11]) 1999 inflows from Japan changed from EUR 3.224 billion to - EUR 2.625 billion due to a revision in UK data.

Figure 2.5.1. EU FDI flows (^{1}) as a % of GDP 1995–2000

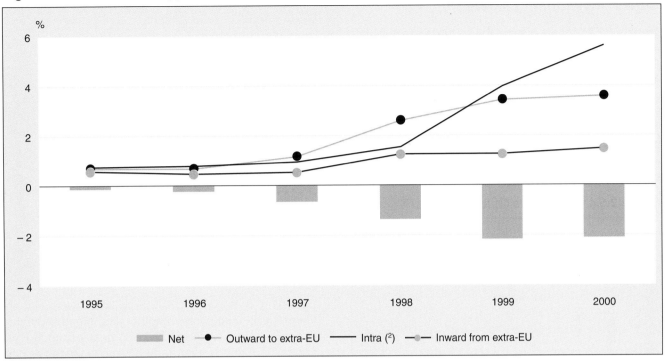

(^{1}) Excluding reinvested earnings.
(^{2}) Average of inward and outward intra-EU.
Source: Eurostat.

The comparison with data for the United States reveals that, in terms of GDP, FDI inflows to the US market clearly exceeded FDI inflows to the EU markets during the second half of the nineties. Moreover, a large part of these FDI flows to the US market were made by investors from the EU although this share decreased between 1999 and 2000.

The breakdown of flows by extra- or intra-EU origin shows that especially the ingoing FDI were typically made by investors from inside the European Union. In 2000, about 80 % of all inflows originated from one of the 15 EU Member States.

Figure 2.5.2. Trend in FDI (^{1}) as a % of GDP EU and United States

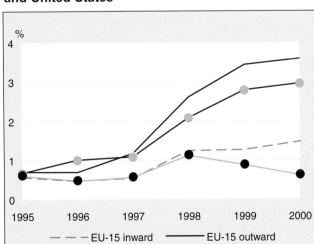

(^{1}) Excluding reinvested earnings.
(^{2}) *Source:* (FDI) United States: Bureau of economic analysis.

Figure 2.5.3. Breakdown of EU-15 FDI by intra-extra flows (^{1})

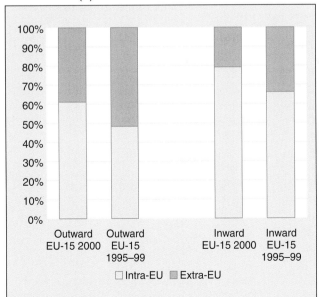

(^{1}) Excluding reinvested earnings.
Source: Eurostat.

Significant differences in the EU Member States' investment climate

The 2000 FDI figures confirm the fact that direct investments are still being unequally distributed within the European Union. They also point to the fact that significant differences in the investment climates might exist among EU Member States. During recent years, ingoing FDI have been economically most important in some small Member States, such as Belgium/Luxembourg, the Netherlands and Ireland. Sweden also recorded FDI inflows in terms of GDP well above the EU-15 average between 1995 and 2000.

Figure 2.5.4. FDI inflows (¹) as a % of GDP

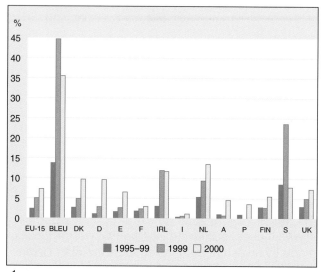

(¹) Sum of extra- and intra flows, excluding reinvested earnings.
Source: Eurostat.

Figure 2.5.5. FDI outflows (¹) as a % of GDP

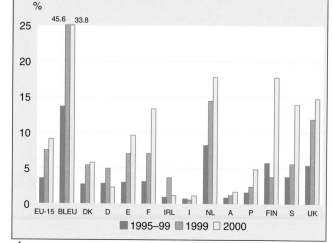

(¹) Sum of extra- and intra flows, excluding reinvested earnings.
Source: Eurostat.

Excluding a nearly EUR 200 billion investment in Germany in 2000 from another EU Member State, direct investments in the EU's largest economy still appear subdued. Germany primarily receives its investments from other EU Member States. Incoming FDI to Germany from other extra-EU partners than the United States are virtually non-existent. Direct investors very much continued to pass-by the Italian market where inflows in recent years only reached a fraction of the average EU level.

The exceptionally high outward and inward flows for Belgium/Luxembourg might partly be the result of mergers and acquisitions involving holding companies

Table 2.5.2. EU FDI flows (excluding reinvested earnings) in 2000, by major source and destination, million EUR

Year: 2000	Outward flows to						Inward flows from					
	World	EU	Non-EU	United States	Japan	Canada	World	EU	Non-EU	United States	Japan	Canada
EU-15	771 677	462 992	304 355	147 317	4 569	33 033	620 495	489 247	125 053	97 836	101	2 584
B/L	90 063	63 191	26 861	15 595	− 688	434	94 570	74 321	18 409	9 654	− 149	160
DK	10 156	3 515	2 321	2 683	− 54	174	17 078	10 236	2 522	2 630	13	− 13
D	47 205	3 339	43 866	26 804	529	165	195 590	193 056	2 533	− 990	786	261
EL	− 147						267					
E	58 302	22 631	35 671	7 366	31	− 9	39 742	27 033	12 708	11 034	55	− 18
F	186 843						41 422					
IRL	1 226	− 1 584	2 810				12 071	458	11 613			
I	13 410	8 985	4 424	1 870	10	57	14 529	10 346	4 181	2 233	83	294
NL	71 326	28 520	42 807	34 845	216	954	54 205	31 716	22 466	14 935	4 328	155
A	3 481	10	993	2 488	− 2	307	9 508	8 867	641	335	28	− 12
P	5 526	409	5 117	371	0	− 2	4 070	3 909	155	− 45	2	195
FIN	23 427	13 277	10 150	5 045	0	80	7 228	6 928	300	0	0	0
S	34 382	22 648	11 734	3 883	201	− 94	19 128	9 842	9 286	3 178	1 084	31
UK	226 477	181 130	45 347	18 001	1 713	4 314	111 087	74 416	36 671	41 929	− 6 355	1 190

EU-15 aggregate includes partly estimations for Greece, Ireland and France for 1999–2000.
Source: Eurostat.

Figure 2.5.6. FDI outflows ([1]) to extra-EU-15 countries as a % of GDP

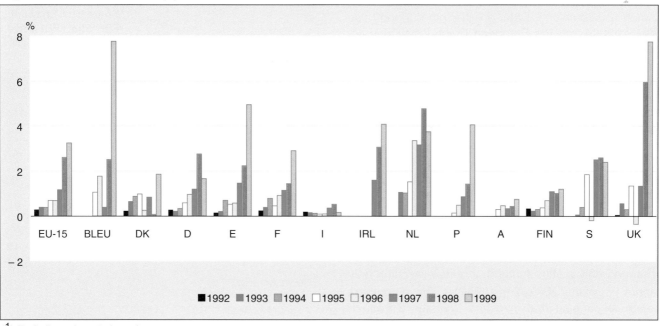

([1]) Excluding reinvested earnings.
Source: Eurostat.

located in Belgium. Moreover, incoming FDI to the four largest EU economies were relatively lower than in the EU as a whole during the period.

EU FDI in major extra-EU areas

The economic importance of direct investment outflows has surged remarkably during the nineties. In 1992, FDI outflows still accounted for less than 0.5 % of total GDP, as compared to the 3.6 % registered in 2000.

The increase in FDI outflows was widespread throughout the EU Member States. The United Kingdom, Neth-

erlands, Spain and Belgium/Luxembourg have, however, been among the main forces powering this expansion of FDI engagements. Also France and Portugal experienced a significant shift in the level of outgoing investments over the period, whereas Italy recorded lower than average values.

The largest part of EU FDI went to the United States

A breakdown on major partners reveals that by far the majority of direct investments from the European Union went to the North American markets and more specifically the United States. This share has been

Figure 2.5.7. Share in extra-EU outflows ([1]) 1992–99 by major partner

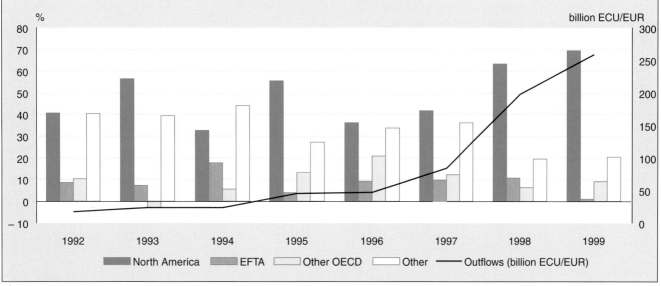

([1]) Excluding reinvested earnings.
Source: Eurostat.

rising significantly, especially since 1996. In 1999, more than 70 % of all extra-EU FDI went to the North American continent. Data on the other hand also demonstrate that the European Union is the primary investor in the United States where on average 54 % of the cumulated 1992–99 flows originated from the EU.

EU investors are taking on an increasing role in globalisation

A closer look at the comparison between the EU and US investment accounts reveals that the United States did not record a rise in foreign direct investments similar to the one we have seen in Europe during recent years. While European investors' engagements abroad have amounted to more than 3.2 % of GDP recently, American investors' foreign participation changed only a little during that period reaching only about 1 % of the US GDP in 1999 ([12]). These numbers seem to suggest that investors from the European Union are more actively taking part in the overall globalisation process.

A regional comparison reveals that the central and eastern European region continues to be the dominant sphere of investors of the European Union and that this dominance has been further emphasised during recent years. From 1995 to 1998, the EU invested almost four times as much FDI capital in this region as its US counterparts, assumably reflecting the forthcoming admission and accession of up to 13 new Member States to the European Union.

The table indicates that EU direct investors have shifted their focus during recent years. While extra-EU-15 European countries only hosted 17 % of total assets in 1998 they received more than 21 % of cumulated EU FDI flows during the 1992-98 period.

It appears that this increased focus primarily concerned some of the leading candidate countries including the Czech Republic, Hungary and Poland.

The continent which appears to have lost most market shares is Asia where close to 10 % of all FDI stocks were recorded at the end of 1998. The Asian region only received about 6.7 % of cumulated FDI flows during the 1992–98 period. This diminishing focus on Asia seems to be widespread among the region's markets though certain countries appear to have faced serious and dramatic withdrawal of EU FDI capital during recent years.

Table 2.5.3. EU FDI position by continent, 1998

	Assets 1998	Share of FDI 1998 assets	Share of FDI flows 1992–98
	(Million ECU)	(As a %)	(As a %)
Extra-EU-15 Europe	138 536	17.0	21.0
of which			
Switzerland	70 903	8.7	7.7
Norway	9 137	1.1	2.1
Turkey	4 017	0.5	0.7
Russian Federation	2 803	0.3	1.0
Asia	75 417	9.2	6.7
of which			
Japan	12 710	1.6	0.7
Singapore	10 923	1.3	– 1.2
Hong Kong	11 814	1.4	0.6
North America	422 354	51.7	52.5
of which			
United States	399 774	48.9	51.4
Canada	22 580	2.8	1.1
Central America	44 100	5.4	4.0
of which			
Mexico	7 924	1.0	1.4
South America	71 424	8.7	11.4
of which			
Brazil	35 535	4.3	5.9
Africa	23 758	2.9	2.6
of which			
North Africa	6 656	0.8	0.6
Rep. of South Africa	5 428	0.7	0.8
Australia and Pacific	30 975	3.8	1.3
of which			
Australia	24 868	3.0	1.3
New Zealand	4 153	0.5	0.0
Total extra EU-15	817 018	100	100

Source: Eurostat.

EU direct investors have also, to a great extent, bypassed Australia and the Pacific region since 1992. Direct investments in this region were already very moderate representing only about 3.8 % of total stocks in 1998. Cumulated FDI flows during the nineties were even more insignificant amounting to only about 1.3 % of extra-EU-15 flows. The continent, which appears to have gained most market shares, is South America where just about 8.7 % of all EU stocks were placed in 1998. The region, however, received 11.4 % of cumulated EU FDI flows between 1992 and 1998. Finally FDI

([12]) The incidence of reinvested earnings is, however, important in this case, as they represent about 20 % on average of EU flows and about 50 % of US flows. This difference is likely to be linked to the lower intensity of EU FDI.

outflows to Africa remained relatively stable representing only about 3 % of FDI assets and cumulated flows during the 1992-98 period.

Figures therefore appear to describe a situation where direct investors have been shifting focus towards new accession countries as well as towards the South American continent. This shift has taken place at the cost of the Asian and Pacific regions and to a lesser extent Central America. North America has kept its privileged position as most preferred market for EU direct investments abroad.

Table 2.5.4. EU FDI outward flows to major partners (equity and other capital, million ECU/EUR)

	Outward flows							
	1992	1993	1994	1995	1996	1997	1998	1999
Extra-EU-15 Europe	4 293	5 585	8 044	7 910	10 479	18 908	37 566	15 149
of which								
Norway	299	359	1 133	964	759	2 876	2 785	4 101
Switzerland	1 210	1 392	3 099	780	3 588	5 553	18 439	− 1 553
Turkey	369	280	398	317	415	126	1 006	947
Russian Federation	:	125	376	312	524	1 811	1 060	567
Asia	1 596	933	3 417	5 018	8 122	8 115	2 565	13 466
of which								
Japan	445	− 1 229	272	854	2 159	446	338	8 275
Singapore	232	− 62	384	654	442	2 193	− 9 338	− 7 653
Hong Kong	− 299	130	− 334	671	458	80	1 972	3 423
North America	7 237	13 629	7 873	25 298	17 146	35 380	125 617	180 092
of which								
United States	6 941	13 789	7 426	24 534	17 272	35 335	122 028	178 277
Canada	296	− 159	443	767	− 124	47	3 588	1 812
Central America	1 911	1 876	1 805	1 112	1 664	6 242	3 196	11 032
of which								
Mexico	235	88	383	1 010	449	2 696	1 162	1 510
South America	1 064	659	2 976	2 594	6 021	12 367	24 791	35 168
of which								
Brazil	166	195	281	798	2 592	4 270	17 742	10 968
Africa	702	108	556	1 146	1 895	3 575	3 478	2 319
of which								
North Africa	11	234	177	162	436	720	990	− 1 061
Rep. South Africa	341	135	75	420	158	1 411	1 008	2 389
Australia and Pacific	1 325	97	− 517	2 573	1 772	49	573	2 062
of which								
Australia	961	271	− 674	2 571	1 571	323	759	1 424
New Zealand	103	− 36	132	− 200	207	99	− 259	424
Total extra-EU-15	17 828	24 157	24 129	45 580	47 412	84 730	198 235	259 320

Source: Eurostat.

Figure 2.5.8. Cumulated 1995–99 FDI outflows ([1]) to extra-EU and extra-US markets (billion ECU)

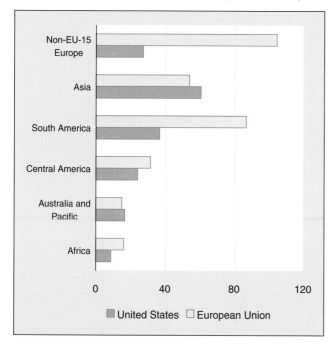

([1]) Excluding reinvested earnings.
Source: Eurostat.

Figure 2.5.9. 1998 FDI assets in extra-EU and extra-US markets (billion ECU)

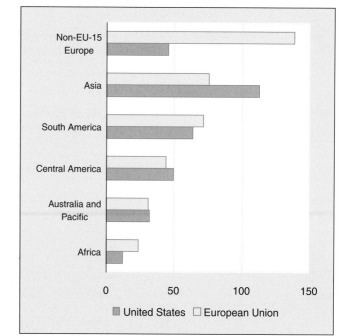

Source: Eurostat.

FDI into EU Member States: major partners

The role of the United States in direct investments going to EU countries is still more predominant than in EU outflows.

North America provided more than three quarters of FDI capital entering the EU in 1999. Over the 1992-99 period, it has always provided the main share of extra-EU FDI. Its share has fluctuated between the highest in 1999 (77 % of extra-EU inflows) and the lowest in 1994 (45 %).

Figure 2.5.10. EU FDI inflows ([1]): major partners

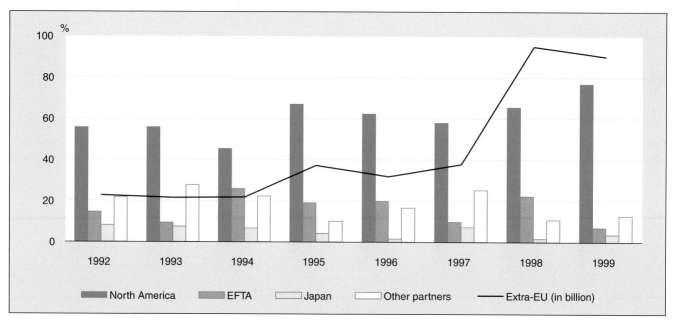

Source: Eurostat.

The second most important source of FDI capital between 1992 and 1997 have been EFTA countries, with an average share of 16 % of total. In 1998, they accounted for more than 22 % of extra-EU inflows but other European countries overtook their position in 1999 with an 11 % share.

On the other hand, the Asian component shrank heavily: in 1999 Asian direct investment companies retrieved capital from their EU affiliates (mainly in the United Kingdom). Central and South America picked up the four percentage points they had lost in 1998 and continued the volatile movements observed over the past years. Besides, Oceania gained 2 percentage points compared to 1998. Less than 1 % of extra-EU inflows came from Africa, which has never represented more than 1.5 %.

Major destinations of FDI in the Union

The European Union still occupies a major role as recipient of direct investments in the world by the end of the nineties, but the allocation of FDI flows into the European Union markets was reshaped during the 1992–99 period.

The United Kingdom has been the most attractive EU location for foreign direct investors since 1992, with a share accounting for more than one quarter of cumulated extra-EU inflows between 1992 and 1996 (see table "Extra-EU inflows excluding reinvested earnings" below). During this period, it recorded 36 % of US FDI inflows and received respectively 14 % and 13 % of the capital invested by Swiss and Japanese direct investors in the European Union. In 1997 and 1998, the United Kingdom consolidated its position as main EU FDI partner for American and Swiss investors with shares noticeably above the 1992–96 average.

Nevertheless, the United Kingdom lost a good deal of its relative importance in extra-EU flows in 1999 to the benefit of Germany and Belgium/Luxembourg: Swiss and, to a lesser extent, US investors slowed down their FDI activities in the United Kingdom. It is important to note that for two consecutive years Japanese investments into the European Union were mostly concentrated in the United Kingdom while at the same time important dis-investments from Asian investors have been recorded.

Approximately 17 % of extra-EU inflows were directed to France between 1992 and 1996. While France maintained its position as the second most important EU location in 1997 with a 15 % share, it recorded only 5 % of extra-EU inflows for two consecutive years. In fact the amounts of extra-EU capital invested in France these last two years were very close to the 1992–96 average of ECU 4.6 billion. Since 1992, more than 70 % of extra-EU FDI made in France are linked to only two countries: the United States and Switzerland.

Figure 2.5.11. Extra-EU inflows (¹) by country of destination

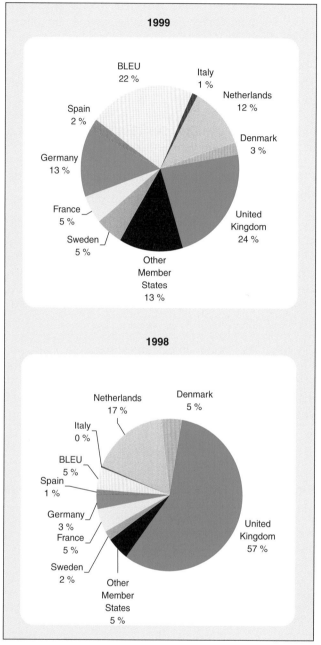

(¹) Excluding reinvested earnings.
Source: Eurostat.

Between 1992 and 1996, the Netherlands, directly followed by Germany, was the third most prominent home country in terms of extra-EU FDI. In 1998, and after having experienced important dis-investment from their Swiss partner the previous year, it overtook France as the second most attractive EU location for FDI. This was particularly true for Canada whose companies invested exceptionally high levels of capital in the country. In 1999, while extra-EU inflows slowed down in the Netherlands, investment from the United States represented more than four fifths of the total.

In 1997, US FDI inflows to Germany decreased considerably and amounted to less than half the 1992–96 average. In 1999, they reached the level of the 1992–96 cumulated flows while investment from Switzerland to Germany offset the dis-invesment recorded the previous year.

The remaining extra-EU inflows were mainly directed to Belgium/Luxembourg (22 % in 1999 compared to 5 % a year earlier), Sweden (5 % in 1999 compared to 2 % in 1998) and Denmark (3 % in 1999 compared to 5 % the previous year) — see also Table 2.5.5.

FDI in Portugal, France and Denmark were made relatively recently

Flow/stock ratios for foreign-owned direct investments in the European markets show that Germany and Finland rank as the oldest as a majority of them were established long before 1992. Nevertheless, while Germany was domicile for about 16 % of all extra-EU foreign-held assets at the end of 1998, Finland recorded less than 1 % of them.

On the other hand, direct investments in Portugal, France, Denmark and the United Kingdom were established much more recently but their weight in total extra-EU liabilities was also considerably different at year-end 1998.

Figure 2.5.12. Flow/stock ratio 1992–98 FDI inflows (¹) as a % of 1998 liabilities

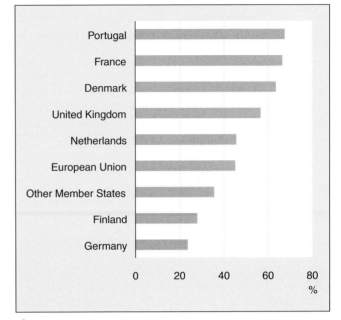

(¹) Excluding reinvested earnings.
Source: Eurostat.

Finally, Figure 2.5.13 illustrates that the real economic importance of extra-EU inflows to Italy, Germany, Finland and Austria during the nineties was lower than in the other EU Member States.

Figure 2.5.13. Extra-EU inflows (¹) to Member States as a % of GDP, 1992–99

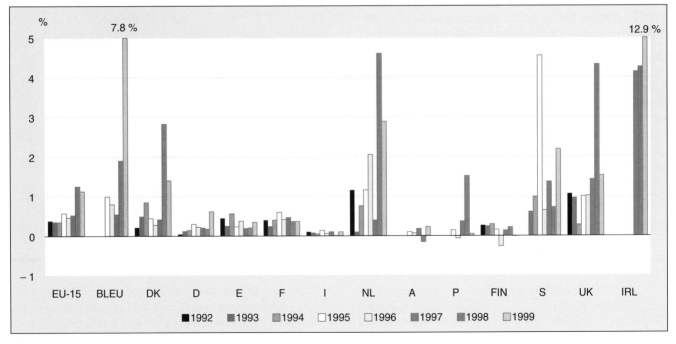

(¹) Excluding reinvested earnings.
Source: Eurostat.

Table 2.5.5. Extra-EU FDI inflows excluding reinvested earnings with major partners: share of total generated by the Member States

	Extra-EU	United States	Switzerland	Japan	Other partners
1992–96 cumulated EU inflows					
European Union	135 126	78 210	18 511	6 915	31 489
of which:					
United Kingdom	27 %	36 %	14 %	13 %	19 %
France	17 %	16 %	30 %	19 %	13 %
Netherlands	12 % (¹)	11 % (²)	11 %	22 %	12 %
Germany	11 %	11 %	14 %	12 %	8 %
Sweden	9 %	:	9 %	2 %	:
BLEU	8 %	8 %	– 1 %	9 %	11 %
Spain	6 %	5 %	10 %	12 %	6 %
Italy	3 %	2 %	4 %	3 %	4 %
Denmark	2 %	1 %	2 %	0 %	5 %
Other Member States	4 %	:	7 %	8 %	:
1997 EU inflows					
European Union	37 784	19 986	2 546	2 729	12 523
of which:					
United Kingdom	44 %	60 %	73 %	31 %	15 %
France	15 %	11 %	74 %	9 %	10 %
Netherlands	10 %	4 %	44 %	26 %	8 %
Germany	8 %	:	– 26 %	1 %	:
Sweden	3 %	9 %	– 60 %	4 %	8 %
BLEU	3 %	– 6 %	– 18 %	7 %	22 %
Spain	3 %	0 %	17 %	2 %	4 %
Italy	2 %	3 %	1 %	6 %	2 %
Denmark	2 %	1 %	– 3 %	0 %	3 %
Other Member States	10 %	:	– 2 %	13 %	:
1998 EU inflows					
European Union	95 014	52 669	19 854	1 515	10 047
of which:					
United Kingdom	57 %	57 %	98 %	74 %	38 %
France	17 %	13 % (³)	10 %	10 %	73 %
Netherlands	5 %	7 %	– 3 %	7 %	12 %
Germany	5 %	8 %	2 %	– 6 %	1 %
Sweden	5 %	7 %	1 %	:	:
BLEU	3 %	7 %	– 15 %	7 %	26 %
Spain	2 %	1 %	3 %	– 6 %	3 %
Italy	1 %	1 %	0 %	– 3 %	5 %
Denmark	0 %	0 %	2 %	5 %	1 %
Other Member States	5 %	0 %	1 %	:	:
1999 EU inflows					
European Union	90 072	67 210	4 260	3 224	15 377
of which:					
United Kingdom	23 %	37 %	12 %	53 %	– 42 %
France	22 %	6 %	16 %	1 %	96 %
Netherlands	13 %	13 %	45 %	16 %	5 %
Germany	12 %	13 %	2 %	5 %	12 %
Sweden	5 %	:	– 26 %	– 4 %	:
BLEU	5 %	3 %	38 %	11 %	5 %
Spain	3 %	2 %	6 %	1 %	3 %
Italy	2 %	2 %	– 2 %	– 2 %	4 %
Denmark	1 %	1 %	5 %	6 %	0 %
Other Member States	13 %	:	5 %	14 %	:

(¹) 1992: Extra-EU-12 and Sweden.

(²) 1995 inflows from United States including reinvested earnings.

(³) 1998 inflows from United States including reinvested earnings.

Source: Eurostat.

FDI between Member States

Although neutral to the EU balance of payments as a whole, data on intra-EU FDI are very interesting because they provide one measure of the extent and pace of economic and financial integration inside the EU. Moreover, they give indications on the regional patterns followed by the process of integration. More specifically, they reflect a long-term dimension of integration that is linked to firms' strategic policies adopted for competing in the single market and internationally. These policies are mainly carried out through mergers and acquisitions, which in fact constituted a large fraction of intra-EU FDI transactions in recent years [14].

Intra-EU FDI growth shows impressive acceleration between 1997 and 2000, particularly in northern Member States.

After stagnating at about 0.7 % of GDP between 1992 and 1996, in 1997 intra-EU FDI flows started growing faster, reaching 3.7 % of GDP in 1999 and 5.6 % in 2000.

1992–99 figures also show that FDI relationships between Member States tend to concentrate in northern European countries. Looking at the shares of flows over this period, it emerges that only six Member States (the United Kingdom, Germany, France, Belgium/Luxembourg and the Netherlands) supplied 80 % and received 70 % of cumulated flows. Instead, the shares of countries such as Italy and Spain diminished considerably on both accounts, reaching their lowest values in 1999. Among Scandinavian countries, Sweden particularly gained in importance, especially as concerns incoming FDI funds received.

While the various countries' absolute dimension influences the comparison among shares of EU total, comparing FDI in GDP terms shows that the general upswing in intra-EU FDI occurring in recent years affected most Member States, but with different intensity.

In particular, a group of small-medium sized countries (Belgium/Luxembourg, the Netherlands, Ireland, Sweden and, to a lesser extent, Denmark and Finland) recorded higher than average percentages, reaching record levels in 1999 under the influence of some large transactions.

Figure 2.5.14. Suppliers and recipients of intra-EU FDI (Shares of 1992–99 flows)

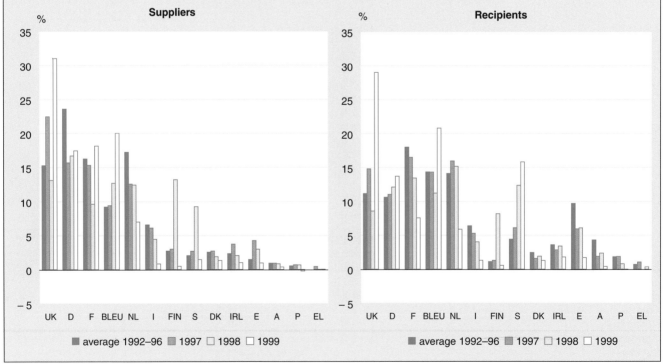

Source: Eurostat.

---

[14] See Unctad World investment report, 2000.

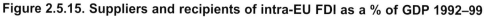

Figure 2.5.15. Suppliers and recipients of intra-EU FDI as a % of GDP 1992–99

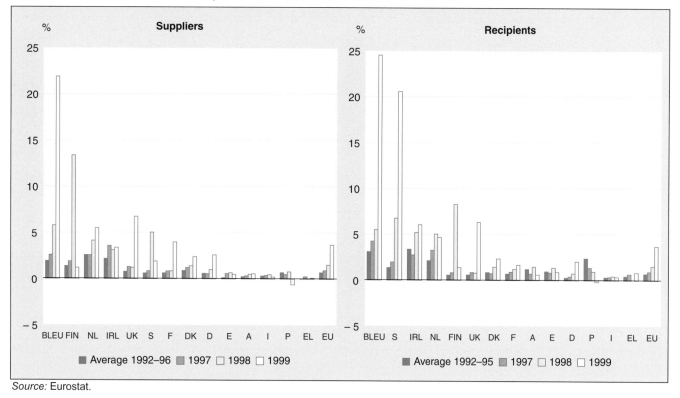

Source: Eurostat.

Big countries naturally tend to concentrate around the average, with two major exceptions: the United Kingdom, that in 1999 reached nearly 7 % of GDP on both accounts, and Italy which remained below 0.5 % between 1992 and 1999.

3. Enterprises in the Union

3.1. Structural development

The annual structural statistics on enterprises provide results obtained from the manufacturing industry, the production and distribution of electricity, gas and water, the construction industry, wholesale and retail trade and market services (excluding financial services) in the Member States.

General trend

Enterprises in the main sectors of economic activity in the European Union recorded solid overall growth between 1995 (taken as the reference year) and 1999.

As Table 3.1.1 shows, construction was the sector in the European Union that posted the biggest increase in terms of turnover, with an increase of 46.4 % compared with 1995, followed by services (+ 36.6 %) and manufacturing (+ 33.8 %).

In the case of the other variables under consideration (value added at factor cost and apparent labour productivity) and for the figures that are available, it is manufacturing that is ahead of the rest.

The variables that are analysed to reveal trends are:

1. **turnover**, comprising amounts invoiced per unit of observation during the reference period, i.e. market sales of goods and services to others;

2. **value added at factor cost**, meaning the difference between the value of what is produced and intermediate consumption in production, adjusted for production subsidies, costs and taxes;

3. **apparent labour productivity**, defined as value added per employee; this variable endeavours to measure the amount of wealth created in an industry by a given number of workers.

The analysis detailed below is based on the first-digit level of NACE rev.1 economic classification and covers:

— Section D: manufacturing;
— Section E: production and distribution of electricity, gas and water;
— Section F: construction;
— Section G: wholesale and retail trade;
— Section H: hotels and restaurants;
— Section I: transport and communications;
— Section K: real estate, renting and business services

Analysis by Member State

The analysis by Member State shows that the growth in the construction sector, where turnover is concerned, is mainly the result of exceptional growth in the United Kingdom (315.5 %), followed by Portugal (225.7 %) and France (181.5 %).

Depending on the sectors analysed, the trends in turnover recorded in the Member States are somewhat different. The figures show some geographical similarity in the manufacturing sector and in the production and distribution of electricity, gas and water, whereas the three other sectors reveal a more diverse geographical pattern.

For example, Portugal — which shows only slight changes for manufacturing and for the production and distribution of electricity, gas and water — is the only country that posts an exceptional increase in wholesale and retail trade (142 %) and services (239.4 %). Austria, too, records a big rise in turnover (211.9 %) in the services sector.

Apparent labour productivity, which establishes a link between value added at factor cost and the number of employees (and which can thus be regarded as an indicator of a country's performance), shows different patterns of development in the Member States, depending on the sector. The production and distribution of electricity, gas and water is the sector in which virtually all the Member States record positive figures, with the United Kingdom showing the biggest increase (160 %).

Table 3.1.1. Main economic variables, 1995–99, by major sector of activity (1995 = 100)

	Manufacturing	Electricity, gas, water	Construction	Wholesale and retail trade	Market services
Turnover	133.8	121.4	146.4	118.0	136.6
Value added	111.0	110.1	100.0	:	:
Productivity	111.7	106.3	100.5	:	:

Source: Eurostat.

Figure 3.1.1. Percentage change in turnover, apparent labour productivity and value added at factor cost in manufacturing, 1995–99

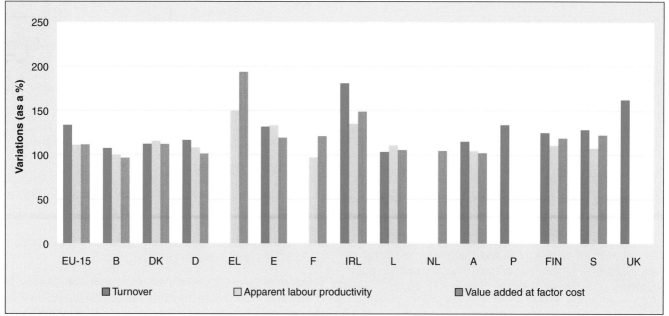

Source: Eurostat.

Figure 3.1.2. Percentage change in turnover, apparent labour productivity and value added at factor cost in production and distribution of electricity, gas and water, 1995–99

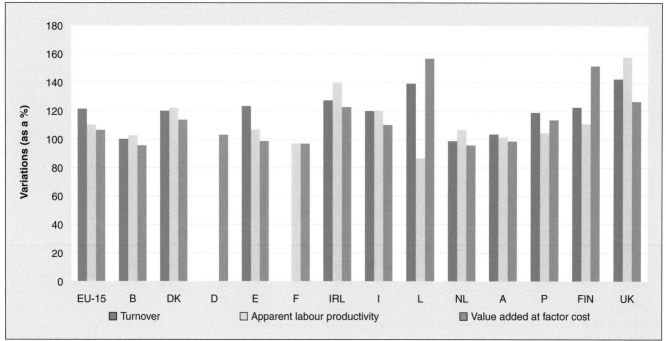

Source: Eurostat.

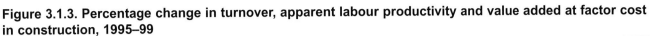

Figure 3.1.3. Percentage change in turnover, apparent labour productivity and value added at factor cost in construction, 1995–99

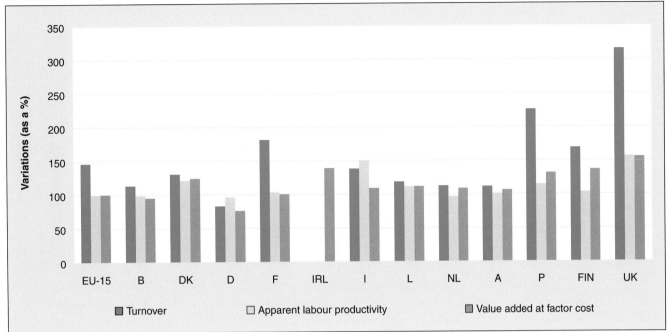

Source: Eurostat.

Figure 3.1.4. Percentage change in turnover, apparent labour productivity and value added at factor cost in wholesale and retail trade, 1995–99

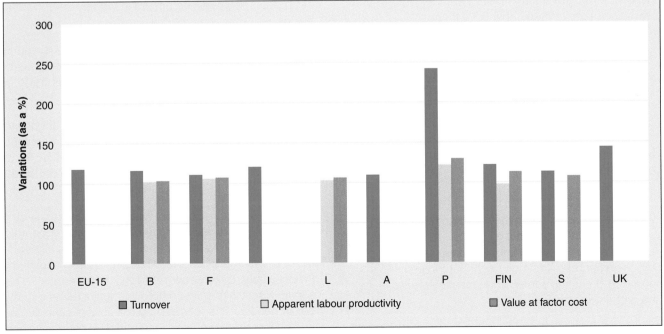

Source: Eurostat.

Figure 3.1.5. Percentage change in turnover, apparent labour productivity and value added at factor cost in services, 1995–99

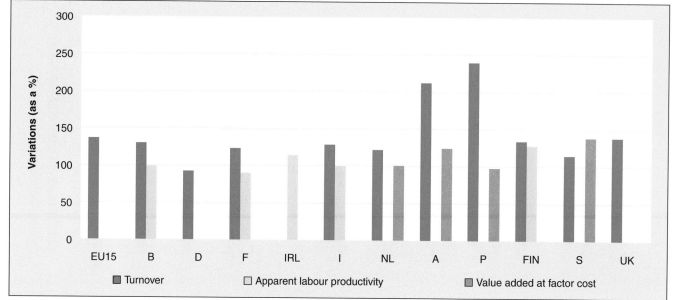

Source: Eurostat.

Performance of European enterprises in 1999

Using the structural statistics for 1999, it is possible to draw up a table for enterprises in the Member States that reveals how wholesale and retail trade dominates employment and shows the performance of manufacturing in terms of the gross operating rate (see Tables 3.1.2 and 3.1.3).

Indeed, the gross operating rate (see box) records its highest figures in the capital-intensive sectors and in the countries where capital has the major role in final production results (see Table 3.1.2).

> The gross operating rate is defined as the ratio between gross operating surplus and turnover. Gross operating surplus is the surplus that results from operating activities after the labour force has been paid. It is the balance available that allows investors and fund providers to be paid, as well as enabling taxes to be paid and providing finance for all or part of investments.

It is for this reason that in the manufacturing sector the economic activities relating to the manufacture of radio, television and communications equipment post very high figures. It can be seen that Finland — home to one of the world's telecommunication giants — has the highest figure (25.3 %).

As for the production and distribution of electricity, gas and water, every Member State records good results.

This can be attributed to the results achieved in both of the sector's two activities: the production and distribution of electricity, gas and heat and the collection, purification and distribution of water. It is only in France that there is a sharp difference between the gross operating rates for the production and distribution of electricity, gas and heat (26 %) and the collection, purification and distribution of water (4.9 %).

Where services are concerned, those involving leasing without operator perform better than the others, with Austria achieving the highest figure (63.8 %). The lowest gross operating rate occurs in wholesale and retail trade.

Employment in the EU (see Table 3.1.3), measured in terms of the number of persons employed, emphasises the predominance of wholesale and retail trade in relation to manufacturing.

The importance of the sector is mainly due to the activities relating to the retail trade and repairs to domestic appliances; in EU-15 these activities account for 52 % of those employed in the wholesale and retail trade sector.

As for the other sectors analysed, the services sector has a major role in employment. Indeed, economic activities relating to non-financial services are the leading job providers in five Member States: Belgium, France, Italy, Luxembourg and the Netherlands. The services sector is in fact employing an increasing number of people. It is followed by the construction sector and by the production and distribution of electricity, gas and water.

Table 3.1.2. Gross operating rates by branch (as a %), 1998

	EU-15	B	DK	D	EL	E	F	IRL	L	NL	A	P	FIN	S	UK
Industry															
Food	*8.6*	7.9	9.4	*7.4*	*14.3*	9.2	:	15.1	:	:	:	9.4	8.7	:	13.5
Tobacco		6.1	12.5	*5.0*	*12.5*	7.7	:	10.5	:	:	:	19.6	6.8	:	11.5
Textiles	*8.9*	8.8	9.9	*6.8*	*14.4*	11.1	6.6	10.5	:	11.6	11.0	11.3	16.3	8.1	10.2
Clothing	*8.6*	7.3	9.7	*5.7*	*10.6*	9.1	4.2	18.0	32.5	6.3	8.0	7.6	9.4	2.2	14.5
Leather and footwear	*6.8*	9.4	10.3	*5.2*	*11.1*	6.4	7.3	2.9	:	8.7	5.6	6.5	11.3	8.1	9.9
Wood processing and manufacture of articles in wood	*8.9*	9.7	10.9	*7.5*	*14.9*	10.0	7.3	10.3	5.0	12.1	10.4	9.0	9.9	7.9	14.5
Paper and paperboard		11.4	11.7	*9.7*	*14.1*	14.1	7.1	18.0	:	13.0	14.5	18.4	17.4	16.8	12.3
Publishing, printing, etc		11.3	11.3	*10.5*	*10.5*	14.9	6.9	18.3	:	17.5	13.3	15.8	15.0	8.7	20.6
Nuclear fuels, coking, etc	*6.1*	7.7	13.6	*4.4*	*16.9*	8.5	4.6	:	:	7.9	:	10.0	3.7	19.1	5.2
Chemicals	*12.3*	13.7	19.0	*7.7*	*13.6*	12.4	9.6	47.2	17.5	11.9	13.2	12.9	17.8	18.2	15.7
Rubber and plastics	*11.3*	10.1	13.8	*9.6*	*16.4*	11.4	8.4	16.9	12.6	14.2	11.3	16.3	16.9	12.0	14.9
Non-metallic mineral products	*13.6*	12.0	16.3	*10.9*	*22.4*	16.6	9.6	20.7	23.1	17.3	13.3	20.6	17.9	10.6	18.1
Metallurgy	*8.3*	7.8	8.5	*7.6*	*11.5*	11.1	6.3	7.8	6.4	13.0	11.4	8.3	12.3	9.2	8.5
Metalworking	*10.7*	10.0	12.6	*8.2*	*16.1*	11.2	7.6	14.6	11.2	11.6	11.4	11.8	14.3	9.3	17.6
Machinery and equipment	*8.8*	9.7	10.0	*7.1*	*11.7*	10.2	6.6	17.8	14.0	10.1	9.0	11.8	9.9	9.3	12.4
Computer and office equipment	*6.9*	6.8	4.5	*6.6*	*15.0*	9.7	4.4	7.7	:	9.4	8.1	6.2	− 0.2	11.1	8.8
Electrical appliances	:	9.6	9.7	*5.0*	*15.7*	11.4	7.3	21.7	10.9	11.3	10.5	10.8	13.3	8.6	10.9
Radio, etc, equipment	:	7.1	9.4	*3.8*	*23.2*	7.3	3.9	23.4	:	:	8.0	9.7	25.3	6.7	14.8
Medical equipment, etc	:	7.2	18.8	*7.9*	*9.8*	11.2	5.7	23.0	:	:	12.6	12.9	17.4	11.6	15.2
Car industry	:	6.1	9.7	*4.4*	*6.3*	8.1	6.9	12.7	:	9.2	9.7	7.3	11.7	14.7	7.4
Other transport equipment	:	9.6	5.4	*4.9*	*9.8*	4.8	5.9	15.4	:	9.1	5.8	7.4	7.6	8.0	12.9
Furniture, other	:	7.2	:	*7.5*	*16.8*	9.3	7.1	:	21.5	12.7	12.0	9.5	12.0	3.8	16.3
Recycling	:	6.0	:	*6.3*	*2.1*	8.3	5.7	14.1	4.8	12.0	:	9.5	4.6	10.1	11.0
Electricity, gas and water															
Productivity and distribution electricity	:	16.2	21.4	:	:	38.7	26.4	27.8	16.9	19.7	23.4	31.1	22.4	21.8	21.2
Collection, purification, distribution of water	:	20.6	16.1	:	:	21.9	4.9	:	22.9	39.9	38.5	44.9	56.3	41.4	50.2
Construction															
Construction	:	10.1	10.7	5.2	:	:	5.5	:	13.9	6.5	11.9	8.8	:	10.5	15.1
Wholesale and retail trade															
Car sales and repairs	:	2.8	:	:	:	:	2.8	:	5.4	3.6	4.4	3.7	5.3	3.6	7.6
Wholesale trade	:	3.5	4.5	:	:	7.5	2.7	:	5.3	:	4.6	5.3	4.9	4.0	6.5
Retail sales and repairs of household goods	:	6.6	6.1	:	:	:	5.4	:	7.6	8.7	6.4	6.3	6.5	4.2	8.5
Services (excluding financial services)															
Hotels and restaurants	:	15.1	:	:	:	17.8	11.0	:	16.6	18.6	17.1	:	12.2	9.9	16.2
Land transport	:	16.3	:	:	:	:	1.3	:	12.5		22.4	:	24.7	8.2	18.3
Water transport	:	− 0.3	:	:	:	:	0.4	:	:	:	22.5	4.9	15.4	7.4	:
Air transport	:	3.5	6.1	:	:	9.9	4.6	:	20.0		10.6	:	10.6	7.8	:
Auxiliary transport services	:	6.6	:	:	:	:	7.4	:	5.5	21.8	6.1	:	8.1	5.9	8.8
Post and telecommunications	:	24.4	31.9	:	:	:	21.0	:	47.7	30.6	27.3	:	24.2	19.2	:
Real estate	:	28.1	:	:	:	:	17.2	:	18.3	41.4	33.7	:	25.5	44.7	:
Leasing without operator	:	33.9	:	:	:	:	44.8	:	49.2	40.6	63.8	:	38.7	26.7	43.9
Computer activities	:	13.0	:	:	:	12.4	6.8	:	− 5.8	8.6	16.0	:	15.8	9.7	30.6
Research and development	:	6.2	:	:	:	28.9	0.2	:	8.0	:	− 8.8	:	3.0	2.9	0.4
Business services	:	12.4	:	:	:	:	6.6	:	14.3	15.9	17.5	:	24.8	10.2	23.0

NB: Data for EU-15 are estimations.
Data in italics (data on industry for EU-15, D and EL) refer to enterprises with more than 20 employees.
Source: Eurostat, SBS database.

Table 3.1.3. Number of employees (1000) by branch, 1999

	EU	B	DK	D	E	F	IRL	I	L	NL	A	P	FIN	S	UK
Industry															
Food	3 715	99	89	894	376	619	46	423	:	:	79	108	42	64	:
Tobacco	60	3	2	13	8	:	1	9	:	6	:	1	0	:	:
Textiles	1 109	43	10	135	108	128	7	323	1	:	22	104	7	9	:
Clothing	1 052	13	6	89	140	111	8	343	0	11	13	144	7	4	:
Leather and footwear	499	3	2	27	70	48	1	230	0	3	7	73	3	1	:
Wood processing and manufacture of articles in wood	867	14	17	188	100	92	5	181	0	20	38	58	29	37	:
Paper and paperboard	:	15	8	148	52	92	5	86	:	26	17	14	41	42	:
Publishing, printing, etc	:	36	55	404	127	215	19	173	:	92	26	40	33	48	:
Nuclear fuels, coking, etc	:	6	0	19	8	30	:	:	0	8	:	3	4	2	:
Chemicals	1 745	68	27	538	134	286	21	205	1	71	26	24	18	38	:
Rubber and plastics	1 399	29	20	396	110	226	10	212	4	34	28	23	16	24	:
Non-metallic mineral products	1 275	35	22	296	176	148	10	250	3	:	34	73	16	16	:
Metallurgy	907	41	10	243	71	125	2	147	7	27	32	14	17	32	:
Metalworking	3 057	65	47	801	299	443	13	653	4	103	67	81	35	85	:
Machinery and equipment	3 044	43	71	1 063	171	323	15	581	3	92	75	47	61	102	:
Computer and office equipment	:	1	2	45	8	46	16	23	:	8	1	1	2	4	:
Electrical appliances	1 374	26	19	532	91	171	15	205	0	23	28	32	16	22	:
Radio, etc, equipment	:	20	14	163	30	145	13	98	:	39	29	18	35	46	:
Medical equipment, etc	:	8	15	299	27	146	16	121	:	24	16	6	11	25	:
Car industry	:	58	8	870	159	274	3	174	:	28	28	24	7	75	:
Other transport equipment	:	10	10	123	53	123	4	95	:	28	5	14	12	19	:
Furniture, other	1 417	28	:	267	165	166	:	306	1	42	51	71	17	30	:
Recycling	:	4	:	12	1	:	0	10	0	3	1	1	0	1	:
Electricity, gas and water															
Productivity and distribution electricity	:	21	16	:	42	163	10	133	1	31	34	16	16	25	:
Collection, purification, distribution of water	:	7	3	:	19	33	0	18	0	8	2	2	2	1	:
Construction															
Construction	:	243	175	1 135	:	1 398	:	1 338	25	442	242	365	113	182	:
Wholesale and retail trade															
Car sales and repairs	3 264	82	:	:	327	431	:	465	6	139	77	114	35	63	:
Wholesale trade	7 380	218	180	:	931	971	:	1 061	12	431	193	277	84	190	:
Retail sales and repairs of household goods	11 367	279	198	:	1 467	1 507	:	1 707	17	662	268	469	113	180	:
Services (excluding financial services)															
Hotels and restaurants	:	156	:	999	975	705	:	805	12	246	202	250	51	77	:
Land transport	:	126	:	:	497	664	:	572	10	184	138	84	52	99	:
Water transport	:	1	:	:	8	15	:	22	:	16	0	2	8	13	:
Air transport	:	13	11	:	43	63	:	23	2	:	8	10	10	14	:
Auxiliary transport services	:	51	:	:	172	252	:	207	2	:	34	6	22	45	:
Post and telecommunications	:	78	58	:	184	460	:	279	4	118	64	37	48	0	:
Real estate	:	22	:	:	184	308	:	182	1	62	25	26	20	45	:
Leasing without operator	:	10	:	:	64	71	:	16	1	23	7	6	3	8	:
Computer activities	:	39	:	:	113	262	:	229	3	94	28	11	25	71	:
Research and development	:	5	:	:	22	25	:	18	2	31	1	0	1	12	:
Business services	:	318	:	:	1 327	1 749	:	1 265	23	915	183	219	114	224	:

NB: Data for EU-15 are estimations.
Figures for IRL, L, NL refer to 1998.
Source: Eurostat, SBS database.

Structural indicators

At the Lisbon Special European Council in spring 2000, the Union set itself the "strategic goal for the next decade: to become the most competitive and dynamic knowledge-based economy in the world capable of sustainable economic growth with more and better jobs and greater social cohesion" (Paragraph 5 of the Council conclusions). The Council acknowledged the need to regularly discuss and assess progress made in achieving this goal on the basis of commonly agreed structural indicators. To this end it invited (Paragraph 36): " ... the Commission to draw up an annual synthesis report on progress on the basis of structural indicators to be agreed relating to employment, innovation, economic reform and social cohesion".

In the months that followed, the Commission and the Council accelerated their activities in order to define the structural indicators needed for this policy process. Some 35 flagship indicators related to the policy domains listed above were finally officially approved at the European Council in Nice in December 2000. These indicators are listed in the box at the end of this page.

Eurostat has been involved in the process of creating the structural indicators. Eurostat has also compiled the data itself and forwarded this data to the Commission Services (DG ECFIN and General Secretariat) responsible for the synthesis report (which was released in February 2001). A large part of the structural indicators are therefore based on the European statistical system.

The work however continues, on the one hand, on additional structural indicators to be developed on certain policy areas (e.g. social cohesion) which would complement the existing indicators. On the other hand, Eurostat has launched a series of actions which will lead to an upgrading of the quality of the 35 structural indicators and to a better involvement of Member States.

Eurostat has also put in place a system for dissemination of the indicators, both tables and graphs, through an entry on its web page (http://europa.eu.int/comm/eurostat). From May 2001 onwards, this page will be updated monthly (on the 11th of each month).

Structural indicators

(adopted by the European Council of Nice in December 2000)

General economic background indicators

a. GDP per capita (in PPS) and real GDP growth rate
b. Energy intensity of the economy
c. Labour productivity (per person employed and per hour worked)
d. Inflation rate
e. Real unit labour cost growth
f. Public balance
g. General government debt

List of 28 indicators

I. Employment

1. Employment rate
2. Employment growth
3. Female employment rate
4. Employment rate of older workers
5. Unemployment rate
6. Tax rate on low-wage earners
7. Life-long learning (adult participation in education and training)

II. Innovation and research

1. Public expenditure on education
2. R & D expenditure
3. ICT expenditure
4. Level of Internet access
5. Patents
6. Exports of high-technology products
7. Venture capital

III. Economic reform

1. Trade integration
2. Business investment
3. Relative price levels and price convergence
4. Prices in network industries
5. Public procurement
6. Sectoral and ad hoc State aids
7. Capital raised on stock markets

IV. Social cohesion

1. Distribution of income (income quintile ratio)
2. Poverty rate before and after social transfers
3. Persistence of poverty
4. Jobless households
5. Regional cohesion (variation in unemployment rate across regions)
6. Early school-leavers not in further education or training
7. Long-term unemployment

3.2. Short-term developments

The indices for total industry ([1]) are based on the components of intermediate goods, capital goods, durable consumer goods and non-durable consumer goods, also called the main industrial groupings (MIGs).

The production index measures the volume of output and the activity of the industrial sector. Figure 3.2.1 shows that production in total industry has increased by 17.9 % since 1995, followed closely by the intermediate goods sector that had a growth of 16.8 %. The production of capital goods continued its steady upward trend and the sector has grown remarkably, reaching index values above 130 (31.4 % increase). Furthermore, durable consumer goods expanded by 22 % since 1995. The previously mentioned sectors have experienced especially rapid growth during 1999-2000. Non-durable consumer goods saw more moderate increases: 7.8 % during the past six years.

Figure 3.2.2 relates the Member States average rate of change in total industrial production during 1995-2000 with the respective weight of the country in the European aggregate. The weights are based in 1995 and calculated on the share of the European total value added at factor cost ([2]) that each Member State demonstrated during 1995. The four largest countries; Italy, France, the United Kingdom and Germany account for 75 % and the remaining 11 countries share 25 % of the weight in the European aggregate for total industry. Spain has a weight of 6.2 % and the rest of the countries have less than 5 % each.

All countries have recorded positive growth rates, but a general remark is that the small countries have increased more rapidly than the larger countries. Most notable is Ireland with an average increase of production of 15.1 % per year. The growth rates of Finland (7.5 %) and Austria (6.1 %) also deserve attention. The United Kingdom has the lowest average annual growth in production of the Member States, with 1.0 %, accompanied by Italy with 1.5 % per year.

Figure 3.2.1. Production index by main industrial groupings for EU-15 ([1])

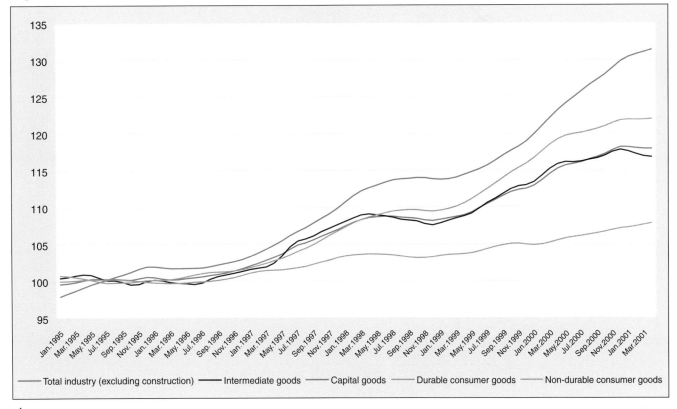

([1]) The comparisons are made between the base year value 1995 = 100 and the latest index value available, here April 2001 (extracted in June 2001).
Source: Eurostat.

([1]) Total industry does not include construction.
([2]) Total value added at factor cost for sections C, D and E (Industry) of NACE Rev.1.

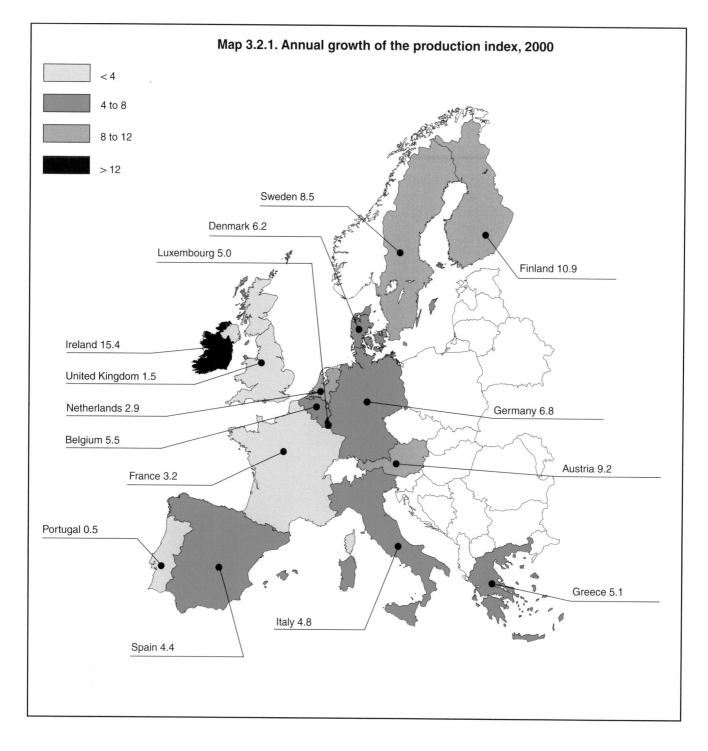

Map 3.2.1. Annual growth of the production index, 2000

< 4
4 to 8
8 to 12
> 12

Sweden 8.5
Denmark 6.2
Luxembourg 5.0
Ireland 15.4
United Kingdom 1.5
Netherlands 2.9
Belgium 5.5
France 3.2
Portugal 0.5
Spain 4.4
Italy 4.8
Finland 10.9
Germany 6.8
Austria 9.2
Greece 5.1

Figure 3.2.2. Average growth 1995–2000 of total industrial production and weight of each country in the European Union's total

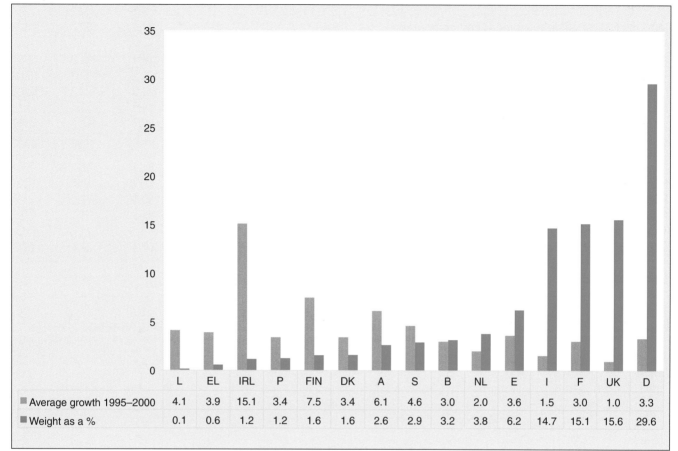

	L	EL	IRL	P	FIN	DK	A	S	B	NL	E	I	F	UK	D
■ Average growth 1995–2000	4.1	3.9	15.1	3.4	7.5	3.4	6.1	4.6	3.0	2.0	3.6	1.5	3.0	1.0	3.3
■ Weight as a %	0.1	0.6	1.2	1.2	1.6	1.6	2.6	2.9	3.2	3.8	6.2	14.7	15.1	15.6	29.6

Source: Eurostat.

The map indicates the growth of the production index during the year 2000 compared to 1999.

Especially Ireland (15.4 %) and Finland (10.9 %) have increased strongly their production levels for total industry. Austria has expanded production by 9.2 % during the year 2000 and Sweden by 8.5 %. Portugal's index augmented only slightly by 0.5 % and the United Kingdom has also announced rather slow growth (1.5 %). In addition, the growth rates of the Netherlands (2.9 %), Spain (4.4 %), France (3.2 %) and Luxembourg (5.0 %) were somewhat below the European average (5.1 %).

However, there are similar trends in the European Union and in general, the same industrial sectors are increasing production in the different Member States.

If we look at the development of the European index values since 1995, we see that it is in particular the manufacture of office machinery and computers and the manufacture of radio, television and communication equipment and apparatus that have the highest growth, with 78.0 % and 74.7 % respectively.

Recycling is the third fastest growing sector since 1995. Mining of coal and lignite; extraction of peat is the sector with the lowest index value in 2000. Manufacture of wearing apparel, etc., mining of uranium and thorium ores and mining of metal ores have fallen from the European level by more than 20 % since 1995.

Table 3.2.1. Industries with the highest/lowest index values in the European Union (1995 = 100)

Industries with the highest index values	1996	1997	1998	1999	2000
Manufacture of office machinery and computers	104.0	120.9	142.5	152.7	178.0
Manufacture of radio, television and communication equipment and apparatus	106.1	114.7	129.4	141.8	174.7
Recycling	109.7	123.4	128.2	132.2	150.6
Manufacture of motor vehicles, trailers and semi-trailers	102.7	110.7	123.0	127.3	138.5
Manufacture of medical, precision and optical instruments, watches and clocks	103.3	105.9	109.7	112.1	125.0
Industries with the lowest index values	**1996**	**1997**	**1998**	**1999**	**2000**
Mining of coal and lignite; extraction of peat	94.3	91.3	81.9	78.7	73.4
Manufacture of wearing apparel; dressing and dyeing of fur	94.8	91.3	88.9	79.6	76.2
Mining of uranium and thorium ores	92.6	89.8	80.5	77.0	77.3
Mining of metal ores	94.1	91.1	90.4	81.1	79.8
Tanning and dressing of leather; manufacture of luggage, handbags, saddlery, harness and footwear	96.1	97.2	92.3	89.4	87.7

Source: Eurostat.

Figure 3.2.3. Number of persons employed in the European Union by main industrial groupings ([1])

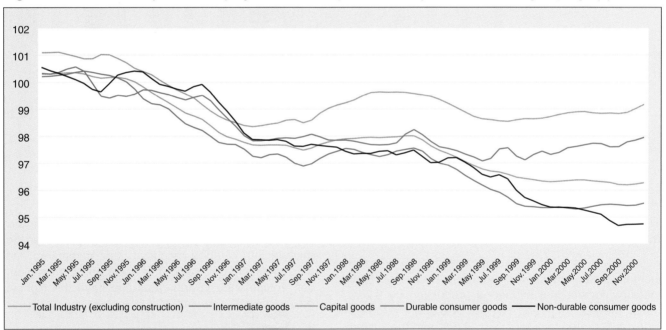

(Total Industry (excluding construction) — Intermediate goods — Capital goods — Durable consumer goods — Non-durable consumer goods)

([1]) The employment data come from business statistics in the Member States. The comparisons are made between the base year value
      1995 = 100 and the latest index value available, here March 2001.
Source: Eurostat.

The number of persons employed in industry has slowly decreased since 1995 in every main industrial grouping on the European level. The most marked fall has occurred in the sector "non-durable consumer goods", which has decreased by 5.2 % since 1995. Employment in capital goods, which is a sector where production has increased remarkably, has only decreased by 0.7 %.

The sectors of the employment index in industry follow more or less the same pattern as the production index. Recycling is the industry with the highest growth since 1995, with 23.2 %. Manufacture of motor vehicles, trailers and semi-trailers have the second highest index value in 2000 (106.1). Similarly, the employment in mining of coal and lignite; extraction of peat has had the most significant decrease of all the sectors, by 41.1 %.

Table 3.2.2. Industries with the highest/lowest employment index values in the European Union, 2000 (1995 = 100)

Industries with the highest index values	
Recycling	123.2
Manufacture of motor vehicles, trailers and semi-trailers	106.1
Manufacture of radio, television and communication equipment and apparatus	104.6
Manufacture of rubber and plastic products	102.9
Extraction of crude petroleum and natural gas, etc.	102.5
Industries with the lowest index values	
Mining of coal and lignite; extraction of peat	58.9
Manufacture of wearing apparel; dressing and dyeing of fur	77.0
Manufacture of coke, refined petroleum products and nuclear fuel	81.8
Electricity, gas, steam and hot water supply	85.0
Manufacture of textiles	87.4

Source: Eurostat.

Figure 3.2.4. Number of persons employed in industry, growth rates

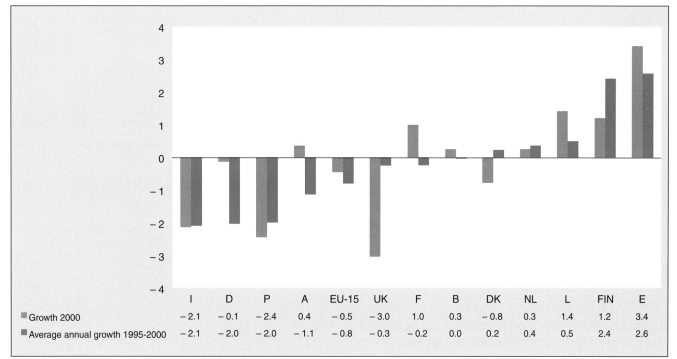

	I	D	P	A	EU-15	UK	F	B	DK	NL	L	FIN	E
Growth 2000	− 2.1	− 0.1	− 2.4	0.4	− 0.5	− 3.0	1.0	0.3	− 0.8	0.3	1.4	1.2	3.4
Average annual growth 1995-2000	− 2.1	− 2.0	− 2.0	− 1.1	− 0.8	− 0.3	− 0.2	0.0	0.2	0.4	0.5	2.4	2.6

Source: Eurostat.

The employment index for industry had a very varied development in the different Member States during 1995–2000. In Italy, Germany and Portugal, employment fell by around 2 % per year. Employment in the United Kingdom decreased by 3 % in 2000 only, however the average decrease during the last six years was less important, namely 0.3 %. Finland and Spain recorded the highest average growth rates (2.4 % and 2.6 % respectively) and Spain's index increased by 3.4 % in 2000.

The index of domestic output prices brings into view the transaction prices for domestic economic activities and is as such an indication of inflationary pressures. The level of industrial domestic output prices was kept fairly stable during the years 1995–99, but has increased more rapidly in 2000. This is a trend apparent in all Member States, however the magnitude has varied. Looking at the MIGs on the European level, the series for intermediate goods has proven to be particularly volatile, varying between index values 94.2 in February 1999 and 112.7 in November 2000. The price index for capital goods presents a relatively steady evolution with a total increase of 3 % since 1995.

Figure 3.2.5. Index of domestic output prices by main industrial groupings

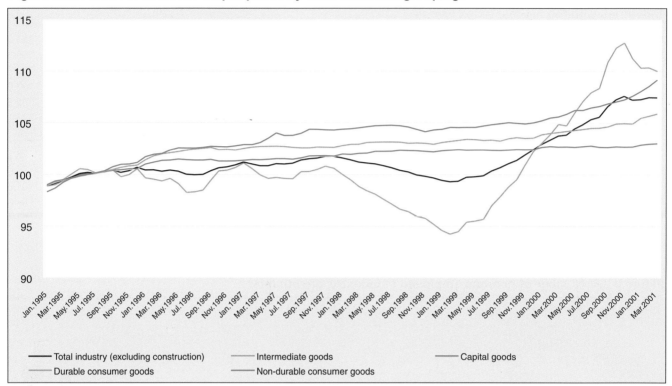

Legend:
- Total industry (excluding construction)
- Intermediate goods
- Capital goods
- Durable consumer goods
- Non-durable consumer goods

Source: Eurostat.

The European aggregate for total industry has augmented by 5.3 index points in total since 1995 and the largest annual rise, of 4.8 index points, took place in 2000. Focusing on a five-year period, Germany and the United Kingdom show the most stable price levels with a rise of 1.8 % and 2.0 % respectively. Greece's price level has had the highest increase among the Member States, reaching an index level of 126.0 in 2000. Moreover, Portugal's price index has risen by 20.3 % since 1995 and a very large part of this increase was developed during 2000.

Employment in construction has shown a steady upward trend since 1995, gaining 9.4 % since 1995 and with an average annual increase of 1.8 %. Production faltered slightly in 1996 with a drop of − 1.8 %, but has thereafter gradually recuperated and the production level in 2000 was 4.1 % higher than 1995.

Figure 3.2.7 displays a comparison between the average annual growth rate of the total retail trade for each Member State over the period 1995 to 2000 and the annual growth rate for 2000.

Germany's average annual growth rate in retail trade during the last five years was 0.02 % and 1.1 % for 2000 compared to 1999. Only Italy registered negative growth for 2000 (− 0.4 %) and the country had a low average growth rate (0.8 %) as well. At the other end of the spectrum, Ireland had both the highest average

Table 3.2.3. Index of domestic output prices (1995 = 100)

	1996	1997	1998	1999	2000
EU-15	100.4	101.3	100.7	100.5	105.3
B	100.6	102.3	101.1	100.6	109.3
DK	101.5	103.3	102.9	104.1	109.2
D	98.8	99.9	99.5	98.5	101.8
EL	106.2	110.4	113.3	117.0	126.0
E	101.7	102.7	102.0	102.7	108.3
F	100.2	100.3	98.6	98.4	103.8
IRL	101.8	101.9	101.9	102.8	109.1
I	101.9	103.2	103.3	103.1	109.3
L	95.7	98.5	101.1	99.0	105.1
NL	101.6	104.3	103.0	102.7	112.2
P	103.8	106.1	102.2	103.6	120.3
FIN	99.1	100.4	99.0	97.8	105.1
S	100.6	101.7	101.3	101.4	105.6
UK	100.5	100.1	100.1	100.4	102.0

Source: Eurostat.

annual growth (7.1 %) and the most rapid expansion for 2000 (9.1 %). Portugal too showed a high average growth of 5.2 % per year and registered in 2000 a rise of 3.5 %. Sweden and Belgium both attained high gains in 2000, with 6.5 % and 6.2 % respectively. The EU average growth reached 2.3 % per year and in 2000, retail trade grew by 2.8 %.

Figure 3.2.6. Employment and production in the construction sector in the Union

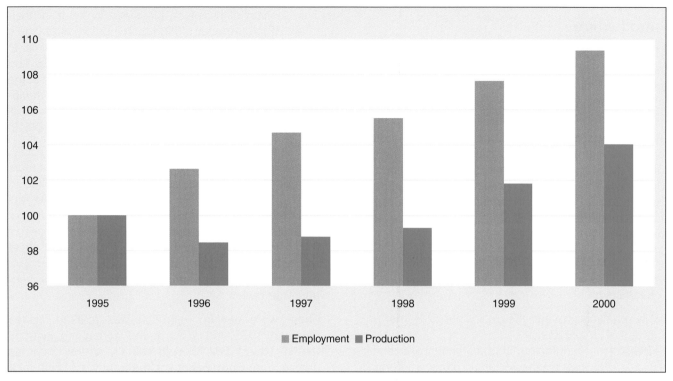

Source: Eurostat.

Figure 3.2.7. Deflated turnover in retail trade

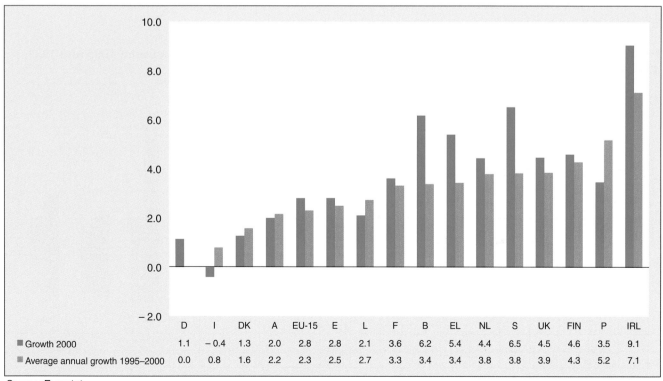

	D	I	DK	A	EU-15	E	L	F	B	EL	NL	S	UK	FIN	P	IRL
■ Growth 2000	1.1	− 0.4	1.3	2.0	2.8	2.8	2.1	3.6	6.2	5.4	4.4	6.5	4.5	4.6	3.5	9.1
■ Average annual growth 1995–2000	0.0	0.8	1.6	2.2	2.3	2.5	2.7	3.3	3.4	3.4	3.8	3.8	3.9	4.3	5.2	7.1

Source: Eurostat.

3.3. High-tech industries

Introduction

With the advancing globalisation of the economy, technology is a key factor in boosting the growth and competitiveness of businesses. This section analyses the industrial sectors whose main activity is highly technology-intensive (high-tech sectors).

An OECD classification (see box) is used to classify a sector as high-tech. The four sectors analysed distinguish themselves from other sectors of economic activity by the highly technology-intensive nature of their industrial production process, as measured by their expenditure on R & D (research and development)

The criteria applied for classifying a sector as belonging to the high-tech industries are based on an OECD classification ([3]).

This analysis covers the following divisions and groups of NACE Rev. 1:
- **DG24.4:** Manufacture of pharmaceuticals, medicinal chemicals and botanical products ("pharmaceutical industry")
- **DL 30:** Manufacture of office machinery and computers
- **DL 32:** Manufacture of radio, television and communication equipment and apparatus ("manufacture of electronic and communication equipment")
- **DM 35.3:** Manufacture of aircraft and spacecraft ("aerospace industry")

The turnover of high-tech sectors

The position of high-tech industries in terms of their share of the turnover of high-tech industry as a whole is shown in Table 3.3.1. One of the main facts to emerge from the analysis is that between 1995 and 1999 there was an increase in the predominance of the manufacture of electronic and communication equipment (NACE Rev. 1 DL 32), which accounted for 43 % of the turnover of high-tech industry as a whole in 1999.

This growth in relative importance, seen in most Member States but above all in Finland (from 70.5 % to 87.6 % between 1995 and 1999), is due to the fact that there are major producers in this sector in Europe, particularly in Finland and Sweden. With increases of 8.3 points and 6.4 points in Portugal and Ireland respectively, the importance of this industry far outstripped that of the pharmaceutical industry in the period under review.

There were upward, although less marked, trends between 1995 and 1999 in the aerospace industry (NACE Rev. 1 DM 35.3) in virtually all the countries analysed. At European level, the turnover of high-tech industry increased by 4.7 points in the period under review. The greatest increase was in France (+ 10.8 percentage points); the pharmaceutical industry also lost ground on the French high-tech market.

The pharmaceutical industry (NACE Rev. 1 DG24.4) and the manufacture of office machinery and computers (NACE Rev. 1 DL 30) showed pockets of economic success.

Figure 3.3.1. Variation of turnover in manufacturing and in high-tech industries between 1995 and 1999, 1995 = 100

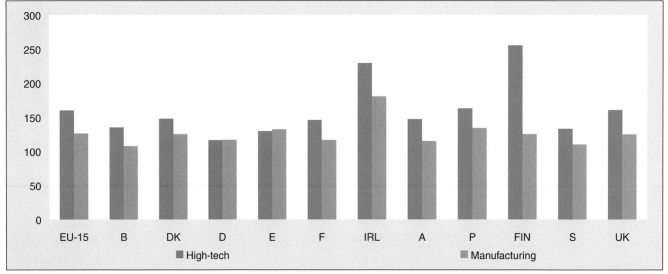

Source: Eurostat.

([3]) DSTI Working Document 1997/2-OECD/GD(97)216 "Revision of the classifications of sectors and high-tech products".

Table 3.3.1. Turnover of high-tech subsectors as a percentage of total high-tech turnover, 1995 and 1999

	Pharmaceuticals (DG 24.4)		Office machinery and computers (DL30)		Electronics and communications (DL32)		Aerospace (DM35.3)	
	1995	1999	1995	1999	1995	1999	1995	1999
EU-15	26.6	21.9	22.5	17.6	38.1	43.0	12.8	17.5
B	50.5	46.9	3.1	1.6	40.1	40.7	6.3	10.8
DK	59.8	60.2	6.5	3.8	33.7	36.0	:	:
D	27.4	32.3	23.2	13.5	37.6	39.1	11.8	15.1
EL	:	:	:	:	:	:	:	:
E	46.2	42.7	20.7	20.2	27.3	29.1	5.8	8.0
F	34.3	27.9	18.6	17.8	29.2	29.6	17.9	28.7
IRL	18.6	15.4	66.2	63.0	15.2	21.6	:	:
I	37.2	40.8	22.7	14.6	30.5	34.7	9.6	9.9
L	:	:	:	:	:	:	:	:
NL	:	:	:	:	:	:	:	:
A	21.1	19.0	0.6	7.7	78.1	73.0	0.2	0.3
P	36.3	26.5	1.6	2.8	60.2	68.5	1.9	2.2
FIN	11.7	4.9	16.9	7.1	70.5	87.6	0.9	0.5
S	25.2	19.8	5.3	2.9	69.5	71.3	8.4	7.6
UK	18.8	20.0	27.9	18.8	31.4	34.7	21.9	26.5

NB: DK, IRL: DM 35.3 not available; France and the Netherlands: data refer to 1998 instead of 1999; United Kingdom: data refer to 1996 instead of 1995. For Sweden, the comparison for the sector DM 35.3 is between figures for 1997 and 1998.
Source: Eurostat.

In Denmark and Italy, the pharmaceutical industry was increasingly important on the high-tech market, since it achieved 60.2 % and 40.8 % respectively in 1999. However, this industry lost ground in terms of relative value in the Member States as a whole, as highlighted by the drop of 4.7 points in turnover.

At European level, the manufacture of office machinery and computers showed the greatest reduction on the high-tech market (– 4.9 points) between 1995 and 1999. In Ireland, although declining since 1995, this sector remains the key industry of the high-tech industries, with a relative share of 63 % in 1999.

A more thorough analysis of the above industries with declining turnover reveals that the two industries are comparable in structure, since each is composed of two similar subsectors (classes of NACE Rev.1) (see Table 3.3.2).

As regards the manufacture of office machinery and computers, the share of the manufacture of computers (including other IT equipment), which accounted for more than 80 % of this industry's turnover, rose slightly between 1995 and 1999, while the relative value of office machinery fell in the same period.

The computer sector distinguishes itself from the office machinery sector by the degree and level of technological innovation in its production process. Innovation is reflected in the former in the novelty of the (highly

Table 3.3.2. Turnover in the subsectors of the pharmaceutical industry and the manufacture of office machinery and computers (as a % of total sector)

Subsector		1995	1999
Pharmaceuticals	Basic pharmaceuticals	20.3	12.7
	Manuf. of preparations	79.7	87.3
Office machinery and computers	Office machinery	16.9	15.6
	Computers, IT equipment	83.1	84.4

Source: Eurostat.

technology-intensive) products placed on the market and in the latter in the improvement of existing products.

There is a similar situation in the pharmaceutical industry. The production of pharmaceutical preparations (which includes medicaments, vaccines, etc.) far outstripped that of the basic pharmaceutical industry. In terms of relative importance, the former increased considerably in the period under review at the expense of the latter. The aspect of innovation and product novelty is vital and obvious for the pharmaceutical preparations sector and important for its economic success.

Employment in high-tech industries

Volume

At European level, employment in the high-tech sector accounted for 7.7 % of employment in the manufacturing industry in 1999. As Figure 3.3.2 shows, this figure rose slightly (+ 1.6 points) in the period under review. Of the countries analysed, Ireland achieved the highest growth (+ 9.1 points) between 1995 and 1999. There was also growth in Finland (+ 7.5), Sweden (+ 2.2) and Belgium (+ 0.7), while in the other countries employment in the sectors under review remained stable or fell slightly.

With regard to the distribution of employment by sector, the manufacture of electronic and communication equipment (NACE Rev.1, DL 32) was the European leader, as it was for turnover. 46.9 % of people employed in high-tech industries in Europe were employed in this industry (see Figure 3.3.3).

An analysis by country reveals that the countries where the influence of this sector was greatest in terms of number of people employed were Finland (80.1 % of high-tech jobs) and Austria (76.3 %) (see Table 3.3.3).

Figure 3.3.3. Distribution of employment in the high-tech sector, EU, 1999

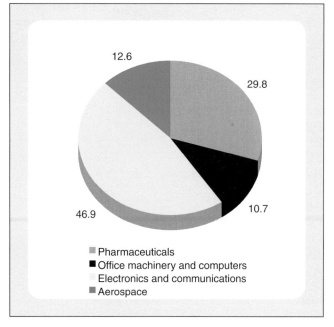

- Pharmaceuticals
- Office machinery and computers
- Electronics and communications
- Aerospace

NB: EU-15 total calculated without data for F, NL and UK.
Source: Eurostat, SBS database.

Figure 3.3.2. Employment in the high-tech sector in manufacturing industry in 1995 and 1999 (as a % of employment in manufacturing)

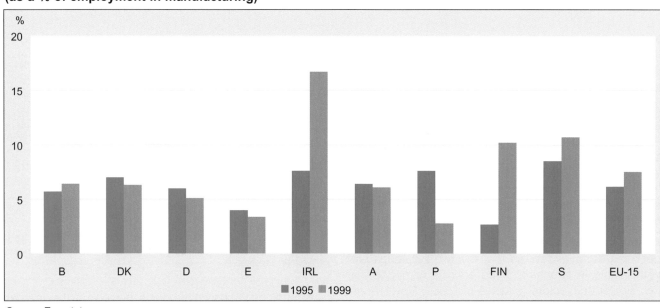

Source: Eurostat.

Table 3.3.3. Employment in the electronics and communications sector, 1999 (as a % of total high-tech employment)

	B	DK	D	E	F	IRL	I	NL	A	P	FIN	S	UK
Electronics and communications	45.9	44.8	42.0	35.1	:	31.2	45.0	:	76.3	64.3	80.7	59.3	:

Source: Eurostat, SBS database.

However, this industry also accounted for a large share of employment in the high-tech sector in the other Member States. The lowest figure was recorded in Ireland, but it still represented 31.2 % of employment in the high-tech industry.

A more detailed analysis of the three subsectors (classes of the NACE Rev.1) which make up the manufacture of electronic and communication equipment shows that for most of the countries observed employment was distributed fairly evenly among these subsectors (see Table 3.3.4). In some countries, however, there was specialisation in a particular economic activity. Table 3.3.4 shows the relative importance of the subsector "Manufacture of television and radio transmitters and apparatus for line telephony and line telegraphy" (NACE Rev. 1 DL 32.2) in Finland (84 %) and Sweden (77 %).

Trends

In most of the countries observed, there was marked or even exceptional growth in employment in high-tech industry between 1995 and 1999, while employment in manufacturing industry remained practically unchanged at European level during the same period (see Table 3.3.5). Ireland saw the highest growth in employment in the high-tech industries (+ 49.3 %). This was due to the good performance of all the industries covered by this analysis. It should be noted that Ireland also achieved very high growth in employment (+ 12.2 %) in manufacturing industry as a whole.

The greatest decrease in the period under review was in Italy, where employment fell by 10.5 % as a result of the downward trend in all the high-tech industries, but particularly as a result of a decrease of 30.6 % in employment in the manufacture of office machinery and computers. Employment in this sector also fell considerably throughout Europe (– 12.8 %) in the period under review, but was also geographically concentrated. While the number of people employed in this industry declined between 1995 and 1999 in most of the countries, there was particularly high growth in Ireland and Austria (+ 39.2 % and + 73.1 % respectively).

Table 3.3.4. Distribution of employment in the sub–sectors of the electronics and communications industry in 1999 (as a % of the total)

	B	DK	D	E	F	IRL	I	L	NL	A	P	FIN	S	UK
dl32.10/dl32	20.8	27.4	39.7	39.0	:	63.1	31.9	:	:	32.0	24.0	12.7	14.2	:
dl32.20/dl32	44.0	23.8	32.6	38.3	:	29.6	58.5	:	:	52.2	34.1	84.0	77.0	:
dl32.30/dl32	35.2	48.8	27.7	27.8	:	7.3	9.6	:	:	15.8	41.9	3.3	8.8	:

Source: Eurostat, SBS database.

Table 3.3.5. Variation in the number of persons employed in high-tech industries and in manufacturing between 1995 and 1999 (as a %)

	Pharmaceuticals	Office machinery and computers	Electronics and communications	Aerospace	High-tech	Manufacturing
EU	5.4	– 12.8	:	2.1	:	0.1
B	4.8	– 25.2	3.2	59.0	8.8	– 2.3
DK	22.4	– 9.0	19.7	:	18.7	– 3.6
D	10.0	– 32.0	– 1.7	– 2.0	– 3.7	10.7
E	– 8.2	– 18.5	3.4	6.7	– 3.7	12.6
F	3.9	16.7	0.2	– 1.3	2.6	– 1.4
IRL	48.0	39.2	69.4	:	49.3	12.2
I	– 2.3	– 30.6	– 8.3	– 13.8	– 10.5	:
A	1.1	73.1	– 10.6	52.0	– 7.3	– 2.7
P	– 17.0	– 10.3	19.2	39.6	7.1	3.2
FIN	– 7.2	– 46.0	58.1	– 20.3	31.8	9.4
S	29.3	– 16.7	22.8	:	39.6	4.8

NB: For France, the comparison is between 1996 and 1998.
Source: Eurostat, SBS database.

Concentrations of employment in some countries are also evident in other high-tech industries, thus high-lighting the specialisation of these Member States in the various high-tech sectors.

In Finland, employment in the aerospace industry fell by more than 20 % between 1995 and 1999, while this industry now employs many more people in Belgium (+ 59 % between 1995 and 1999), Austria (+ 52 %) and Portugal (+ 39.6 %).

There was an upward trend in employment in the man-ufacture of electronic and communication equipment in most of the countries observed. It was very marked in Ireland (+ 69.4 % between 1995 and 1999) and Finland (+ 58.1 %). In contrast, employment in this industry fell considerably in Austria (– 10.6 %) and Italy (– 8.3 %) in the period under review.

Apparent labour productivity

In virtually all the Member States, apparent labour pro-ductivity (value added per person employed) in high-tech industry highlights the performance of this sector.

The figures recorded for productivity in high-tech industry exceed those of the manufacturing industry in all the countries observed, the greatest differences being in Finland and Denmark (see Table 3.3.6).

In terms of absolute values, Finland and Ireland are the countries with the highest productivity (respective-ly ECU 100 300 and ECU 103 900 per person employed).

In a large majority of the countries observed there was an upward trend in productivity in high-tech industry; Finland was in the lead with an increase of ECU 40 800 between 1995 and 1998. However, in the Netherlands and Ireland apparent labour productivity in high-tech industry fell between 1995 and respec-tively 1997 and 1998.

Manufacturing industry, on the other hand, increased its productivity in all the countries observed, although at a much more modest rate.

A more thorough analysis of the various industries which make up high-tech industry reveals that the manufacture of electronic and communication equip-ment (NACE Rev. 1 DL 32) had the lowest figure for

Table 3.3.6. Apparent labour productivity in high-tech industries and in manufacturing between 1995 and 1998 (1 000 ECU)

	1995		1996		1997		1998	
	High-tech	Manufacturing	High-tech	Manufacturing	High-tech	Manufacturing	High-tech	Manufacturing
B	81.5	59.5	82.3	56.8	88.6	59.0	81.4	59.5
DK	60.3	40.1	68.4	42.2	60.7	43.5	69.2	46.4
D	53.3	50.4	55.9	52.2	61.5	53.0	64.1	54.7
EL	23.1	20.0	24.1	20.0	34.0	30.0	38.4	30.0
E	52.2	30.0	58.2	30.0	58.6	30.0	59.4	40.0
F	:	:	61.2	44.9	67.5	46.3	69.1	48.1
IRL	114.1	64.8	95.7	69.5	108.2	82.9	103.9	87.6
I	47.7	30.0	51.9	40.0	53.3	40.0	:	:
L	:	57.7	:	56.9	:	62.0	:	64.0
NL	68.9	55.7	59.8	56.1	69.8	:	:	:
A	63.8	49.0	:	:	63.4	48.4	75.8	51.2
P	:	:	26.6	15.1	31.8	16.2	33.9	17.1
FIN	59.5	53.5	60.9	52.7	80.3	56.7	100.3	59.3
S	61.5	50.9	67.6	52.7	105.0	56.7	76.7	54.7
UK	:	:	52.6	40.1	67.5	49.1	:	:

NB: The 1995 figures for the Netherlands are estimates.
Source: Eurostat, SBS database.

productivity, with ECU 55 400 per person employed. Product innovation in this sector and the recent success of its products on the market mean large numbers of jobs but also increasing standardisation of technologies, accessible to an ever-increasing number of manufacturers, which results in reduced value added. These two factors combined explain the level of productivity in this sector.

The pharmaceutical industry, with ECU 80 200, had the highest productivity (see Table 3.3.7). The productivity of the four industries analysed increased to varying degrees between 1996 and 1998, the greatest increase being in the aerospace industry — from ECU 45 000 in 1996 to ECU 70 400 in 1998.

Table 3.3.7. Apparent labour productivity in high-tech subsectors and in manufacturing in the EU

	Pharmaceuticals	Office machinery and computers	Electronics and communications	Aerospace	High-tech	Manufacturing
1998	80.2	74.6	55.4	70.4	68.9	51.4
1997	81.2	67.5	58.4	60.3	66.1	47.6
1996	77.8	67.4	44.8	45.0	56.1	42.5

Source: Eurostat, SBS database.

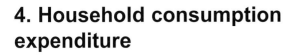

4. Household consumption expenditure

4.1. Overview

Consumption is certainly an important variable in determining the economic performance of a country. In this respect, it has been presented in Chapter 1. But in addition, consumption also reflects social conditions, in particular related to the welfare of a country.

In 2000, households in the EU spent EUR 4 956 billion (at current prices) for their consumption. When calculating per capita figures, the average spending of households in the EU in 1999 was EUR 13 120 per head. In order to better compare Member States, consumption per head has been calculated in purchasing power standards (1) (PPS). In 2000, the United Kingdom, alongside Luxembourg, stands out as having per capita figures well above the average of other Member States: + 34 % for Luxembourg and + 16 % for the United Kingdom. The lowest figures have been registered in Portugal (20 % below the EU value), Spain and Greece (both 18 % under the EU average).

These figures relating to total consumption have already been presented in Section 1.3 (see Table 1.3.1 and Figure 1.3.1). But even if consumption, as a total, has a relevant role in the determination of economic results, when splitting household consumption into different items according to purpose, further interesting conclusions become available. This chapter aims at determining consumption patterns, finding differences and similarities between them and pointing out the evolution over time of the spending behaviour of EU households (2).

When considering the structure of consumption in Figure 4.1.1, a first relevant observation is that three items take up the largest part of household consumption, defining clearly the "basic" consumption items in the EU: nearly half of the total consumption expenditure is spent for food, housing and transport. Around one quarter of household consumption is dedicated to more "recreational" items. The remaining part is spent for minor sub-items of consumption.

Breakdown of consumption by purpose

Household final consumption expenditure is broken down by consumption purpose using the Coicop classification ("classification of individual consumption by purpose"). The following 2-digit Coicop items will be distinguished here:

— Food and non-alcoholic beverages
— Alcoholic beverages, tobacco and narcotics
— Clothing and footwear
— Housing, water, electricity, gas and other fuels
— Furnishings, household equipment and routine household maintenance
— Health
— Transport
— Communication
— Recreation and culture
— Education
— Restaurants and hotels
— Miscellaneous goods and services

Figure 4.1.1. Structure of consumption expenditure in EU-15, 1999 (as a % of total consumption)

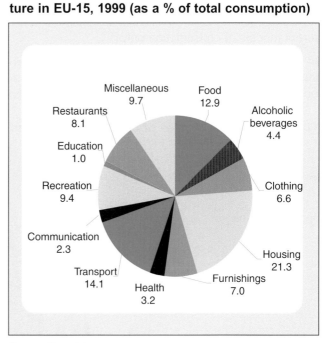

Source: Eurostat.

---

(1) Purchasing Power Standards are calculated on the base of Purchasing Power Parities (PPP). These PPP represent the relationship between the amounts of national currency needed to purchase a comparable, representative basket of goods in the country concerned. PPPs are calculated for total consumption only; thus no per head figures for specific items of consumption will be presented.

(2) The latest year for which these breakdowns of household consumption by purpose is available is 1999.

Looking at the temporal trend in consumption items in Table 4.1.1, the first evidence is that the share of food consumption in household spending is getting lower over time. This is a natural evolution in developed countries, as the EU Member States. Housing is generally becoming the single most important item in household spending for consumption, followed by expenses for transports.

Moreover, the differences in the structure among EU countries (see Figure 4.1.3) give a quite good indication of the existing models of consumption. The relationship between a country's welfare and the pattern of consumption is confirmed by the fact that Greece and Portugal, which show the smallest GDP per capita figures (used here as an indication of a country's welfare), also show the largest shares of consumption dedicated to food. As well, though somewhat less unambiguous, at least an indication of a certain preference in the pattern of consumption is given by the fact that the largest shares of food consumption are recorded in Mediterranean countries. Households in northern countries, on the other hand, dedicate the largest parts of their consumption to housing. Since consumption expenditure is influenced by a large range of factors that make figures not easily comparable, the figures here should be considered as a simple indication of different models of consumption only.

In terms of growth, expenditure for food and for housing has been rather steady, while spending for transport showed higher growth rates. The most dynamic

Table 4.1.1. Structure of consumption expenditure in the EU-15, 1995–99
(as a % of total consumption)

	1995	1999
Food and non-alcoholic beverages	14.2	12.9
Alcoholic beverages, tobacco	4.2	4.4
Clothing and footwear	7.0	6.6
Housing, water, electricity, gas	21.4	21.3
Furnishings, household equipment	7.1	7.0
Health	3.4	3.2
Transport	13.5	14.1
Communication	2.0	2.3
Recreation and culture	9.0	9.4
Education	0.9	1.0
Restaurants and hotels	8.0	8.1
Miscellaneous	9.2	9.7

Source: Eurostat.

item of consumption in the EU has been expenditure for communication, but these still represent only a minor part of total spending (2.3 % in 1999). Among Member States, the highest growth rates have been recorded in the Netherlands and in Finland. Other items of consumption showing particular dynamic growth have been those for recreation and for transport.

Figure 4.1.2. Growth rates of consumption expenditure by item in the EU-15, 1996–99 (as a %)

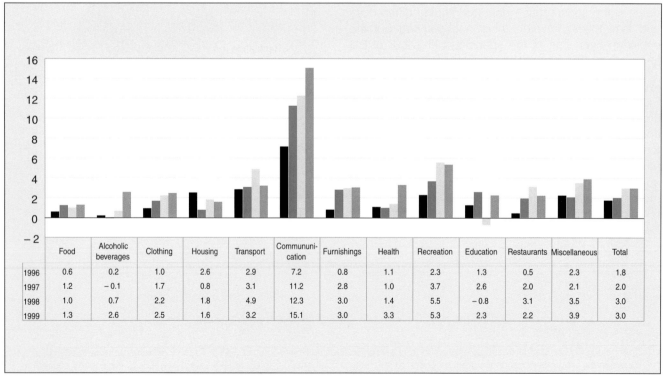

	Food	Alcoholic beverages	Clothing	Housing	Transport	Communication	Furnishings	Health	Recreation	Education	Restaurants	Miscellaneous	Total
1996	0.6	0.2	1.0	2.6	2.9	7.2	0.8	1.1	2.3	1.3	0.5	2.3	1.8
1997	1.2	– 0.1	1.7	0.8	3.1	11.2	2.8	1.0	3.7	2.6	2.0	2.1	2.0
1998	1.0	0.7	2.2	1.8	4.9	12.3	3.0	1.4	5.5	– 0.8	3.1	3.5	3.0
1999	1.3	2.6	2.5	1.6	3.2	15.1	3.0	3.3	5.3	2.3	2.2	3.9	3.0

Source: Eurostat.

Figure 4.1.3. Shares of the most important items of consumption expenditure among Member States, 1999 (as a % of total consumption)

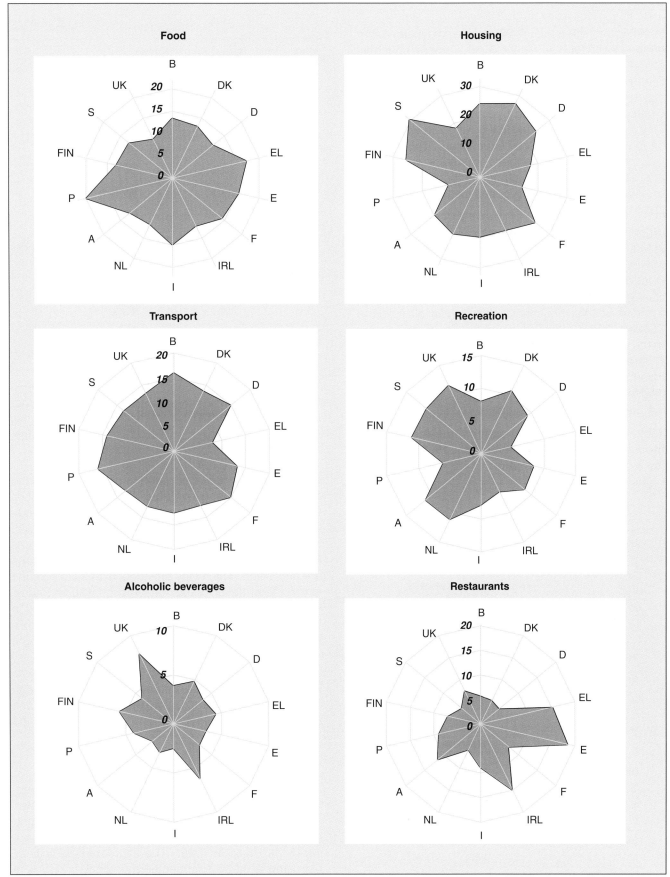

Source: Eurostat.

4.2. Analysis by purpose

Food

In 1999, the highest figures for household expenditure on food were recorded in the Mediterranean countries of the EU. Portugal came first among the Member States, with food and non-alcoholic beverages accounting for 20.1 % of total expenditure. Next came Greece (17.2 %), followed by Italy and Spain (around 15 %). Households in the United Kingdom spent least on food: only 9.8 % of total expenditure. The figure in Germany and the Netherlands was somewhat higher at above 11 %, and in the other Member States the figures were fairly closely grouped between 12 % and just over 14 %.

When the structure of expenditure in 1999 (the most recent year for which data are available) is compared with the figures for 1995 (the first year for which data compiled according to the ESA 95 are available), it can clearly be seen that expenditure on food is declining as a share of total household spending in all Member States. This is normal in countries where living standards are high and where spending is thus channelled in other directions. The biggest reductions occurred in Ireland, where spending on food as a percentage of total expenditure fell by 3.7 points, and Spain (down by 2.4 points).

Table 4.2.1. Consumption expenditure for food and non-alcoholic beverages, 1995–99 (as a % of total consumption)

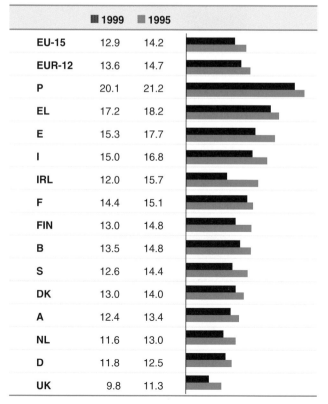

	1999	1995
EU-15	12.9	14.2
EUR-12	13.6	14.7
P	20.1	21.2
EL	17.2	18.2
E	15.3	17.7
I	15.0	16.8
IRL	12.0	15.7
F	14.4	15.1
FIN	13.0	14.8
B	13.5	14.8
S	12.6	14.4
DK	13.0	14.0
A	12.4	13.4
NL	11.6	13.0
D	11.8	12.5
UK	9.8	11.3

Source: Eurostat.

Table 4.2.2. Consumption expenditure for food and non-alcoholic beverages, growth index for volume and prices, 1999

	(1996 = 100)	
	■ Volume	■ Price
EU-15	103.6	102.6
EUR-11	103.7	102.7
P	113.3	106.2
EL	106.7	111.4
FIN	105.6	102.8
E	105.5	101.8
NL	104.4	105.2
F	104.2	103.6
DK	103.4	104.8
D	103.1	101.1
S	102.9	103.8
I	102.4	101.7
UK	102.4	101.2
IRL	101.4	108.9
A	101.2	102.5
B	99.9	104.1

Source: Eurostat.

Growth indices were calculated in order to assess the absolute variation (see Table 4.2.2). These indices show how much the volume of consumption expenditure went up between 1996 and 1999, based on 1996 as the reference year. In addition, the growth indices for consumer prices for the consumption item at hand are presented, which may provide a useful background to the interpretation of the consumption volume trends. In 1999, the biggest absolute growth was recorded in Portugal, where spending on food and non-alcoholic beverages was up by 13.3 % in comparison with the reference year. As a rule, the variations were not very large, and in Belgium in particular the 1999 figure was basically the same as that for the reference year. Overall in the European Union, the 1999 figure for food and non-alcoholic beverages was 3.6 % above the 1996 figure.

Housing

The single biggest share of total household consumption in the European Union is used for housing, water, electricity, gas and other fuels. This heading accounted for just over a fifth (21.1 %) of all household spending in the Union in 1999. The figure was particularly high among the Nordic members of the EU: 30.6 % in Sweden, 27.3 % in Denmark and 25.5 % in Finland.

Corresponding strong deviations from the average show at the other end of the scale, where particularly in Portugal housing, water, electricity, gas and other fuels accounted for only a very small percentage of total household expenditure (10.9 %). All in all, there are thus two distinct geographic groups: on the one side there is the Nordic group (Denmark, Finland and Sweden) where the figures are high; on the other side, there are three Mediterranean countries — i.e. Portugal, Greece and Spain — where the figures are low.

When changes in the structure of household consumption are compared over the period from 1996 to 1999, it can be seen that spending as a percentage on housing, water, electricity, gas and other fuels stayed more or less the same. There was very little change in the percentage figure between 1995 and 1999, with a reduction of only 0.1 percentage points from 21.4 to 21.3 %. In virtually every Member State the change was negligible over the period under review, the exceptions being Ireland and Sweden. There was a significant change, where spending on housing increased its share by 3.6 percentage points, and in Sweden, the Member State that spends most on housing, water, electricity, gas and other fuels as a percent-

age of total household consumption, where however the share fell by 1.9 points.

Lastly, as a way of indicating absolute changes in volumes and prices during the review period, Table 4.2.4 shows the growth indices. In 1999, expenditure volumes for housing, water, electricity, gas and other fuels were up by 4.2 % compared with the reference year, whereas prices showed a somewhat bigger increase (+ 5.5 %) in comparison to 1996. The strongest increases in the volume of expenditure on housing were observed for Ireland and Portugal, whereas this volume remained virtually unchanged in Sweden.

Table 4.2.4. Consumption expenditure for housing, water, electricity, gas and other fuels, growth index for volume and prices, 1999

	(1996 = 100)	
	■ Volume	■ Price
EU-15	104.2	105.5
EUR-11	104.5	105.3
IRL	120.5	101.9
P	113.3	107.8
E	108.9	107.1
FIN	107.1	106.4
EL	106.2	106.3
F	105.1	102.0
B	104.7	104.1
A	104.1	105.4
D	103.9	105.1
UK	103.6	105.2
NL	103.0	110.9
DK	102.7	109.9
I	102.3	108.1
S	100.1	103.9

Source: Eurostat.

Transport

Transport is the third big consumption item for households in the European Union, together with housing and food: in 1999, transport accounted for 14.1 % of total consumption in the Union, a share bigger now than that of household spending on food. The highest relative rates of household spending on transport, at around 16 %, were recorded in Belgium and Portugal. In Greece (9.1 %), on the other hand, transport is relatively less significant as a consumption item. The low share of household expenditure on transport in Greece stands apart from the values observed in the other EU countries.

Table 4.2.3. Consumption expenditure for housing, water, electricity, gas and other fuels, 1995–99 (as a % of total consumption)

	(As a % of total consumption)	
	■ 1999	■ 1995
EU-15	21.3	21.4
EUR-11	21.5	21.3
S	30.6	32.5
DK	27.3	27.4
FIN	25.5	25.3
B	24.4	24.3
F	23.9	23.8
D	24.3	23.4
NL	20.8	21.4
I	19.8	19.4
UK	18.2	19.1
A	19.7	18.8
EL	17.5	17.6
IRL	19.5	15.9
E	14.5	14.7
P	10.9	11.0

Source: Eurostat.

Over the period under review, there was only modest change in the percentage of expenditure devoted to transport in the Union (+ 0.6 percentage points between 1995 and 1999) or in most Member States. Belgium is conspicuous, in that household expenditure on transport soared over the period: in 1999 it was 3 % higher than in 1995 and the highest on record in the EU. The rates rose in Spain and Finland, too, albeit more moderately. Greece is unique, in that the share of spending on transport did not grow.

The extraordinary growth in spending on transport in some EU countries is all the more visible in view of the growth indices: in 1999, expenditure volumes for transport in Ireland were higher by more than one third in comparison to those recorded in 1996 (+ 35.6 %), and spending on transport (at constant prices) grew by 31.4 % in Spain, by 20.5 % in Belgium and by 20.0 % in Finland.

Table 4.2.5 Consumption expenditure for transport, 1995–99 (as a % of total consumption)

	(As a % of total consumption)	
	■ 1999	■ 1995
EU-15	14.1	13.5
EUR-11	14.0	13.4
P	16.0	15.2
F	15.0	14.6
D	15.1	14.2
UK	14.5	14.2
DK	13.8	13.5
B	16.1	13.1
FIN	14.0	12.8
A	12.7	12.6
I	12.6	12.3
NL	12.4	12.2
S	13.2	12.1
E	13.4	11.6
IRL	12.3	11.4
EL	9.1	9.2

Source: Eurostat.

Table 4.2.6 Consumption expenditure for transport, growth index for volume and prices, 1999

	(1996 = 100)	
	■ Volume	■ Price
EU-15	111.6	104.9
EUR-11	111.8	103.9
IRL	135.6	106.4
E	131.4	104.8
B	120.5	104.4
FIN	120.0	104.5
S	118.2	102.8
NL	117.0	104.2
P	115.1	110.2
I	112.3	105.0
EL	111.9	106.5
UK	110.2	109.6
D	108.9	104.0
A	107.6	101.9
DK	106.1	107.2
F	105.5	102.2

Source: Eurostat.

Recreational items

As has been pointed out, nearly half of all household consumption focuses on the three components of expenditure that have just been described. In the European Union in 1999, households spent 48.3 % of total expenditure on housing, water, electricity, gas and other fuels, transport and food and non-alcoholic beverages.

If we regard these headings as items of "basic" consumption, it is then possible to identify those items that can be better described as "recreational". As a convention, when speaking of recreational consumption expenditure, this covers the items recreation and culture, restaurants and hotels and alcoholic beverages and tobacco. When the figures for these three headings of household consumption are added together, we find that in the EU in 1999 recreational spending accounted for 21.9 % of total expenditure, or well below half of the figure for basic consumption spending.

Table 4.2.7 Consumption expenditure for "recreational" items, 1995–99 (as a % of total consumption)

	Recreation		Restaurants		Alcoholic beverages		Total "recreational"	
	1995	1999	1995	1999	1995	1999	1995	1999
EU-15	9.0	9.4	8.0	8.1	4.2	4.4	21.2	21.9
EUR-11	8.7	8.8	8.3	8.4	3.5	3.5	20.5	20.6
B	8.5	8.1	6.0	5.8	3.8	3.9	18.4	17.8
DK	10.6	10.8	5.4	5.4	5.0	4.9	21.0	21.0
D	9.4	9.3	5.5	5.0	3.9	3.9	18.9	18.2
EL	4.3	4.7	14.7	15.4	4.2	4.5	23.2	24.6
E	8.5	8.4	18.9	18.6	2.7	3.4	30.1	30.5
F	8.5	8.7	7.3	7.4	3.4	3.4	19.2	19.5
IRL	7.7	6.5	14.5	15.0	6.6	6.3	28.8	27.7
I	7.3	7.9	8.7	8.9	2.5	2.5	18.5	19.2
L	:	:	:	:	:	:	:	:
NL	11.0	11.1	5.8	5.9	3.5	3.2	20.4	20.2
A	11.0	11.2	12.0	11.5	2.7	2.8	25.7	25.5
P	5.6	6.1	9.0	8.9	4.3	4.1	18.9	19.2
FIN	11.0	11.1	7.2	7.1	6.1	5.7	24.2	23.9
S	10.2	11.0	4.6	5.1	4.6	4.1	19.4	20.2
UK	10.3	11.7	7.1	7.6	8.6	8.0	26.0	27.3

Source: Eurostat.

Table 4.2.7 gives the figures for recreational consumption. A closer look at the European figures reveals that in 1999 households in the European Union spent 9.4 % of their total expenditure on recreation and culture, 8.1 % on restaurants and hotels and 4.4 % on alcoholic beverages and tobacco, totalling the 21.9 % just mentioned. It can further be seen that in 1999 households in Spain and Ireland stood out for their high levels of recreational consumption. For both, this is primarily due to a high share of consumption expenditure for restaurants and hotels. Belgium and Italy, on the other hand, showed the lowest consumption shares for recreational items. Belgium was, in fact, below the EU average for all three sub-items.

The highest figures for percentage spending on recreation and culture in the EU was recorded in the United Kingdom (11.7 %), followed by Austria, Finland and the Netherlands, with figures of around 11 %. Greece was at the other extreme, with a figure of 4.7 %.

For restaurants and hotels, it is Spain that is well ahead of the other Member States, with Spanish households devoting 18.6 % of their total expenditure to this heading in 1999. Next come Greece and Ireland, with figures of 15.4 % and 15.0 % respectively. The countries where households spend least on restaurants and hotels are Germany and Sweden, where the figure is about 5 %.

In order to give a general impression, Figure 4.2.1 shows the changes in volume by country for each of the three sub-headings, with the countries presented in the order of the magnitude of growth. It can be seen that in the United Kingdom consumption in volume terms for recreation and culture grew by one third in the review period. In the Union as a whole, the figure showed a rise of 15.3 %, and there were substantial rises in most Member States. The smallest changes were in France, Belgium and Germany.

The changes were generally less marked in the case of restaurants and hotels, for which in the EU as a whole the increase over the period was 7.5 %. There was a big rise only in Ireland, where the figure for restaurants and hotels posted an increase of 27.8 % in relation to the reference year. In Germany, on the other hand, the 1999 figure was actually slightly down on the 1996 figure.

The changes were even smaller for alcoholic beverages and tobacco, which recorded an increase of only 3.1 % in the EU during the review period. The highest growth indices were achieved in Spain and Ireland, but increases were much less marked in the other Member States. Indeed, in the United Kingdom and Sweden the 1999 figures were down on those of the reference year.

115

Figure 4.2.1. Consumption expenditure for "recreational" items, volume growth index, 1999 (1996 = 100)

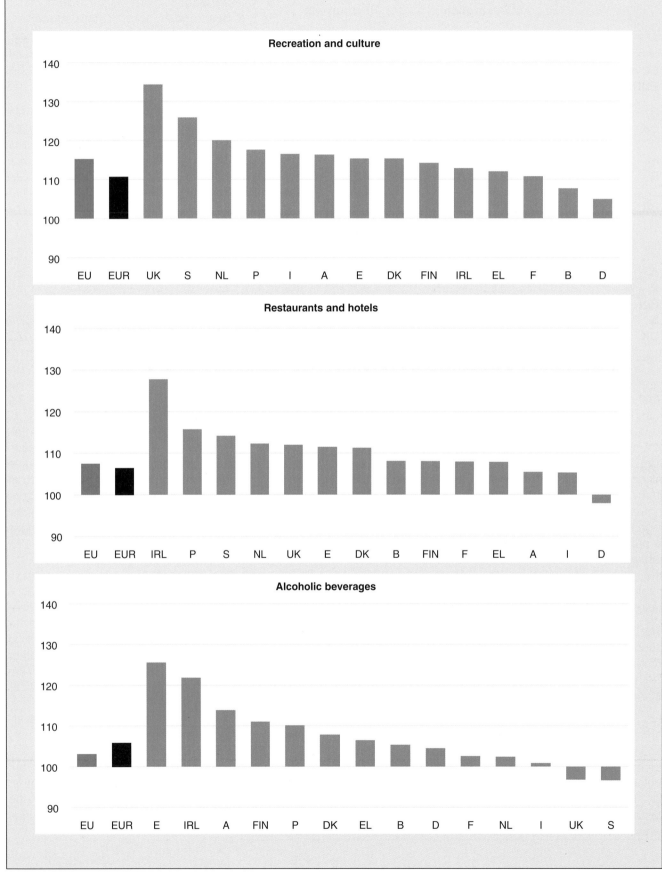

Source: Eurostat.

Others

In this section we describe the remaining items of consumption. These have been grouped together for being of minor importance in total consumption or for lack of consistency among data. Altogether, these six items of consumption accounted for less than one third of total expenditure of households for consumption in the EU. In the following section a short description of the expenses for clothing and footwear (6.6 % of total private consumption expenditure in the EU, 1999), for furnishings, household equipment and routine maintenance of the house (7.0 %) and for communication (2.3 %) will be given. As for the remaining three headings, health (3.2 %), education (1.0 %) and other goods and services (9.7 %), no further discussion will be provided. In fact, because of their peculiar characteristics, those three functions could not be compared among countries and over the time.

In 1999, expenditure for clothing and footwear in the European Union was 6.6 % of total consumption. Among Member States in three southern countries the expenditure for clothing and footwear was proportionally the highest: Greece (10.7 %), Italy (9.2 %) and in Portugal (8.3 %). At the opposite end, households in Finland (4.6 %) and Denmark (5.0 %) spent the smallest shares on this item. Over the period under review all Member States reduced the proportion spent on clothing and footwear (see Table 4.2.8). Considering the absolute growth over the period considered (1996 = 100) in Table 4.2.9, in the EU spending at constant prices for buying clothing and footwear increased by 6.5 %, while the corresponding prices had a smaller variation of 1.6 % only. Among Member States, in Ireland, spending on this item had the most substantial increase and the 1999 figure was 54.5 % higher than the benchmark value. The next largest variations were recorded in Portugal and the United Kingdom (around + 16 %). It should be noted that in those three countries, concurrent with the large increase in spending volume, prices recorded a contraction.

Spending for furnishings, household equipment and routine maintenance of the house in 1999 took a share of 7.0 % in total consumption — this item thus being slightly ahead of clothing and footwear. Households in Italy (9.4 %) and in Austria (8.6 %) dedicated the largest parts of total spending to this item, while their counterparts in Sweden (4.8 %) and Finland (4.6 %) spent the smallest shares. Over last five years this figure for the EU as a whole reduced only marginally. Specifically, among the four biggest economies, in Germany and Italy this item lost importance, whilst in France and the United Kingdom the quota increased. In no Member State did this item see radical changes, and variations in the quotas were fairly modest (see Table 4.2.8). When considering the absolute growth of

household spending for furnishings, household equipment and routine maintenance of the house the variations are more important: in 1999 spending in Sweden (+ 22.3 %), Ireland (+ 21.3 %) and the United Kingdom (+ 21.2 %) was much higher than the same figure recorded in 1996 (the reference year). Prices tended to increase in all Member States, the only exception being in Sweden.

As a percentage of total consumption, the households in the Union dedicated 2.3 % of their total consumption to communication. Dutch and Swedish households showed the largest quotas (respectively with 3.2 % and 3.0 %), while in Belgium and Portugal this item accounted for a rather negligible part of total consumption. Over the period under consideration (1995/1999) this item expanded its importance in almost all Member States; the exceptions being Belgium and Portugal. In particular, the part of consumption dedicated to communication increased strongly in the Netherlands, in Italy, in Austria and in Finland — in those countries the quota increased by roughly one percentage point. Albeit relatively small in absolute terms, communication has been the most dynamic item in household consumption: in the EU in 1999 spending for communication grew by 15.1 % while prices dropped. Considering absolute growth over the 1996/99 period the spending in the EU in 1999 was 43.7 % higher than the benchmark figure. In the Netherlands spending nearly doubled over the ref-

Table 4.2.8 Consumption expenditure for "other" items, 1995–99 (as a % of total consumption)

	Clothing		Furnishings		Communications	
	1995	1999	1995	1999	1995	1999
EU-15	7.0	6.6	7.1	7.0	2.0	2.3
EUR-11	7.2	6.8	7.4	7.3	1.9	2.4
B	6.8	5.7	6.7	5.8	0.1	0.1
DK	5.2	5.0	5.8	5.6	1.7	1.8
D	7.1	6.5	7.6	7.2	2.0	2.3
EL	10.9	10.7	6.6	6.4	1.5	1.8
E	6.8	6.5	6.2	6.1	1.8	2.1
F	5.5	5.2	6.3	6.4	1.8	1.9
IRL	7.3	6.5	7.0	6.8	1.8	2.0
I	9.6	9.2	9.6	9.4	2.1	2.9
L	:	:	:	:	:	:
NL	6.5	6.2	7.4	7.4	2.1	3.2
A	7.1	6.7	8.9	8.6	2.0	2.8
P	8.4	8.3	6.8	7.0	0.2	0.2
FIN	4.8	4.6	4.5	4.6	1.9	2.7
S	5.4	5.4	4.6	4.8	2.3	3.0
UK	6.7	6.2	5.9	6.2	2.1	2.2

Source: Eurostat.

erence period, in Finland it increased by 76.0 % and in Ireland by 64.6 %. The smallest variation has been recorded in France, where spending in 1999 was higher than in the reference year by only 16.5 %. Also considering prices, communication recorded an extraordi-

nary development in EU countries: Prices actually tended to fall, with the exception of Spain (+ 4.7 % in 1999), Sweden (+ 3.2 %), and Greece and Italy, where prices remained stable (see Table 4.2.9).

Table 4.2.9 Consumption expenditure for 'other' items, growth index for volume and prices, 1999

	Clothing			Furnishings			Communications	
	(1996 = 100)			(1996 = 100)			(1996 = 100)	
	volume	price		volume	price		volume	price
EU-15	106.5	101.6	**EU-15**	109.1	103.2	**EU-15**	143.7	93.9
EUR-11	104.6	103.4	**EUR-11**	107.0	103.6	**EUR-11**	145.8	93.5
IRL	154.5	82.7	**S**	122.3	99.2	**NL**	190.7	96.2
P	116.8	95.6	**IRL**	121.3	107.7	**FIN**	176.0	98.2
UK	116.4	88.8	**UK**	121.2	101.6	**IRL**	164.6	85.8
FIN	113.9	99.0	**FIN**	118.5	101.5	**A**	158.2	95.8
NL	111.5	104.3	**P**	116.8	105.5	**I**	154.9	99.5
E	111.3	106.7	**NL**	116.4	104.9	**D**	154.7	87.4
S	110.3	102.1	**E**	114.5	107.7	**UK**	141.0	93.0
DK	110.1	92.0	**DK**	108.7	104.8	**B**	136.5	97.9
EL	107.2	117.2	**EL**	108.1	114.7	**E**	127.5	104.7
A	106.7	99.4	**A**	108.0	104.4	**S**	126.9	103.2
F	106.4	100.4	**I**	107.6	106.1	**P**	125.9	95.4
I	103.1	107.4	**F**	107.3	102.0	**DK**	122.6	94.2
D	100.2	101.1	**B**	102.6	101.9	**EL**	118.2	100.2
B	93.8	102.6	**D**	102.5	102.2	**F**	116.5	94.1

Source: Eurostat.

5. General government in the Union

This section sets out to provide an overview of the size and structure of the public sector in the various Member States (see box entitled "Definition of general government"). After outlining the importance of general government in national economies with the help of the major aggregates of the national accounts, it will first consider the revenue, in particular taxes, and the expenditure of general government and then the difference between the two that amounts to public surplus/deficit.

Definition of general government

According to the "European system of national and regional accounts in the Community" (ESA 95), the general government sector includes "all institutional units which are other non-market producers whose output is intended for individual and collective consumption, and mainly financed by compulsory payments made by units belonging to other sectors, and/or all institutional units principally engaged in the redistribution of national income and wealth". General government is divided into four subsectors: central government, State government, local government and social security funds.

5.1. Major aggregates of general government

In the Union and in the euro-zone, general government output accounts for slightly less than a fifth of GDP (see Table 5.1.1). If intermediate consumption – 6.1 % of GDP in the Union, on average — is disregarded, the gross value added of the sector amounted to 12.3 % of GDP in the Union, and 12.6 % in the euro-zone, in 1999. It ranged in the Member States between 8.9 % and 19.7 %.

Table 5.1.1. Main aggregates of general government, 1999 (as a % of GDP)

	P1	P2	D1	P3	P51
	Output	Intermediate consumption	Compensation of employees	Final consumption expenditure	GFCF
EU-15	18.4	6.1	10.4	20.0	2.3
EUR-11	17.3	4.7	10.7	20.0	2.5
B	16.4	3.1	11.6	21.4	1.8
DK	27.3	7.9	17.1	25.5	1.7
D	13.6	3.9	8.3	19.0	1.8
EL	16.6	4.8	11.5	15.0	4.1
E	16.0	4.0	10.5	17.3	3.3
F	21.8	5.5	13.7	23.6	2.9
IRL	14.1	5.2	8.2	14.0	2.6
I	17.4	4.9	10.6	18.0	2.5
L	15.0	3.4	8.7	17.5	4.5
NL	18.9	6.2	10.2	22.8	3.0
A	18.2	5.8	11.4	19.8	1.8
P	20.3	4.0	14.4	19.8	4.1
FIN	25.4	9.2	13.6	21.5	2.8
S	29.3	9.6	16.5	26.9	2.8
UK	20.6	11.5	7.5	18.5	1.1

Source: Eurostat.

General government compensation of employees in the Union and the euro-zone amounted to 10.4 % and 10.7 % of GDP respectively in 1999, with figures in individual Member States ranging from 7.5 % in the United Kingdom to 16.5 % in Sweden and 17.1 % in Denmark.

Final consumption expenditure of general government in the Member States ranged between 14.0 % (Ireland) and 26.9 % (Sweden) of GDP in 1999, the Community average being 20.0 %. As for gross fixed capital formation, it accounted for between 1.1 % (United Kingdom) and 4.5 % (Luxembourg) of GDP in 1999. The average for the Union as a whole was 2.3 %, and for the euro-zone 2.5 %.

5.2. General government revenue and expenditure

On 10 July 2000, the European Commission adopted Regulation (EC) No 1500/2000 implementing Council Regulation (EC) No 2223/96 (the "ESA 95 regulation") with respect to general government expenditure and revenue.

The culmination of the work of a task force that brought together Eurostat, the 15 Member States, the European Central Bank and the ECFIN Directorate-General, the regulation offers for the first time a common definition of total general government revenue and expenditure and provides one of the first components of a complete and consistent set of harmonised accounts relating to the public sector in Europe.

It should be noted that according to the regulation, the difference between the total revenue and the total expenditure must be equal to the surplus/deficit of general government (see Section 5.3).

General government revenue

In 2000, total general government revenue (see Table 5.2.1) varies between 39.5 % (Spain) and 62.5 % (Sweden) of GDP, depending on the Member State. By way of comparison, the overall figure for government revenue in the United States and Japan varies between 33 % and 35 % of GDP.

Taxes and social security contributions account for about 90 % of general government revenue in the Union. Other sources (property income, other current transfers, capital transfers) are of minor importance (see Figure 5.2.1). It is worth noting that the Union's own resources (agricultural levies, customs duties, VAT revenue) appear in the accounts according to the ESA as direct payments to the rest of the world and are not therefore included under either revenue or expenditure of general government.

Taxes and social security contributions are thus the main source of general government revenue in the Union.

Taxes on production and imports and taxes on income and wealth reached 13.9 % and 14.5 % of GDP in the Union (see Table 5.2.2). The figures for the euro-zone were 13.7 % and 13.1 % respectively. The range for taxes on production and imports (from 11.6 % in Spain to 17.0 % in Denmark) was narrower than for taxes on income and wealth (from 10.5 % in Greece and Spain to 28.7 % in Denmark).

Social security contributions accounted for a significant percentage of GDP in 2000: 14.4 % in the Union

Table 5.2.1. Total general government revenue (as a % of GDP)

	1995	1996	1997	1998	1999	2000
EU-15	46.3	47.0	47.1	46.8	47.2	47.1
EUR-11	46.6	47.4	47.7	47.2	47.7	47.5
B	48.6	49.3	49.7	50.0	50.0	50.3
DK	58.0	58.8	58.3	58.0	58.5	55.7
D	46.1	46.8	46.5	46.6	47.2	47.0
EL	40.3	41.8	43.4	44.9	46.5	:
E	38.4	38.8	39.1	39.2	39.6	39.5
F	49.7	51.4	51.9	51.2	51.9	51.4
IRL	39.4	39.5	38.5	37.7	37.6	:
I	45.8	46.1	48.4	46.8	47.1	46.1
L	48.3	47.9	47.0	46.4	47.3	46.5
NL	47.3	47.8	47.1	46.4	47.5	:
A	52.1	52.8	52.2	52.0	51.6	50.7
P	40.4	41.6	41.7	41.8	42.7	43.9
FIN	56.2	56.8	55.3	54.5	53.6	55.1
S	60.0	62.2	61.6	62.9	62.1	62.5
UK	40.1	39.8	40.0	41.2	41.4	42.1

Source: Eurostat.

and 16.4 % in the euro-zone. Here, too, there were big differences between Member States, since for example actual social contributions as a percentage of GDP ranged from 2.2 % in Denmark to 17.6 % in Germany.

Because of the changeover from ESA 79 to ESA 95, it is still hard this year to calculate the compulsory levy ratio (total taxes and social security contributions in relation to gross domestic product). On account of the

Figure 5.2.1. Main categories of general government revenue, 2000 (as a % of total)

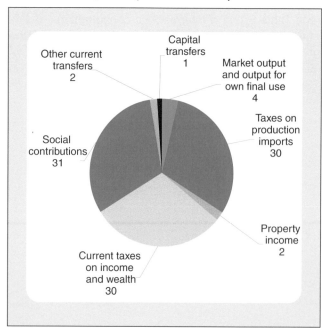

Source: Eurostat.

lack — until very recently ([1]) — of a common methodology and the discrepancies observed among the Member States with regard to the format of data and the length of series concerning GDP, taxes and social security contributions, it was felt that it would be better to forgo this exercise so that there would be no risk of misinterpreting the results.

Table 5.2.2. Main categories of taxes and social contributions, 2000 (as a % of GDP)

	D2	D5	D91	D2	D2	Total
	T.P.I	C.T.I.W.	C.T.	A.S.C.	I.S.C.	([1])
EU-15	13.9	14.5	0.3	13.4	1.0	43.1
EUR-11	13.7	13.1	0.3	15.3	1.1	43.5
B	13.4	17.6	0.5	14.3	2.0	47.8
DK	17.0	28.7	0.2	2.2	1.0	49.1
D	12.0	12.5	0.1	17.6	1.0	43.2
EL ([2])	15.2	10.5	0.3	11.7	2.0	39.7
E	11.6	10.5	0.4	12.5	0.9	35.9
F	15.5	12.3	0.6	16.5	1.8	46.7
IRL ([2])	13.1	13.8	0.5	4.4	1.4	33.2
I	15.1	14.6	0.1	12.4	0.3	42.5
L	14.9	16.1	0.1	10.7	0.9	42.7
NL ([2])	12.2	12.2	0.3	16.0	1.1	41.8
A	14.7	13.2	0.1	15.0	2.1	45.1
P	14.9	10.9	0.1	11.2	0.8	37.9
FIN	13.3	21.0	0.3	12.1	0.0	46.7
S	14.7	22.5	0.1	15.6	0.7	53.6
UK	14.1	16.9	0.2	7.0	0.6	38.8

([1]) The rate of compulsory levies ("fiscal burden") cannot be calculated directly from the data in this table as internal consolidation would first be required.

([2]) Greece, Ireland, Netherlands: 1999.
Source: Eurostat.

Functional taxation approach

In order to be able to compare countries, tax revenue is usually expressed as a percentage of GDP. It may also be expressed as a percentage of total levies. However, there is a third indicator that proves particularly useful: the statistical tax ratio or implicit tax rate (see box). Due to a lack of basic figures, the analysis

covers series ending in 1997. Nevertheless, the trend over the last three decades is sufficiently significant for the analysis to be presented here.

Since 1970, tax on consumption (as measured by the implicit tax rate) has remained fairly stable, at around 16-17 % (see Table 5.2.3). Taxes on the other factors of production (capital, energy, etc.) rose until 1980 (36.6 % of GDP) but subsequently declined to settle at just over 30 % of GDP. Taxes on employed labour have steadily increased, however, with the implicit tax rate rising from less than 30 % in the early 1970s to 35 % at the beginning of the 1980s and edging over 40 % from the mid-1990s.

More and more tax on employed labour

Taxes on labour (non-wage labour costs) are defined as taxes and social contributions which in some way or other discriminate against the use of the labour factor in the official (visible) sector of the economy. More specifically, taxes on employed labour primarily include social security contributions payable by employers and employees as well as income tax, that is taxes which discourage an employee from working more or an unemployed person from accepting a job instead of receiving social benefits or moonlighting.

In 1997, taxes and social contributions in relation to employed labour accounted for a half (49.9 %) of all levies in the Union and just over a fifth (21.2 %) of GDP (see Table 5.2.4). While a greater tax burden on employed labour has been a fairly common feature of virtually every tax system in the Union over the last three decades, there have been some slight exceptions to the general pattern in the last 20 years.

Between 1980 and 1990 deductions increased as a percentage of GDP in 11 countries, but as a percentage of all levies in only eight. Between 1990 and 1997 there were 10 countries that were increasing taxation on employed labour. Of the four Member States — Luxembourg, Netherlands, United Kingdom and Germany — that had set out to reduce taxation on employed labour in the 1980s, only the first two have maintained the policy until now. When deductions are

Table 5.2.3. Implicit tax rates

	1970	1975	1980	1985	1990	1991	1992	1993	1994	1995	1996	1997
Consumption	17.6	15.5	16.0	15.6	16.2	16.2	16.2	16.1	16.5	16.7	16.7	16.8
Labour employed	28.9	32.2	35.1	37.1	37.5	38.3	39.0	39.7	40.2	41.7	42.0	41.9
Other factors of production	26.2	34.7	36.6	32.3	31.5	31.9	32.2	32.2	30.3	29.4	30.5	31.1

Source: Eurostat, DG TAXUD (provisional estimates).

([1]) In June 2001, the Member States and Eurostat agreed on a common methodology for the calculation of this compulsory levies ratio ("tax burden"), so that from next year onwards, official harmonised figures will be published again.

Table 5.2.4. Taxes on employed labour

	As a % of GDP					As a % of total taxes				
	1980	**1985**	**1990**	**1995**	**1997**	**1980**	**1985**	**1990**	**1995**	**1997**
EU-15	19.7	20.1	20.1	21.4	21.2	51.3	49.8	49.5	51.1	49.9
EUR-11	19.9	20.8	20.5	22.1	22.1	51.7	51.6	50.8	52.2	51.3
B	22.2	23.9	22.4	23.2	22.8	50.3	50.6	50.5	50.4	48.9
DK	21.3	23.8	24.1	25.0	24.6	46.8	48.4	49.4	48.8	47.6
D	21.4	22.1	20.9	24.0	23.2	51.4	53.2	52.9	56.0	55.5
EL	3.9	7.7	12.1	15.2	16.0	34.5	31.7	41.2	45.4	46.1
E	14.7	14.7	16.1	16.8	17.2	57.4	49.0	46.5	49.1	48.4
F	20.8	22.2	21.9	23.2	23.5	50.0	50.0	50.0	51.7	50.6
IRL	14.0	16.3	14.6	13.3	12.9	40.3	42.0	41.0	39.5	38.0
I	16.0	17.8	19.2	18.8	20.9	52.1	51.3	49.5	45.9	47.4
L	21.7	18.1	16.6	16.2	16.3	46.8	39.2	39.8	37.4	37.3
NL	26.7	26.5	25.8	25.0	23.9	58.1	58.3	57.1	55.4	52.2
A	19.0	19.9	19.3	22.1	22.3	46.4	46.4	46.7	51.2	49.7
P	9.4	10.6	12.6	14.5	15.4	36.7	36.1	39.0	40.8	41.4
FIN	21.4	23.8	26.5	27.2	26.6	58.1	58.3	58.4	58.8	56.6
S	33.2	31.5	35.8	31.9	34.7	67.6	63.0	64.1	63.7	63.9
UK	16.7	14.8	14.3	14.9	14.5	45.5	38.3	37.8	40.4	39.0

Source: Eurostat, DG TAXUD (provisional estimates).

considered as a percentage of all levies, the lower figures recorded by eight Member States between 1990 and 1997 can be explained in the case of six of them by an increase in total levies, rather than by the emergence of any real trend.

It is possible to give a little more detail to the analysis by dividing deductions on employed labour between those borne by employers and those paid by employees.

At the beginning of the 1970s the figure for both types of contributor was 7.3 % of GDP. Since 1973, employees have had to bear almost the full brunt of increased taxation on employed labour. The gap between employers and employees has steadily widened, with the result that the former now provide only two fifths of deductions while employees account for three fifths.

Figure 5.2.2. Taxes on employed labour (as a % of GDP)

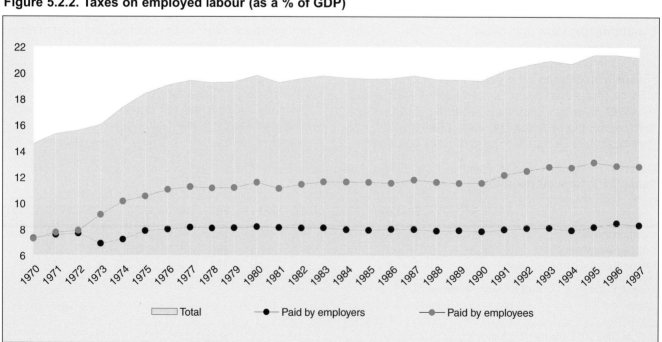

Source: Provisional estimates, Eurostat, DG TAXUD.

Implicit tax rates

There are two main methods that are used to calculate tax rates. The microeconomic method compares the internal rate of an activity with and without taxation, thereby giving the actual marginal tax rate. The main aim of this method is to construct a specimen operator (household, investor, etc.) using data from household surveys, business statistics or other sources and to apply the tax rules (rates, rules governing tax relief, etc.) in order to work out the tax burden normally borne by the economic operator that has been defined. The advantage of the microeconomic model is that it reveals the actual tax burden on the economic operator and not *ex post* results. The method is hampered, however, by major problems in connection with the availability of data.

In macroeconomic terms, it is possible to calculate a tax rate by dividing the taxes imposed on a specific activity or good by a suitable matching tax base. This gives an average tax rate or implicit tax rate (ITR). Determining this kind of rate requires fewer statistical data and less complicated calculations. However, it provides very reliable results, that are often very similar to those obtained using the microeconomic method.

In collaboration with the TAXUD (Customs and Indirect Taxation) Directorate-General, Eurostat has for some years published various implicit tax rates defined as follows:

— implicit tax rate on consumption = taxes on consumption divided by private consumption in the economic territory (excluding general government compensation of employees);
— implicit tax rate on employed labour = taxes on employed labour divided by compensation of employees;
— implicit tax rate on other factors of production = taxes on self-employed persons plus taxes on capital divided by the net operating surplus of the economy plus consolidate government interest payments.

General government expenditure

Total general government expenditure in the Union (see Table 5.2.5) accounts on average for 46.4 % of GDP in 2000, although the range of figures is fairly wide, from about 35 % in Ireland to 58.1 % in Sweden. By way of comparison, overall government spending accounts for about 34–35 % of GDP in the United States and 37–38 % in Japan.

There is clearly a strong correlation between the overall amount of public spending — which goes hand-in-hand with a high level of revenue — and the general degree of economic development, which is normally matched by wider social benefits (see Table 5.2.6).

Table 5.2.5. Total general government expenditure (as a % of GDP)

	1995	1996	1997	1998	1999	2000
EU-15	53.5	51.2	49.5	48.5	47.8	46.4
EUR-11	54.1	51.6	50.3	49.3	48.9	47.3
B	53.0	53.0	51.6	50.9	50.7	50.3
DK	60.3	59.8	58.0	56.9	55.4	53.3
D	56.1	50.3	49.2	48.6	48.6	45.6
EL	50.5	49.2	47.4	47.4	48.3	:
E	45.0	43.7	42.2	41.8	40.8	39.9
F	55.2	55.5	55.0	53.9	53.5	52.8
IRL	41.6	39.7	37.8	35.6	35.8	:
I	53.4	53.2	51.1	49.6	48.9	46.5
L	45.1	45.4	43.4	43.2	42.6	41.2
NL	56.4	49.6	48.2	47.1	46.5	:
A	57.2	56.6	53.9	54.3	53.7	51.9
P	44.9	45.6	44.4	44.1	44.8	45.3
FIN	59.9	59.9	56.8	53.2	51.8	48.4
S	67.6	65.3	63.2	60.8	60.4	58.1
UK	45.8	44.2	42.0	40.7	40.1	40.1

Source: Eurostat.

The main component by far of general government expenditure (see Figure 5.2.3) comprises social benefits other than social transfers in kind (38 % of all expenditure). This is followed by compensation of employees in the public sector (just over 24 %), intermediate consumption (14 %) and property income (9 %). Finally, gross fixed capital formation accounts for 5 % of general government expenditure in the Member States.

Figure 5.2.3. Main categories of general government expenditure, 2000 (as a % of total)

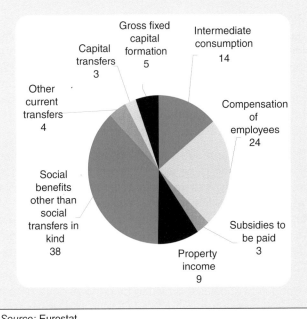

Source: Eurostat.

Some important functions

Among the main items accounting for government expenditure, there are some that merit special attention. Accounting for around one sixth of GDP in 1999, social benefits (excluding social transfers in kind) — which include pensions, health care, unemployment benefits, etc. — represent the main item of expenditure (see Table 5.2.6). Depending on the Member State, they range between 10.2 % and 18.9 % of GDP. Topping the table in this are Sweden, Germany, Austria and France. The countries where such expenditure is proportionally the lowest are Ireland and Portugal.

Table 5.2.6. Social benefits paid by general government — other than social transfers in kind (as a % of GDP)

	1995	1996	1997	1998	1999
EU-15	17.2	17.4	17.2	16.6	16.5
EUR-11	17.3	17.7	17.6	17.1	17.1
B	16.6	16.6	16.3	16	15.7
DK	20.4	19.8	18.8	18.1	17.5
D	18.1	19.3	19.3	18.9	18.9
EL	15.1	15.4	15.6	15.6	15.8
E	13.9	13.8	13.3	12.8	12.4
F	18.5	18.7	18.8	18.4	18.4
IRL	11.8	11.6	10.9	10.3	10.2
I	16.7	16.9	17.3	16.9	17.3
L	16.5	16.4	15.7	15.4	15.1
NL	15.3	14.8	13.9	13	12.5
A	19.5	19.5	18.9	18.6	18.6
P	11.8	11.8	11.7	11.7	11.7
FIN	22.2	21.5	19.9	18.4	17.9
S	21.3	20.3	19.6	19.3	18.9
UK	15.4	14.9	14.4	13.7	13.5

Source: Eurostat.

While the provision of social benefits to households represents a traditional function of allocation among the various categories of the population (active population, pensioners, unemployed, sick, etc.), general government of course provides a whole range of other functions for the benefit of the community, for example national defence and public security, education, transport, communications, cultural and leisure facilities.

By virtue of the production and consumption activities that these entail, general government has an influence on the economy that varies from country to country but which is never insignificant. While compensation of employees and intermediate consumption are the major items of general government expenditure, subsidies paid to businesses and gross fixed capital formation also figure strongly.

Production subsidies provided by general government in 1999 amounted to 1.4 % of GDP in the Union (see Table 5.2.7). The countries that provide most help to businesses are Sweden, Denmark and Austria; those that provide the least help are Greece, the United Kingdom and Ireland.

Table 5.2.7. Subsidies paid by general government (as a % of GDP)

	1995	1996	1997	1998	1999
EU-15	1.6	1.6	1.4	1.4	1.4
EUR-11	1.7	1.7	1.5	1.5	1.5
B	1.5	1.6	1.4	1.5	1.5
DK	2.5	2.6	2.4	2.3	2.3
D	2.1	2.0	1.8	1.8	1.7
EL	0.4	0.5	0.2	0.1	0.2
E	1.1	1.0	0.9	1.1	1.2
F	1.5	1.5	1.5	1.4	1.3
IRL	1.0	1.0	1.0	0.8	0.7
I	1.5	1.5	1.2	1.3	1.3
L	1.8	2.0	1.8	1.8	1.5
NL	1.1	1.2	1.5	1.5	1.6
A	2.9	2.6	2.6	2.8	2.6
P	1.4	1.5	1.1	1.1	1.0
FIN	2.8	2.1	1.9	1.7	1.6
S	3.8	3.3	2.7	2.2	2.0
UK	0.7	0.8	0.6	0.5	0.6

Source: Eurostat.

On average, government investment in fixed capital goods (see Table 5.2.8) amounts in 1999 to 2.3 % of GDP in the Union. The figures differ widely, however, ranging from 1.1 % in the United Kingdom to 4.5 % in Luxembourg. While four countries — Germany, France, Austria and the United Kingdom — have steadily reduced government investment these last five years, the trend in many other Member States has fluctuated up and down.

Table 5.2.8. General government gross fixed capital formation (as a % of GDP)

	1995	1996	1997	1998	1999
EU-15	11.2	11.1	10.8	10.5	10.4
EUR-11	11.2	11.2	11.0	10.7	10.7
B	12.0	11.9	11.8	11.7	11.6
DK	17.3	17.3	17.1	17.3	17.1
D	9.0	8.9	8.7	8.4	8.3
EL	11.3	10.7	11.6	11.7	11.5
E	11.3	11.3	10.9	10.7	10.5
F	13.7	13.9	13.8	13.7	13.7
IRL	10.2	9.7	9.2	8.8	8.2
I	11.2	11.5	11.6	10.7	10.6
L	9.6	9.6	9.3	9.1	8.7
NL	10.8	10.4	10.2	10.2	10.2
A	12.6	12.3	11.5	11.3	11.4
P	13.7	13.7	13.8	14.1	14.4
FIN	15.4	15.6	14.6	13.9	13.6
S	17.3	17.8	17.4	16.8	16.5
UK	8.8	8.3	7.8	7.4	7.5

Source: Eurostat.

5.3. Public debt and deficit

Depending on whether or not a country's revenue covers its expenditure, there will be a surplus or a deficit in its budget. If there is a shortfall in revenue, the government is obliged to borrow. Expressed as a percentage of GDP, a country's annual (deficit) and cumulative (debt) financing requirements are significant indicators of the burden that government borrowing places on the national economy. These are in fact two of the criteria used to assess the government finances of the Member States that are referred to in the Maastricht Treaty in connection with qualifying for the single currency (see box).

The general reduction of public deficit ...

Public deficit (see Table 5.3.1) is defined in the Maastricht Treaty as general government's net borrowing according to the European system of accounts (see box). In 2000, nine Member States achieved a surplus in the budget (net lending), while in all the others the deficit was less than 1.4 % of GDP. Apart from Denmark — which has, however, been recording a surplus for several years — every country reduced its deficit or increased its surplus in 2000. The general improvement is thus continuing. The budget restrictions introduced in recent years are clearly bearing fruit.

The average figures for the Union and the euro-zone improve steadily throughout the five years under review, and at the end of 2000, for the first time since the adoption of the Maastricht Treaty, the Union's and the euro-zone averages are positive, that is 1.2 % and

Table 5.3.1. General government deficit (as a % of GDP)

	1996	1997	1998	1999	2000
EU-15	− 4.2	− 2.4	− 1.5	− 0.6	1.2
EUR-11	− 4.2	− 2.6	− 2.1	− 1.2	0.3
B	− 3.8	− 1.9	− 0.9	− 0.7	0.0
DK	− 1.0	0.4	1.1	3.1	2.5
D	− 3.4	− 2.7	− 2.1	− 1.4	1.3
EL	− 7.4	− 4.6	− 3.2	− 1.8	− 0.9
E	− 5.0	− 3.2	− 2.6	− 1.2	− 0.3
F	− 4.1	− 3.0	− 2.7	− 1.6	− 1.3
IRL	− 0.2	0.7	2.1	2.1	4.5
I	− 7.1	− 2.7	− 2.8	− 1.8	− 0.3
L	2.6	3.6	3.2	4.7	5.3
NL	− 1.8	− 1.1	− 0.7	1.0	2.0
A	− 3.8	− 1.7	− 2.3	− 2.1	− 1.1
P	− 4.0	− 2.7	− 2.2	− 2.0	− 1.4
FIN	− 3.2	− 1.5	1.3	1.8	6.7
S	− 3.4	− 1.5	1.9	1.8	4.0
UK	− 4.4	− 2.0	0.4	1.3	4.4

Source: Eurostat.

0.3 % of GDP respectively. In 1996 they had both been − 4.2 % (see Figure 5.3.1).

... and public debt continues

Public debt (see Table 5.3.2) is defined in the Maastricht Treaty as total general government gross, nominal and consolidated debt outstanding at the end of the year.

At the end of 2000, nine countries had a level of public debt below the 60 % threshold, and three others are

Figure 5.3.1. Variation of general government net lending/net borrowing in the euro-zone (as a % of GDP)

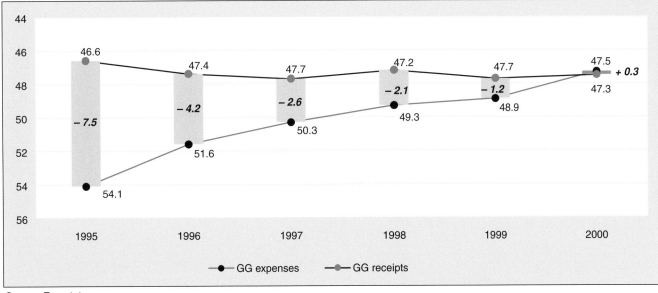

Source: Eurostat.

not very far from this percentage. Three Member States — Italy, Belgium and Greece — were still above 100 %, but the figure has been dropping every year since 1995.

At the end of 2000, the average debt ratio for the 15 Member States stood at 64.2 %, with a figure of 69.7 % for the countries in the euro-zone.

Table 5.3.2. General government debt (as a % of GDP)

	1996	1997	1998	1999	2000
EU-15	72.6	71.0	68.9	68.0	64.2
EUR-11	74.5	74.2	73.5	72.0	69.7
B	130.9	125.3	119.8	116.4	110.9
DK	65.1	61.4	55.8	52.6	47.3
D	59.8	60.9	60.7	61.1	60.2
EL	111.3	108.3	105.5	104.6	103.9
E	68.2	66.7	64.7	63.4	60.6
F	57.1	59.3	59.7	58.7	58.0
IRL	74.3	65.1	55.0	50.1	39.1
I	122.1	120.1	116.2	114.5	110.2
L	6.2	6.0	6.4	6.0	5.3
NL	75.2	70.0	66.8	63.2	56.3
A	69.1	64.7	63.9	64.7	62.8
P	62.7	59.1	55.3	55.0	53.8
FIN	57.1	54.1	48.8	46.9	44.0
S	76.0	73.0	71.8	65.2	55.6
UK	52.7	51.1	48.1	45.7	42.9

Source: Eurostat.

Budgetary discipline and notification of public debt and deficit

The Maastricht Treaty states that the Member States are required to avoid excessive public deficits. To this end, they must fulfil two conditions. Firstly, the ratio of government deficit to GDP must not exceed a reference value (3 %), unless the ratio has declined substantially and continuously and reached a level close to the reference value, or that the reference value has been exceeded only exceptionally and temporarily and the ratio is close to the reference value. Secondly, the ratio of government debt to GDP must not exceed a reference value (60 %), unless the ratio is diminishing sufficiently and approaching the reference value at a satisfactory pace.

At the Madrid Summit in December 1995, the European Council stressed the need for budgetary discipline both before the introduction of monetary union and after the start of stage three on 1 January 1999. This determination was reflected in the Growth and Stability Pact, which is intended to prevent any country, no longer able to rely on exchange rates and interest rates, to resort to budgetary policy to revive its economy, since such a solution could very quickly have a negative effect on its public deficit, thereby prompting a rise in interest rates which would be detrimental to all the participants in EMU.

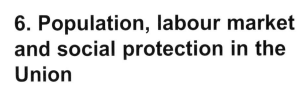

6. Population, labour market and social protection in the Union

6.1. Population

The EU, the world's third most populous economic area

Having 377 million inhabitants on the 1 January 2001, the European Union is the third most populous economic area after China (1 273 million) and India 1 030 million, which reached its first billion well before the millennium change. Indeed, after these two giants, its population is almost as large as those of the United States (278 million) and Japan (127 million) together.

The European Union currently covers 70 % of the population of the whole of Europe (excluding most of the former Soviet Union and parts of the former Republic of Yugoslavia). The 10 central European countries plus Cyprus, Malta and Turkey, which are potential future Member States of the Union have a total population of about 176 million people. Turkey is the largest of those countries with a population of 65.8 million, Poland is the second largest with 38.6 million. Romania (22.4 million), the Czech Republic and Hungary (both 10 million) rank in the medium-size group of countries and the remainder have less than 10 million inhabitants.

The six largest EU countries by area (France, Spain, Sweden, Germany, Finland and Italy) occupy nearly 80 % of the total EU territory. The five countries with the highest populations i.e. Germany, the United Kingdom, France, Italy and Spain, represent 80 % of the whole population of the Union. Population density ranges from just 15 per km2 in Finland to nearly 400 per km2 in the Netherlands. The population is most dense in a belt running from northern Italy through south and west Germany and the Benelux countries to southern England. Border regions in all directions tend to be less densely populated. In 1991, more than half of the population of the EU countries lived in urban settlements (defined as compact areas with a population density of at least 500 persons per km2). This percentage ranges, however, from a low of 21 % in Sweden to a high of 77 % in the United Kingdom.

Slow population growth as compared with the United States

Population growth in the EU slowed in the 1970s and 1980s but accelerated in the early 1990s. This was due to a temporary increase in immigration. The long-term trend points to a decline in the growth rate. The United States' population has grown steadily since the 1970s until recently. In Japan, population growth diminished substantially during the same period.

Table 6.1.1 shows the recent development of the components of the population change in 1996–2000. The population of the EU increased in 1999 by 0.28 %, a rate clearly higher than that of Japan (+ 0.18 %), but much slower than that of the United States (+ 0.90 %). Net migration is still the most important source of population growth in the Union. Its share of total population increase was 65 %. In the United States, net migration is also important but the natural increase is the major driving force of the relatively strong population growth. Japan faces a situation of near zero net migration, thus migration having no role in the population growth.

Table 6.1.1. Components of population change, 1996–2000 (as a %)

	Natural increase	+ Net migration	= Population change
EU-15			
2000	0.10	0.18	0.28
1999	0.07	0.20	0.27
1998	0.08	0.14	0.22
1997	0.09	0.14	0.23
1996	0.08	0.20	0.28
EUR-11			
2000	0.10	0.17	0.27
1999	0.07	0.17	0.24
1998	0.07	0.10	0.17
1997	0.09	0.13	0.22
1996	0.07	0.20	0.27
US			
2000	0.55	0.35	0.90
1999	0.56	0.35	0.91
1998	0.59	0.36	0.95
1997	0.59	0.32	0.91
1996	0.60	0.33	0.93
JP			
2000	0.18	− 0.01	0.17
1999	0.19	0.00	0.19
1998	0.20	− 0.04	0.20
1997	0.23	− 0.04	0.19
1996	0.22	− 0.00	0.18

Source: Eurostat.

Increasing share of non-EU nationals

The European Union has witnessed a slow but steady growth in the share of the non-national population during recent decades. The total number of non-nationals has increased from 13.6 million in 1985 to 18.6 million in 1999. In 1999, the share of the non-nationals from other EU countries was 31 % of the total number of non-nationals, and the share of those from outside the Union was 69 %.

Non-EU nationals account for a greater share of the total population in Austria (estimated about 8 %) and Germany (6.7 %) than in any of the other Member States where the equivalent figures range from 1 % and 4 %. As a proportion of the total population, EU nationals of other Member States are most significant in Luxembourg (32 %) and Belgium (5.5 %), the figures in other countries of the Union varying between 0.5 % and 2.5 %.

The share of the non-EU nationals of the EU total population has been growing slowly but steadily from 3.8 % in 1985 to 5.0 % in 1999. This is due to the fact that net migration of the whole EU has exceeded the natural increase since 1989. Also the compositions of inflows (immigration) and outflows (emigration) have favoured non-EU nationals, being on average 55 to 45 in immigration and even 50 to 50 in emigration during the whole period. In 1999, 41 % of immigrants to EU countries were citizens of some EU country. They were either returning to their own country or moving to another EU country. The rest, some 59 %, were nationals of non-EU countries.

Ageing population and labour force

Figure 6.1.1 shows the age and sex structure of the European Union in 1999 in the form of a population pyramid. The pyramid has a broad waist and narrow shoulders. But things will change. The waist will rise upwards and the shoulders will broaden in the coming years. This is because the low fertility continues to decrease the younger age classes and expanding life expectancy tends further to increase the share of the older age classes.

Figure 6.1.1. Age pyramid for the European Union on 1 January 1999

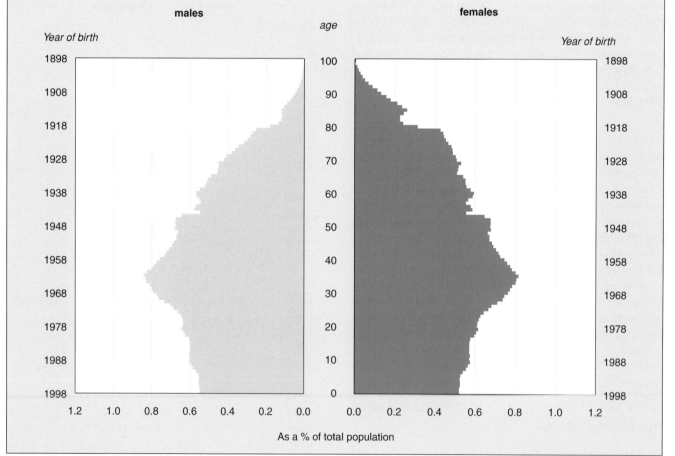

Source: Eurostat.

Long-term changes in fertility of the EU and Japan have been remarkably similar. In 1970, both had total fertility higher than 2 (EU 2.38 and Japan 2.09). After a rapid decrease in the 1970s there was a steady downward slope to the bottom levels 1.42 for EU in 1995 and 1.39 for Japan in 1997, which are well below the level of reproduction. Now, the direction seems to be upwards, the total fertility rate of EU rose from 1.45 in 1999 to 1.53 in 2000, the highest figure in 10 years. A slight rise was also seen in Japan from 1.40 to 1.41. The United States, on the other hand, had the highest level in 1970 (2.48) dropping to nearly 1.7 in the mid-1970s, but turning up again and staying just over 2 in the whole 1990s (2.06 in 2000).

Since 1945, life expectancy at birth in the EU has increased almost continuously. Following an interruption in 1995, the upward trend was resumed in 1996. For the Union as a whole, and based on mortality rates measured in 1999, it is estimated that life expectancy is now at an all-time high: at birth, girls can now expect to live an average of 81.2 years and boys 74.9 years, well over 10 years more than in 1945.

The corresponding figures for the United States were 74.2 for men and 79.7 for women and for Japan 77.4 and 84.8. In most other developed countries, average life spans are shorter than in the EU: the most extreme case appears to be the Russian Federation, where the average man now lives 15 years less than his EU counterpart.

In Table 6.1.2 the population is split into several age groups for 1970 and 1995–99. In all three areas the proportion of young persons (0-14) has declined in the last 25 years. However, in the United States the share of this group remains much higher than in the Union or Japan. Within the European Union, the southern Member States, Spain, Italy and Portugal have experienced the greatest fall in share of young people and this trend is expected to continue. In all three economic areas and especially in Japan, the proportion of elderly people (65 +) increased considerably.

The population of 15-64 year-olds is a good indicator of the actual and potential labour force. In the European Union and United States, this age group accounted for a substantially higher percentage of the population in 1999 than in 1970. In Japan, although there was virtually no change over the same period, the 15-64 cohort remained a larger component of the Japanese population than that in the EU or United States. In recent years (1995-98), the share of this age group has been almost constant in all three countries. However, the internal structure has been changing in all three countries during the 1990s. The share of the older part of the potential labour force (40 to 64 years) increased from 1990 to 1999 in the EU from 44.1 % to 46.4 %, in Japan from 49 % to 50.3 % and in the United States from 38.9 % to 45.3 %. This indicates ageing of the labour force, which will also continue in the coming years.

The old age dependency ratio (65 +/15-64) increased from 1970 in all three areas with more than doubling in Japan which reached the level of EU (24.1 %) as compared with 19.3 % in the United States.

The total age dependency ratio (the number of people aged 0-14 and 65 and over related to the number of people aged 15-64) has dropped substantially since 1970 in the EU and in the United States with the EU being most affected. In Japan, a fall in the proportion of young people was counterbalanced by a rise in that of the elderly. However, during the recent years (1995-98) the ratio has been almost constant in all three economic areas.

Demographic consequences of a possible enlargement of the Union

The candidate countries have clearly younger age structure (more young people and less old ones) than the present. However, because of low fertility and life expectancy, most of the candidate countries have a declining population. So, enlargement of the EU, especially, by the present CEC countries would slightly postpone the ageing trend but hasten starting of the population decline of the Union by a few years.

What concerns the development of the working population, the trends in the candidate countries considered are somewhat different than in the present EU. Nearly all the candidate countries have a total age dependency ratio that is not only lower than the EU-15 average but also declining faster. Only when the small birth cohorts from the 1990s enter the working ages will there be a rapid increase in the total dependency ratio.

Therefore, although enlargement of the European Union would in the medium term lighten the demographic burden on the working population of the Union, it would hardly alter the longer-term decline in this age group.

Table 6.1.2. Population shares in major age groups and age dependency ratios 1970, 1995-1999 (as a %)

	Population shares			Age dependency ratios	
	0–14	15–64	65+	65+/15–64	(0–14 and 65+) /15–64
EU-15					
1999	17.0	66.9	16.1	24.1	49.5
1998	17.1	67.0	15.9	23.7	49.3
1997	17.3	67.0	15.7	23.6	49.3
1996	17.4	67.0	15.6	23.3	49.3
1995	17.6	67.0	15.4	23.0	49.2
1970	24.7	63.1	12.2	19.3	58.5
US					
1999	21.4	65.9	12.7	19.3	51.7
1998	21.5	65.8	12.7	19.3	52.0
1997	21.6	65.7	12.7	19.3	52.2
1996	21.7	65.6	12.7	19.3	52.5
1995	21.8	65.4	12.8	19.6	52.9
1970	28.3	61.9	9.8	15.8	61.2
JP					
1999	15.0	68.5	16.5	24.1	46.0
1998	15.2	68.8	16.0	23.3	45.3
1997	15.4	69.1	15.5	22.4	44.8
1996	15.7	69.3	15.0	21.6	44.3
1995	16.2	69.6	14.2	20.4	43.7
1970	24.0	69.0	7.0	10.1	44.9

Source: Eurostat.

6.2. Employment

Largest rise in employment by 1.8 % since 1995

Employment increased in the European Union by 1.8 % in 2000 compared with 1999, the largest increase since 1995. Although employment rose in all Member States, in many, the growth was less than the previous year. In the euro-zone, employment growth was slightly higher (2 %) because in three of the four Member States outside the EMU (Denmark, Greece and the United Kingdom) the employment growth was only 1 % or less. Ireland and Luxembourg had by far the highest employment growth. Spain, France, the Netherlands and Sweden also had an employment growth above the EU average.

63 % of the population aged 15-64 is employed

At the Lisbon European Council of March 2000 a target was set whereby by 2010 the overall employment rate should stand at 70 % with 60 % for women. Later, in March 2001, the Stockholm European Council set an intermediate target of 67 % for the overall employment rate in 2005. In 2000, the EU employment rate (% of employed persons in the population aged 15-64) was 63 %. This rate is two points more than the employment rate for the euro-zone. Denmark, the Netherlands, Sweden and the United Kingdom have already reached an employment rate of 70 %. Austria, Portugal and Finland have attained the intermediate target of 67 %. However, in Austria, the employment

rate decreased, in particular the full-time employment rate. In Denmark, there was a similar decline.

Compared with 1999, the employment rate increased most in Spain, Ireland and the Netherlands (two points or more). In Spain and Ireland, the rise of the employment rate was almost entirely due to a rise in the full-time employment rate, but in the Netherlands, it was due to a rise in the part-time employment rate.

Table 6.2.2. Employment rates (15–64 years) by full-time/part-time, 2000 growth (as a % of the total population of the same age)

	Total	Full-time	Part-time
EU-15	63.1	51.9	11.1
EUR-11	61.3	51.2	9.9
B	60.9	45.1	11.7
DK	76.4	60.0	16.3
D	65.3	52.9	12.5
EL (1)	55.9	53.4	2.4
E	54.7	50.3	4.4
F	61.7	51.4	10.4
IRL	64.5	53.8	10.7
I	53.4	48.7	4.6
L	62.7	55.7	7.0
NL	72.9	43.0	29.9
A	67.9	56.6	11.3
P	68.1	62.6	5.5
FIN	68.1	60.0	8.1
S	71.1	55.3	15.4
UK	71.2	54.1	17.1

Source: LFS.

Table 6.2.1. Employment and annual employment growth

	x 1000			As a %	
	1998	**1999**	**2000**	**1999/1998**	**2000/1999**
EU-15	159 210	161 744	164 663	1.6	1.8
EUR-11	121 217	123 310	125 806	1.7	2.0
B	3 802	3 851	3 921	1.3	1.8
DK	2 693	2 722	2 742	1.1	0.7
D	37 537	37 944	38 534	1.1	1.6
EL (1)	3 921	3 893	3 920	-0.7	0.7
E	14 664	15 173	15 671	3.5	3.3
F	22 376	22 782	23 317	1.8	2.3
IRL	1 531	1 624	1 701	6.1	4.7
I	22 448	22 686	23 059	1.1	1.6
L	237	249	262	5.1	5.2
NL	7 743	7 935	8 122	2.5	2.4
A	3 956	4 011	4 046	1.4	0.9
P	4 739	4 825	4 909	1.8	1.7
FIN	2 184	2 230	2 264	2.1	1.5
S	4 071	4 166	4 257	2.3	2.2
UK	27 308	27 653	27 938	1.3	1.0

(1) 2000 data: provisional data.
Source: Comparable estimates based on the labour force survey (QLFD).

**Table 6.2.3. Employment rates (15–64 years) by sex and full-time/part-time, 2000
(as a % of the population of the same age and sex)**

	Male			Female		
	Total	**Full-time**	**Part-time**	**Total**	**Full-time**	**Part-time**
EU-15	72.4	68.1	4.2	53.8	35.8	17.9
EUR-11	71.2	67.3	3.7	51.4	35.2	16.1
B	69.8	61.8	3.8	51.9	29.1	19.2
DK	80.7	72.9	7.7	72.1	46.9	25.2
D	72.7	69.5	3.3	57.8	36.0	21.8
EL	71.3	69.6	1.7	41.3	38.2	3.1
E	69.6	67.7	1.9	40.3	33.4	6.9
F	68.8	65.2	3.6	54.8	37.8	17.0
IRL	75.6	70.5	5.1	53.4	37.1	16.3
I	67.6	65.1	2.5	39.3	32.5	6.8
L	75.0	73.7	1.3	50.0	37.1	12.9
NL	82.1	66.6	15.5	63.4	18.7	44.7
A	76.2	73.2	3.0	59.7	40.0	19.6
P	76.2	73.6	2.6	60.4	52.1	8.3
FIN	71.1	65.8	5.3	65.2	54.2	10.9
S	72.6	65.7	6.6	69.7	44.4	24.6
UK	77.9	71.8	6.1	64.5	36.2	28.3

Source: LFS.

Part-time employment rate in the Member States between 2 % and 30 %

In the Netherlands, the part-time employment rate was 30 % following an increase by more than two points. On the other hand, in Greece, Spain, Italy and Portugal, part-time employment is relatively uncommon with a part-time employment rate of less than 6 %. In Greece and Portugal, the part-time employment rate even decreased.

Almost every sixth employed person in the EU is working part-time because they could not find a full-time job. However, involuntary part-time continued to decrease (15.8 % compared with 17.3 % in 1999). In Denmark, the Netherlands and the United Kingdom, where part-time employment is prevalent, as well as in Germany and Austria, involuntary part-time is below EU average. The situation is clearly different for men and women. In general, relatively more men work part-time because they could not find a full-time job. In Denmark, Spain, Portugal, Finland and Sweden relatively more women are involuntary part-time workers.

**Table 6.2.4. Involuntary part-time by sex, 2000
(as a % of part-time employment)**

	Total	**Male**	**Female**
EU-15	15.8	22.5	14.1
EUR-11	17.4	23.7	15.8
B ([1])	22.2	28.5	21.0
DK	13.1	10.1	14.1
D	12.0	16.7	11.2
EL	42.9	48.0	40.2
E	22.8	22.1	22.9
F	26.8	42.1	23.5
IRL	16.0	30.1	11.2
I	35.6	46.3	31.5
L	(7.2)	.	(6.8)
NL	3.5	4.5	3.1
A	10.6	19.0	9.2
P	22.6	14.5	26.3
FIN	34.6	29.5	37.3
S	23.2	22.0	23.5
UK	9.6	19.2	7.2

([1]) Only employees.
Source: LFS.

A slightly narrowed gender gap in employment rates of 18.6 points

The female employment rate is 18.6 points less than the male employment rate in the EU. Compared with 1999, the gender gap narrowed only slightly from 18.9 to 18.6 points. In Greece, Spain, Luxembourg and Italy, this gender gap is much wider, the low female employment rate being related to a low part-time employment rate. On the other hand, the gender gap is much smaller in Sweden, Finland and Denmark. Moreover in Finland, the gap between the female and male full-time employment rate is relatively small compared with all other Member States.

This gender gap is also obvious in part-time work. The female part-time employment rate in the EU is almost 18 % in contrast to the male part-time employment rate of only 4 %. In the Netherlands, female part-time employment is particularly high, with two in three women working part-time. Other Member States with a high female part-time employment are Denmark, Germany, Sweden and the United Kingdom.

Employment growth in highly skilled non-manual occupations

Half of the employment growth was in highly skilled non-manual occupations (managers, professionals and technicians) and another 30 % in low- and medium-skilled non-manual occupations (clerks, services and sales workers). In Germany, Italy, Sweden and the United Kingdom, employment growth was largely concentrated in highly skilled non-manual occupations. In Spain and Austria, employment growth was distributed over highly skilled and low- and medium-skilled non-manual occupations while in Finland, employment growth was distributed over highly skilled non-manual and low- and medium-skilled manual occupations (skilled agricultural workers, craft and trades workers and operators). In France, Ireland and the Netherlands, employment growth was more diverse covering both manual and non-manual occupations.

Table 6.2.5. Annual employment growth by occupation (excluding armed forces)

	Total	Senior officials, managers, professionals and technicians	Clerks, services and sales workers	Skilled agriculture, craft and trade workers, operators	Elementary occupations
EU-15	1.8	1.0	0.6	− 0.2	0.3
EUR-11	2.0	1.1	0.7	− 0.1	0.4
B	1.8	− 0.8	1.6	− 1.4	2.4
DK	0.7	1.4	− 1.3	− 0.6	1.2
D	1.6	1.0	0.4	− 0.1	0.2
EL	0.7	0.0	0.7	0.0	0.1
E	3.3	1.3	1.2	0.5	0.3
F	2.3	0.7	0.8	0.7	0.2
IRL	4.7	1.6	1.5	1.6	0.0
I	1.6	2.4	0.5	− 1.5	0.3
L	5.2	1.3	1.3	0.6	2.0
NL	2.4	0.9	0.9	− 0.4	1.0
A	0.9	0.7	0.8	− 0.1	− 0.5
P	1.7	0.3	0.4	− 0.3	1.3
FIN	1.5	1.2	− 0.3	0.8	− 0.2
S	2.2	1.7	0.0	0.4	0.2
UK	1.0	0.8	0.4	− 0.4	0.2

Source: Eurostat.

6.3. Unemployment

In 2000, the total number of unemployed in the EU averaged 14.2 million or 8.2 % of the labour force, excluding collective households. The unemployment rate for the euro zone is higher than for the entire EU because the unemployment rate in Denmark, Sweden and the United Kingdom is below the EU average. This unemployment rate is the lowest rate since 1992. In six Member States, the unemployment rate is below 5 %. It decreased in all Member States except in Luxembourg, where it remained at a low 2.4 %. The decline was the largest in Belgium, Spain and France.

Table 6.3.1. Unemployment rate (^{1}), yearly average (as a %)

	1999	2000
EU-15	9.1	8.2
EUR-11	9.9	8.9
B	8.8	7.0
DK	5.2	4.7
D	8.6	7.9
EL	11.6	11.1
E	15.9	14.1
F	11.2	9.5
IRL	5.6	4.2
I	11.3	10.5
L	2.4	2.4
NL	3.4	3.0
A	3.9	3.7
P	4.5	4.1
FIN	10.2	9.8
S	7.2	5.9
UK	6.1	5.5

(^{1}) Harmonised unemployment rate.
Source: Eurostat.

Definition of unemployment

Harmonised unemployment rate

Eurostat harmonised unemployment rates are calculated according to the recommendations of the 13th International Conference of Labour Statisticians (1982). According to these recommendations, the unemployed comprise persons aged 15 and over who are without work; are currently available for work and have been actively looking for work or have already found a job to start later.

Counts of the number of persons registered at public employment offices are not suitable for international comparison because of effects of changes in national administrative rules and procedures.

Long-term unemployment

In the coordinated European employment strategy which was launched by the extraordinary Summit of Luxembourg in November 1997, the prevention of long-term unemployment was strongly emphasised. Since 1997, there has been a steady decline and the long-term unemployment rate (unemployed persons looking for a job for one year or longer) reached 3.7 %. Nevertheless, the relatively high long-term unemployment rate remains endemic in Italy and Greece. Although in Spain it was also more than 6 %, the decline for several years was considerable.

Table 6.3.2. Long-term unemployment rate (^{1}), yearly average (as a % of the labour force)

	1999	2000
EU-15	4.2	3.7
EUR-11	4.8	4.2
B	4.9	3.8
DK	1.2	1.0
D	4.4	4.1
EL	6.5	6.3
E	7.9	6.5
F	4.4	3.8
IRL	2.6	1.7
I	6.9	6.4
L	0.7	0.5
NL	1.2	1.0
A	1.1	1.0
P	1.8	1.7
FIN	2.9	2.8
S	2.0	1.5
UK	1.7	1.5

(^{1}) Harmonised unemployment rate — 12 months and more.
Source: Eurostat.

Within the framework of the employment guidelines of the European employment strategy, a different threshold of six months is applied for young people under 25 to define long-term unemployment. The long-term unemployment rate for people under 25 has decreased in all Member States (except in Finland) and reached a low 8.4 % in the EU. In Belgium, Greece, Spain and Italy, it exceeds the EU average.

Table 6.3.3. Youth long-term unemployment rate ([1]) (15–24 years), yearly average (as a % of the labour force of the same age)

	1999	2000
EU-15	9.5	8.4
EUR-11	10.9	9.8
B	14.0	9.6
DK	1.6	0.4
D	4.8	4.4
EL	18.5	15.9
E	21.4	18.6
F	8.8	8.5
IRL	:	:
I	25.6	24.2
L	3.1	1.8
NL	5.9	1.3
A	1.7	1.6
P	4.8	3.7
FIN	2.6	3.1
S	3.7	3.2
UK	4.3	3.9

([1]) Harmonised unemployment rate — 6 months and more.
Source: Eurostat.

Table 6.3.4. Unemployment rate by sex ([1]), yearly average 2000 (as a %)

	Males	Females
EU-15	7.0	9.7
EUR-11	7.3	10.9
B	5.7	8.8
DK	4.2	5.3
D	7.6	8.3
EL	7.3	16.7
E	9.8	20.6
F	7.8	11.5
IRL	4.3	4.2
I	8.0	14.4
L	1.9	3.3
NL	2.3	3.8
A	3.2	4.4
P	3.3	5.1
FIN	9.0	10.6
S	6.0	5.8
UK	6.0	4.9

([1]) Harmonised unemployment rate.
Source: Eurostat.

Higher unemployment among women and young people

The female unemployment rate in the EU was below 10 % for the first time since 1992 but it was still 2.7 points higher than the male unemployment rate. This is a slightly narrower gap than the 2.9 points in 1999. This less favourable situation for women occurs in all Member States except Ireland, Sweden and the United Kingdom. The situation is particularly unfavourable to women in Greece and Spain, where the female unemployment rate is twice the male unemployment rate.

When the unemployment rates are compared by age, the youth unemployment rate in the EU and in most Member States is more than twice the rate of those aged 25 and over. Half of the unemployed young people are looking for their first job. In Belgium, Greece, Italy, Luxembourg and the United Kingdom, the youth unemployment rate is more than three times the rate of those aged 25 and over. The large difference between the youth unemployment rate and the rate of those aged 25 and over is partly due to a low labour participation.

Table 6.3.5. Unemployment rate by age ([1]), yearly average 2000, (as a % of the labour force of the same age)

	Less than 25 years	25 years and over
EU-15	16.2	7.1
EUR-11	17.1	7.7
B	17.7	5.8
DK	7.3	4.3
D	9.1	7.8
EL	29.6	8.6
E	26.2	12.0
F	20.0	8.3
IRL	6.5	3.7
I	30.7	8.0
L	7.3	1.9
NL	5.6	2.4
A	5.3	3.5
P	8.9	3.3
FIN	21.3	8.1
S	11.3	5.3
UK	12.7	4.2

([1]) Harmonised unemployment rate.
Source: Eurostat.

A youth unemployment population ratio, on the other hand, does not depend on the participation rate because the basis is the total youth population instead of the labour force. In the EU, the youth unemployment population ratio is 7.8 %, a decrease of 0.8 points compared with 1999. The youth unemployment population ratio decreased in all Member States except in Germany, Luxembourg and Austria — with already low ratios of less than 5 % — and in Finland where this ratio remained among the highest in the EU.

Higher unemployment among those with a lower level of education

The risk of unemployment is higher among those aged 25-64 with an educational level below upper secondary education. It shows the importance of further education and training in a period of employment growth, job vacancies and decreasing unemployment. In Luxembourg and Austria, the unemployment rate for people with less than upper secondary education was twice the unemployment rate for those with an upper secondary education. The odds of being unemployed for those with less than upper secondary education (compared with upper secondary education) were also high in the Netherlands and the United Kingdom.

Table 6.3.7. Adult unemployment rates (25–64 years) by educational attainment, spring 2000 (as a % of the labour force of the same age and level of education)

	Third level	Upper secondary	Less than upper secondary
EU-15	4.4	6.8	10.7
EUR-11	5.0	7.4	11.2
B	2.4	5.5	9.1
DK	2.6	3.9	6.3
D	4.3	8.0	13.8
EL	7.1	10.9	7.9
E	9.2	11.3	13.8
F	5.1	8.0	13.8
IRL	:	:	:
I	5.9	7.4	9.8
L	1.0	1.6	3.1
NL	1.7	1.8	3.4
A	2.3	4.0	8.2
P	2.3	3.8	3.6
FIN	4.9	8.8	11.9
S	3.0	5.2	8.0
UK	2.2	4.4	8.5

Source: Eurostat.

Table 6.3.6. Youth unemployment population ratio (15–24 years), yearly average 2000 (as a % of the total population of the same age)

EU-15	7.8
EUR-11	7.6
B	6.5
DK	5.3
D	4.6
EL	11.3
E	11.4
F	7.1
IRL	3.3
I	11.8
L	(2.5)
NL	4.0
A	2.9
P	4.2
FIN	11.1
S	5.5
UK	8.3

Source: Eurostat.

6.4. Social protection and pensions

The data on expenditure and receipts of social protection schemes presented here are drawn up according to the "Esspros Manual 1996". Esspros stands for European system of integrated social protection statistics, a harmonised system providing a means of analysing and comparing social protection financial flows.

In this manual, social protection is defined as follows: "Social protection encompasses all interventions from public or private bodies intended to relieve households and individuals of the burden of a defined set of risks or needs, provided that there is neither a simultaneous reciprocal nor an individual arrangement involved.

The list of risks or needs that may give rise to social protection is fixed by convention as follows:

- sickness/health care;
- disability;
- old age;
- survivors;
- family/children;
- unemployment;
- housing;
- social exclusion not elsewhere classified."

Social benefits are recorded without any deduction of taxes or other compulsory levies payable on them by beneficiaries. "Tax benefits" (tax reductions granted to households for social protection purposes) are generally excluded.

6.4.1. Social protection

Expenditure on social protection

In 1998, expenditure on social protection as a percentage of GDP continued to fall in EU-15 (– 0.4 points compared with 1997; – 1.2 compared with 1993). However, the trend in expenditure on social protection was not regular during the period 1990-98. Between 1990 and 1993, there was a considerable increase (+ 3.5 points), which peaked at 28.9 % in EU-15 in 1993. This was due mainly to the slower rate of growth of GDP and the increasing unemployment level.

Between 1993 and 1996, expenditure on social protection as a percentage of GDP showed a slight downward trend, which was due partly to renewed growth in GDP but also to a slowdown in the growth of social protection expenditure (in particular a decrease in unemployment benefits).

These trends quickened in 1997 and 1998, when the expenditure/GDP ratio decreased by 0.5 and 0.4 points respectively. The decrease was most marked in Finland (– 2.3 points in 1997 and – 2.1 points in 1998) and Ireland (– 1.3 and – 1.1 respectively). The Netherlands also saw a noticeable reduction in 1998 (– 0.9 points). Only in Greece and Portugal did the ratio continue to increase. In Norway and Switzerland too, the ratio increased between 1996 and 1998. It should be noted that the significant growth of the GDP in recent years explained a large part of the trend in Ireland.

Figure 6.4.1. Expenditure on social protection in the EU-15 (as % of GDP)

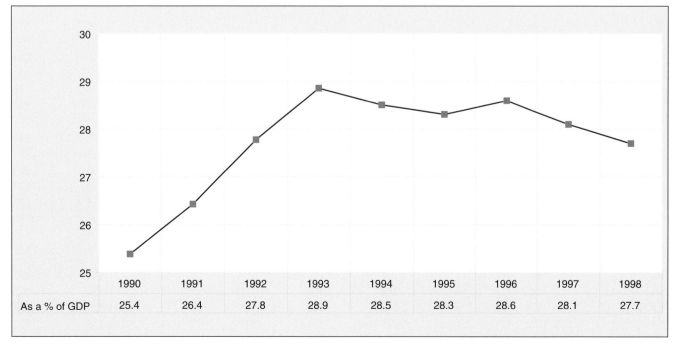

	1990	1991	1992	1993	1994	1995	1996	1997	1998
As a % of GDP	25.4	26.4	27.8	28.9	28.5	28.3	28.6	28.1	27.7

Source: Eurostat, Esspros.

Table 6.4.1. Expenditure on social protection (as a % of GDP)

	1990	1993	1996	1997	1998
EU-15	**25.4**	**28.9**	**28.6**	**28.1**	**27.7**
EUR-11	**25.5**	**28.5**	**28.5**	**28.1**	**27.7**
B	26.4	29.5	28.8	28.1	27.5
DK	28.7	31.9	31.4	30.5	30.0
D	25.4	28.4	30.0	29.5	29.3
EL	23.2	22.3	23.1	23.6	24.5
E	20.5	24.7	22.5	22.0	21.6
F	27.6	30.9	31.0	30.8	30.5
IRL	18.7	20.5	18.5	17.2	16.1
I	24.3	26.2	25.2	25.7	25.2
L	22.6	24.5	25.2	24.8	24.1
NL	32.4	33.5	30.1	29.4	28.5
A	26.7	28.9	29.6	28.8	28.4
P	15.8	21.3	22.0	22.5	23.4
FIN	25.1	34.6	31.6	29.3	27.2
S	33.1	38.6	34.5	33.6	33.3
UK	22.9	29.1	28.0	27.3	26.8
IS	17.1	18.9	18.7	18.4	18.3
NO	26.4	28.8	26.2	25.8	27.9
EEA	**25.4**	**28.8**	**28.5**	**28.1**	**27.7**
CH	20.2	25.1	26.9	27.9	27.9

Source: Eurostat, Esspros.

Expenditure on social protection per capita increased in real terms by about 4.3 % per year during the period 1990–93 in EU-15. The increase was particularly marked in Portugal (13 % per year) and the United Kingdom (9 % per year). Only Greece reduced its per capita expenditure in real terms during this period.

In contrast, during the period 1993–96 there was an average increase of 1.7 % per year for EU-15 as a whole. In Spain, Sweden and the Netherlands expenditure per capita even decreased in real terms. Only Greece and Germany (as well as Iceland) experienced an increase in their real-terms growth. The growth rate then fell to 1.0 % per year between 1996 and 1998 in EU-15. In Finland, the Netherlands, Italy and the United Kingdom, per capita expenditure in real terms stabilised in 1998. Luxembourg, Portugal and Greece had growth rates well above the average in 1998. This was also true of Iceland.

The EU average for social protection expenditure as a percentage of GDP (27.7 % in 1998) conceals major differences between Member States. Sweden (33.3 %), France (30.5 %) and Denmark (30.0 %) had the highest rates, while Ireland (16.1 %) and Spain (21.6 %) had the lowest. In Iceland the ratio was 18.3 %.

Table 6.4.2. Expenditure on social protection per capita at constant prices (index 1990 = 100)

	1991	1992	1993	1994	1995	1996	1997	1998
EU-15	**104**	**110**	**113**	**115**	**117**	**119**	**120**	**122**
EUR-11	**103**	**109**	**111**	**112**	**115**	**118**	**118**	**120**
B	104	107	115	115	115	117	118	119
DK	105	108	113	122	122	122	121	122
D	95	103	104	106	110	114	112	114
EL	96	94	96	97	101	104	111	120
E	110	117	124	119	119	120	121	124
F	103	107	111	112	116	117	118	120
IRL	106	112	119	123	131	133	139	144
I	105	109	109	109	108	113	118	118
L	108	112	120	124	129	134	138	151
NL	101	103	104	102	106	102	103	103
A	104	107	110	115	117	118	118	120
P	112	129	144	149	153	163	174	189
FIN	108	115	116	119	119	122	120	120
S	100	105	108	108	106	106	106	109
UK	110	121	130	130	130	135	135	135
IS	105	103	104	106	110	113	118	127
NO	106	110	113	114	115	119	122	127
EEA	**104**	**110**	**113**	**114**	**117**	**119**	**120**	**122**
CH	105	112	117	118	119	124	130	132

Source: Eurostat, Esspros.

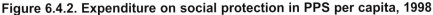

Figure 6.4.2. Expenditure on social protection in PPS per capita, 1998

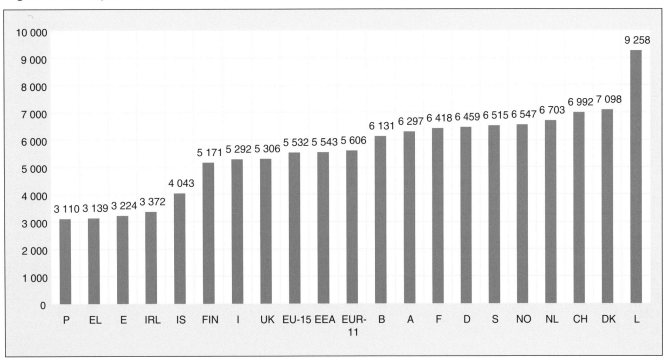

Source: Eurostat, Esspros.

Expressed in PPS (purchasing power standards) per capita, the differences between countries are more marked. Luxembourg spends the most (9 258 PPS per capita), followed by Denmark (7 098 PPS per capita). Portugal and Greece recorded the lowest levels (under 3 200 PPS per capita). The ratio between the country which spends the most and the one which spends the least was thus 3.0 : 1 in 1998 (compared with 3.7 : 1 in 1990).

The differences between the countries reflect the differences in social protection systems, demographic changes, unemployment rates and other social, institutional and economic factors.

Social benefits

In 1998, in most of the Member States, benefits under the old-age and survivors' functions took the lion's share of expenditure on social protection: 45.7 % of total benefits in EU-15 as a whole, or 12.2 % of GDP. This was particularly true for Italy, where over 60 % of total benefits was accounted for by these functions. One of the reasons for this was the proportion of the population in the over-65 age group (18 % compared with an EU-15 average of 16 %).

In Ireland, on the other hand, benefits in respect of the old-age and survivors' functions represented well under 30 %. Ireland is in fact the "youngest" country in Europe, with 32 % of the population aged under 20 in 1998 (compared with an EU-15 average of 23 %) and only 11 % aged 65 and over. In Portugal, Ireland and

Figure 6.4.3. Social benefits by group of functions, EU-15, 1998
(as a % of total benefits and as a % of GDP)

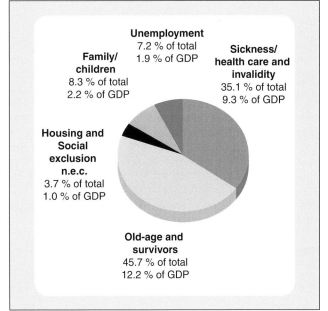

Source: Eurostat, Esspros

Finland, the sickness/health care and disability group of functions had the largest share of total benefits. This was also true for Iceland (more than 50 %) and Norway.

Table 6.4.3. Social benefits by group of functions 1998 (as a % of total social benefits)

	Old-age and survivors	Sickness/ healthcare and disability	Family/children	Unemployment	Housing and social exclusion n.e.c.
EU-15	**45.7**	**35.1**	**8.3**	**7.2**	**3.7**
EUR-11	**46.5**	**34.9**	**8.0**	**7.8**	**2.9**
B	42.8	33.3	8.5	12.7	2.7
DK	38.3	30.8	13.0	11.7	6.2
D	42.3	36.1	10.1	8.7	2.8
EL	52.6	30.4	8.1	4.8	4.2
E	46.1	37.3	2.1	13.5	1.0
F	44.0	34.1	9.8	7.6	4.5
IRL	24.9	41.4	12.7	15.5	5.5
I	64.0	29.5	3.6	2.7	0.1
L	44.2	36.7	14.1	3.5	1.5
NL	41.1	40.3	4.5	7.3	6.8
A	48.2	34.9	10.0	5.5	1.4
P	42.7	45.9	5.3	4.7	1.5
FIN	34.5	37.1	12.8	12.0	3.6
S	39.4	35.0	10.8	9.3	5.5
UK	43.9	36.9	8.6	3.6	7.1
IS	31.7	50.1	12.6	2.6	2.9
NO	32.6	47.9	13.3	2.9	3.3
EEA	**45.5**	**35.3**	**8.4**	**7.1**	**3.7**
CH	49.7	35.8	5.3	5.6	3.6

Source: Eurostat, Esspros.

The family/children function accounted for 8.3 % of total benefits in EU-15, or 2.2 % of GDP. The figure was over 12 % in Luxembourg, Denmark, Finland and Ireland (as well as Norway and Iceland), and under 5 % in Spain, Italy and the Netherlands. There are considerable differences between the Member States in the share of unemployment-related benefits in the total. They represented over 13 % of total benefits in Ireland and Spain and under 3 % in Italy (and Iceland and Norway). It is important to note that the amount of "unemployment" benefits is not always explained by the level of unemployment in the country, since considerable differences remain regarding the coverage and the amount of unemployment benefits.

Between 1990 and 1998, the structure of social benefits showed different rates of growth for the various functions. The variations resulted from evolving needs and changes in social protection legislation.

Between 1990 and 1998, per capita expenditure in EU-15 under the old-age and survivors functions increased very steadily by 22 % in real terms. In the same period, the percentage of the population in the over-65 age group rose from 14.6 % in 1990 to 16.0 % in 1998.

Table 6.4.4. Social benefits per capita at constant prices in the EU-15 (index 1990 = 100)

	1990	1991	1992	1993	1996	1997	1998
Old-age and survivors	100	102	106	109	118	120	122
Sickness/healthcare and disability	100	104	110	111	116	116	118
Family/children	100	104	111	113	127	130	130
Unemployment	100	120	134	148	134	126	123
Housing and social exclusion n.e.c.	100	100	110	120	136	135	135
Total benefits	**100**	**104**	**110**	**113**	**120**	**120**	**122**

Source: Eurostat, Esspros.

Expenditure under the sickness/healthcare and disability group of functions grew at a lower rate than the average increase of 22 % in total benefits. This reflects, *inter alia*, the Member States' efforts to control costs. In contrast, family/children-related expenditure increased at a higher rate than the average. This increase (+ 30 % between 1990 and 1998) was particularly marked in 1996, when Germany introduced reforms and extended the system of family benefits.

The trend in unemployment-related expenditure calls for more thorough analysis. Between 1990 and 1998, it rose by 23 % in EU-15 (similar to total benefits), but it was not a steady increase, since the total level of these benefits depends broadly on the trend in unemployment.

Between 1990 and 1993, these benefits increased very rapidly in EU-15. Their share of total benefits rose from 7.3 % in 1990 to 9.5 % in 1993, since the corresponding figures for unemployment-related expenditure during this period increased in all the countries except Greece (showing a decrease) and Belgium (where the share was stable).

The increase was particularly marked in Finland (from 6.1 % in 1990 to 16.0 % in 1993), where there was a steeper rise in unemployment than elsewhere. Switzerland also experienced a significant increase between 1990 and 1993. From 1993 on, there was a decrease in unemployment-related benefits in EU-15, resulting partly from a gradual improvement in the economic situation and partly from reforms of the payment system (e.g. limitation of the period during which benefits are payable, changes in the conditions of entitlement to benefits) in some countries.

Between 1993 and 1998, the share of unemployment-related expenditure in total benefits fell from 9.5 % to 7.2 % in EU-15. The decrease was more marked in Spain (from 21.7 % to 13.5 %), Denmark (from 17.9 % to 11.7 %), Finland (from 16.0 % to 12.0 %) and the United Kingdom (from 6.8 % to 3.6 %). There was also a significant decrease in Norway.

The financing of social protection

Figure 6.4.4. Receipts of social protection by type EU-15, 1998 (as a % of total receipts)

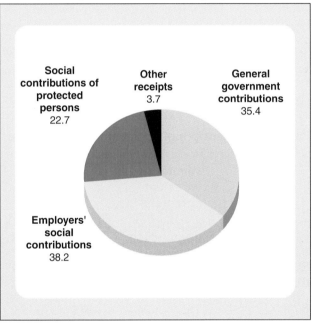

Source: Eurostat, Esspros.

In 1998 for EU-15 as a whole, the main sources of funding for the social protection system were social contributions, which accounted for 60.9 % of total receipts followed by tax-funded general government contributions (35.4 %). Social contributions are paid partly by employers and partly by the protected persons (employees, self-employed, pensioners and others). The European average conceals considerable differences between the countries in the structure of social protection funding. The proportion derived from social contributions is greater in Belgium, Spain, France and Germany, where this type of funding accounts for over 65 % of total receipts.

In contrast, Denmark and Ireland (as well as Norway) finance their social protection systems mainly through taxes, which account for over 60 % of total receipts.

Table 6.4.5. Expenditure on unemployment function (as a % of total social benefits)

	1990	1993	1996	1997	1998
EU-15	7.3	9.5	8.2	7.5	7.2
EUR-11	7.1	9.7	8.5	8.0	7.8
B	13.4	13.4	12.9	12.8	12.7
DK	15.4	17.9	13.8	12.6	11.7
D	6.0	10.6	9.2	8.8	8.7
EL	4.1	3.7	4.2	4.6	4.8
E	18.0	21.7	14.8	14.1	13.5
F	8.3	9.3	8.0	7.8	7.6
IRL	15.8	18.0	18.4	16.9	15.5
I	1.7	2.3	3.2	2.9	2.7
L	3.0	3.1	3.6	3.7	3.5
NL	8.3	9.3	10.0	9.0	7.3
A	4.6	5.6	5.7	5.5	5.5
P	3.4	5.4	5.8	5.0	4.7
FIN	6.1	16.0	14.0	13.3	12.0
S	:	11.7	10.4	10.4	9.3
UK	5.7	6.8	4.9	3.7	3.6
IS	1.9	3.8	3.6	3.2	2.6
NO	6.9	8.6	5.7	4.3	2.9
EEA	7.3	9.5	8.1	7.4	7.1
CH	0.8	6.8	6.0	6.9	5.6

Source: Eurostat, Esspros.

The United Kingdom, Luxembourg and Sweden (as well as Iceland) are also heavily dependent on general government contributions.

During the economic slowdown from 1990 to 1993, general government contributions per capita increased in real terms (+ 20 %) in EU-15 more rapidly than the other sources of funding (+ 9 % for total receipts). In contrast, social contributions showed only a slight increase (+ 4 %).

Table 6.4.6. Receipts of social protection per capita at constant prices in EU-15 (index 1990 = 100)

	1990	1993	1996	1997	1998
General government contributions	100	120	125	127	139
Social contributions	100	104	111	112	111
– by employers	100	102	106	107	109
– by protected persons ([1])	100	108	119	121	113
Other receipts	100	101	105	104	107
Total receipts	**100**	**109**	**115**	**116**	**119**

([1]) Employees, self-employed, pensioners and others.
Source: Eurostat, Esspros.

Between 1993 and 1997, when GDP recovered and public expenditure was put under stricter control, general government contributions increased at a lower rate whereas social contributions grew at a faster rate.

In 1998, there was a decrease in social contributions by protected persons, resulting from, *inter alia*, measures to combat unemployment adopted by several Member States (for example exemption from social contributions, as an incentive to take on workers). This decrease was compensated by a particularly significant increase in general government contributions, especially in France and Italy. For example, in France sickness contributions by protected persons were replaced, in part or in total, by an increase of the "generalised social contributions" (classified under "earmarked taxes" of the Esspros).

Overall, between 1990 and 1998 general government contributions as a proportion of total receipts increased by 5.1 points in EU-15. Particularly in France and Portugal, these contributions increased more rapidly than in the other countries. On the other hand, they accounted for considerably less of the total receipts in Denmark and the Netherlands. Iceland also experienced a significant fall.

Table 6.4.7. Receipts of social protection by type (as a % of total of receipts)

	General government contributions		Social contributions						Other receipts	
			Total		Employers		Protected persons ([1])			
	1990	1998	1990	1998	1990	1998	1990	1998	1990	1998
EU-15	**30.3**	**35.4**	**65.5**	**60.9**	**42.2**	**38.2**	**23.3**	**22.7**	**4.3**	**3.7**
EUR-11	**25.0**	**31.2**	**70.9**	**64.6**	**46.0**	**41.5**	**24.9**	**23.1**	**4.1**	**4.1**
B	23.8	24.4	67.0	73.0	41.5	50.6	25.5	22.4	9.2	2.6
DK	80.1	67.2	13.1	26.6	7.8	8.7	5.3	17.9	6.8	6.3
D	25.2	30.9	72.0	66.1	43.7	37.4	28.4	28.7	2.8	3.0
EL	33.0	29.2	59.0	61.7	39.4	37.6	19.6	24.1	8.0	9.1
E	26.2	27.2	71.3	69.7	54.4	52.2	16.9	17.5	2.5	3.1
F	16.7	30.7	80.8	66.4	52.0	46.5	28.8	19.9	2.5	2.9
IRL	58.9	61.3	40.0	37.5	24.5	23.9	15.6	13.6	1.0	1.2
I	29.0	38.3	67.9	59.5	52.9	44.7	15.0	14.8	3.1	2.2
L	40.6	46.3	51.5	49.3	28.9	25.0	22.6	24.2	7.9	4.4
NL	25.0	15.7	59.0	64.4	20.0	30.1	39.1	34.3	15.9	19.9
A	35.9	34.5	63.1	64.6	38.1	37.5	25.1	27.1	0.9	0.9
P	33.8	42.6	57.0	47.4	36.9	29.5	20.1	17.8	9.2	10.0
FIN	40.6	43.1	52.1	50.1	44.1	36.2	8.0	13.8	7.3	6.8
S	:	45.8	:	48.3	:	39.1	:	9.3	:	5.9
UK	42.4	47.9	55.1	51.4	28.2	27.0	27.0	24.4	2.4	0.7
IS	67.8	52.9	32.2	47.1	24.9	38.9	7.3	8.2	0.0	0.0
NO	63.0	60.7	36.4	38.3	24.0	24.0	12.4	14.3	0.5	1.0
EEA	**30.9**	**35.8**	**64.9**	**60.5**	**41.8**	**37.9**	**23.1**	**22.6**	**4.2**	**3.7**
CH	19.2	19.4	62.7	59.2	31.6	29.4	31.1	29.8	18.1	21.5

([1]) Employees, self-employed, pensioners and others.
Source: Eurostat, Esspros.

Between 1990 and 1998, the share of employers' social contributions fell by 4.0 points in EU-15, decreasing in all the countries except Belgium, the Netherlands and Denmark. There were particularly large reductions in Portugal and Finland. Also, the share of social contributions by protected persons fell slightly between 1990 and 1998 in EU-15 as a whole, from 23.3 % to 22.7 %.

6.4.2. Expenditure on pensions

The Esspros methodology distinguishes between cash benefits and benefits in kind. Cash benefits can be periodic or lump sum. The "pensions" aggregate only includes some periodic cash benefits in the disability, old age, survivors' and unemployment functions. More specifically, the "pensions" aggregate is defined in this publication as the sum of the following social benefits (with the function to which the category of benefit belongs in brackets):

- disability pensions (disability function);
- early retirement benefits due to reduced capacity to work (disability function);
- old age pensions (old age function);
- anticipated old age pensions (old age function);
- partial pensions (old age function);
- survivors' pensions (survivors' function);
- early retirement benefits for labour market reasons (unemployment function).

These benefits are divided into means-tested and non-means-tested benefits. The value of the "pensions" aggregate was calculated for all countries in accordance with the above definition, regardless of national differences in the institutional organisation of social protection systems. Some of the benefits which make up the "pensions" aggregate (for example disability pensions) are paid to people who have not reached the standard retirement age.

The definitions of the different categories of social benefits can be found in the Esspros manual 1996. In accordance with Esspros, pensions are recorded without any deduction of taxes or other compulsory levies payable on them by beneficiaries. On the other hand, the values of pensions do not include the social contributions which pension schemes pay on behalf of their pensioners to other social protection schemes (e.g. health schemes). Esspros records these payments under the heading "re-routed social contributions".

In 1998, expenditure on pensions in EU-15 was equivalent to 12.6 % of GDP. In Italy it amounted to almost 15 % of GDP, and in Austria to more than 14 %. Ireland spends less than 5 % of its GDP on pensions. In Iceland, the percentage is also low (less than 6 %).

Between 1990 and 1998, expenditure on pensions in EU-15 rose by 0.9 GDP percentage points from 11.7 % to 12.6 %. This trend was a generalised one in EU-15 except in the Netherlands and Ireland, both of which recorded a sharp drop due largely to the slow growth in pensions expenditure in the Netherlands and the strong growth in GDP in Ireland during this period. In the Netherlands, where GDP had risen by an annual average of 2.7 % during the period 1990 to 1998, the growth in expenditure on pensions in real terms was the slowest in EU-15, at an annual average of approximately + 0.8 %, compared with + 3.2 % for EU-15.

Figure 6.4.5. Expenditure on pensions, 1998 (as a % of GDP)

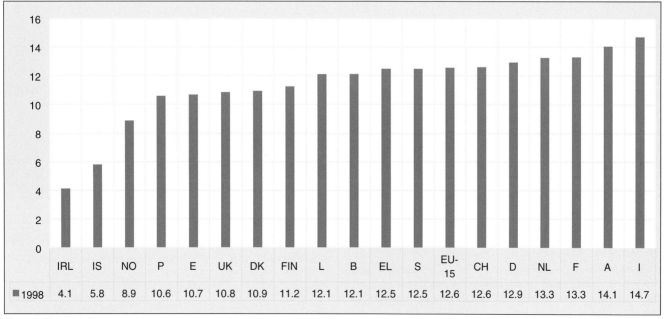

	IRL	IS	NO	P	E	UK	DK	FIN	L	B	EL	S	EU-15	CH	D	NL	F	A	I
■ 1998	4.1	5.8	8.9	10.6	10.7	10.8	10.9	11.2	12.1	12.1	12.5	12.5	12.6	12.6	12.9	13.3	13.3	14.1	14.7

Source: Eurostat, Esspros.

Figure 6.4.6. Expenditure on pensions in the EU-15 (as a % of GDP)

Source: Eurostat, Esspros.

Ireland proved almost symmetrical to the Netherlands, with expenditure on pensions up by some + 3.3 % in real terms as an annual average from 1990 to 1998 and the fastest growth in GDP in the EU, at an annual average of roughly + 6.3 %, compared with approximately + 2.1 % in EU-15.

The increase in the share of GDP accounted for by expenditure on pensions between 1990 and 1998 was particularly marked in Portugal (almost + 3 points), where spending on pensions in real terms rose by some + 7.3 % per annum against an average increase in GDP of about + 2.3 % per annum.

The ratio in Switzerland rose faster than in any EU-15 Member State (by + 3.2 points), where an annual average of 4.0 % more was spent on pensions, compared with an average increase in GDP of only + 0.5 % per annum.

The trend in pensions expenditure was irregular throughout the period 1990–98. The upturn was, in fact, substantial between 1990 and 1993: in EU-15 the rate increased by 1.1 percentage points to reach 12.8 % of GDP in 1993. This was due to a relatively small real rise in GDP (+ 1.6 % as an annual average) coupled with a moderate rise of + 4.9 % per annum in expenditure on pensions expressed in real terms.

The increase in the ratio between 1990 and 1993 was particularly steep in Finland (+ 3.4 GDP percentage points). Finland was in recession during this period, and therefore spent + 4.5 % more in real terms per annum on pensions.

Table 6.4.8. Expenditure on pensions, 1990–98 (as a % of GDP)

	1990	1993	1996	1998
EU-15	**11.7**	**12.8**	**12.8**	**12.6**
B	11.8	13.1	12.2	12.1
DK	9.6	10.1	11.5	10.9
D	12.0	12.5	12.9	12.9
EL	12.1	11.4	11.7	12.5
E	9.4	10.6	10.9	10.7
F	12.2	13.0	13.4	13.3
IRL	5.6	5.6	4.7	4.1
I	13.5	15.1	14.8	14.7
L	12.2	13.1	12.9	12.1
NL	15.3	15.6	14.0	13.3
A	13.7	14.2	14.6	14.1
P	7.7	9.6	10.3	10.6
FIN	10.4	13.8	12.8	11.2
S	:	13.7	12.9	12.5
UK	9.6	11.3	11.1	10.8
IS	4.5	5.5	5.7	5.8
NO	8.6	8.9	8.3	8.9
CH	9.4	11.0	12.0	12.6

Source: Eurostat, Esspros.

EU expenditure on pensions as a percentage of GDP stabilised (12.8 %) between 1993 and 1996 as a result of upturns in both GDP and pensions expenditure. The average rise in GDP in EU-15 from 1993 to 1996 was + 2.2 % per annum, compared with + 2.3 % per annum in pensions expenditure.

Table 6.4.9. Expenditure on pensions at constant prices (index 1990 = 100)

	1990	1993	1996	1998
EU-15	**100**	**115**	**124**	**128**
B	100	115	113	119
DK	100	109	137	138
D	100	125	134	138
EL	100	96	105	122
E	100	117	128	135
F	100	108	116	122
IRL	100	110	117	130
I	100	113	120	126
L	100	124	139	147
NL	100	104	105	107
A	100	109	119	122
P	100	132	157	176
FIN	100	114	122	123
S	100	:	:	:
UK	100	121	130	134
IS	100	118	135	159
NO	100	108	118	129
CH	100	114	125	136

Source: Eurostat, Esspros.

The trend intensified between 1996 and 1998 in EU-15, where the real average growth rate in pensions spending fell to + 1.9 % per annum while that of GDP rose to + 2.6 % per annum. Expenditure on pensions as a percentage of GDP fell from 12.8 % to 12.6 %.

In most EU-15 Member States the rate fell between 1996 and 1998. A notable exception was Greece,

which showed a sharp rise in pensions expenditure in real terms (+ 7.6 % per annum on average).The drop in the ratio was marked (– 1.6 GDP percentage points) in Finland, where there was a renewed upturn in the economy (GDP: + 5.8 % as an annual average) and slower growth in expenditure on pensions (+ 0.6 % per annum) than in the other countries.

In most Member States, pensions were top of the list of social protection expenditure headings in 1998; representing 47 % of the EU-15 total expenditure on social benefits. This applied particularly to Italy, where over 60 % of all social benefits were pensions. In Greece, Portugal, Luxembourg, Austria and Spain, expenditure on pensions represented over 50 % of the total spending on social benefits.

In Ireland and Sweden, expenditure on benefits in kind was higher than expenditure on pensions. This is also true of Iceland and Norway. In Denmark, benefits in kind were equivalent to pensions, at 10.9 % of GDP.

However, in Italy, benefits in kind were equivalent to only 5.5 % of GDP, compared with an EU-15 average of 8.3 %.

Other cash benefits, that is cash benefits excluding pensions, accounted in 1998 for 22 % of all EU-15 benefits, equivalent to 5.8 % of GDP. On the other hand, in Ireland and Belgium they accounted for more than 30 % of the total, but in Portugal and Greece for less than 16 %.

Figure 6.4.7. Social benefits, EU-15, 1998 (as a % of total benefits and of GDP)

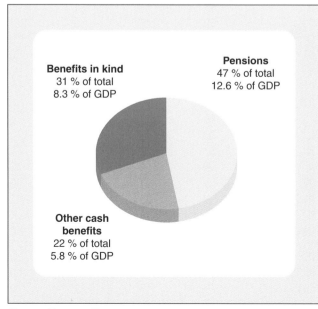

Benefits in kind
31 % of total
8.3 % of GDP

Pensions
47 % of total
12.6 % of GDP

Other cash benefits
22 % of total
5.8 % of GDP

Source: Eurostat, Esspros.

Table 6.4.10. Social benefits, 1998 (as a % of GDP)

	Old-age pensions	Benefits in kind	Other cash benefits	Total benefits
EU-15	**12.6**	**8.3**	**5.8**	**26.6**
B	12.1	6.7	8.1	26.9
DK	10.9	10.9	7.2	29.1
D	12.9	8.6	6.7	28.2
EL	12.5	7.5	3.7	23.7
E	10.7	6.1	4.3	21.0
F	13.3	9.7	5.9	28.9
IRL	4.1	6.2	5.0	15.3
I	14.7	5.5	4.1	24.3
L	12.1	6.4	4.7	23.2
NL	13.3	7.9	5.7	26.8
A	14.1	8.1	5.3	27.5
P	10.6	7.4	2.5	20.4
FIN	11.2	8.6	6.5	26.4
S	12.5	13.3	6.8	32.6
UK	10.8	9.1	6.0	26.0
IS	5.8	9.2	3.2	18.3
NO	8.9	11.8	6.7	27.3
CH	12.6	6.5	6.3	25.4

Source: Eurostat, Esspros.

Table 6.4.11. Social benefits, 1998 (as a % of total)

	Old-age pensions	Benefits in kind	Other cash benefits	Total benefits
EU-15	47	31	22	100
B	45	25	30	100
DK	38	38	25	100
D	46	30	24	100
EL	53	32	15	100
E	51	29	20	100
F	46	34	20	100
IRL	27	40	33	100
I	61	23	17	100
L	52	28	20	100
NL	50	29	21	100
A	51	29	19	100
P	52	36	12	100
FIN	43	33	25	100
S	38	41	21	100
UK	42	35	23	100
IS	32	51	18	100
NO	32	43	24	100
CH	50	26	25	100

Source: Eurostat, Esspros.

In 1998, expenditure on old-age pensions topped the list of pensions expenditures in every country, accounting for 75 % of the total (equivalent to 9.5 % of EU-15 GDP), and for about 80 % in the United Kingdom, France and Germany. The percentage is also high in Sweden, Italy, Spain and Switzerland. Ireland records the lowest value, at 47 %.

The proportion of the population aged 65 or over is the main explanation for the differences. In 1998, over 17 % of the population in Sweden and Italy was aged 65 or over; in Ireland the figure was less than 12 %, and the EU-15 average was 16.0 %.

In the Netherlands and Portugal, over 20 % of all expenditure on pensions consisted of disability pensions in 1998, compared with the European Union average of roughly 9 %. The same is true of Norway and Iceland. On the other hand, France, devotes less than 5 % of its expenditure on pensions to disability pensions. The various rules on benefits linked to disability are one explanation for these figures.

The various rules on benefits linked to disability are one explanation for these figures.

In Denmark, Ireland, Austria and Finland, other pensions account for a very high proportion of pensions expenditure: more than 12 %, compared with the EU-15 average of 5 % and only 1 % in Sweden. The proportion of the population aged 50 to 59 not economically active partly explains the discrepancies between countries. For example, in Ireland and Austria, more

Figure 6.4.8. Breakdown of pension expenditure between categories, EU-15, 1998 (as a % of total pensions and of GDP)

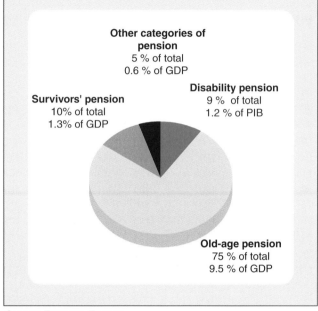

Source: Eurostat, Esspros.

than 40 % of the population aged 50 to 59 is inactive, compared with an EU-15 average of 35.6 % in 1998. In Sweden the figure is less than 15 %.

Table 6.4.12. Breakdown of pension expenditure between categories, 1998 (as a % of total of pensions)

	Old-age pension	Disability pension	Survivor's pension	Other categories of pension
EU-15	75	9	10	5
B	63	11	21	5
DK	62	15	0	23
D	79	9	3	9
EL	69	9	16	6
E	74	13	8	5
F	80	4	12	3
IRL	47	15	22	16
I	74	7	18	2
L	70	20	8	3
NL	60	22	11	7
A	59	9	20	13
P	63	21	12	3
FIN	59	20	9	12
S	75	18	6	1
UK	81	10	8	0
IS	65	25	9	0
NO	67	28	4	0
CH	75	17	8	0

Source: Eurostat, Esspros.

7. Money, interest rates and prices in the Union

7.1. Exchange rates, the euro and EMU

The third stage of economic and monetary union (EMU) began with the introduction of the single currency, the euro, on 1 January 1999. In May 1998, the European Council announced the 11 countries that would be part of economic and monetary union from the outset: Austria, Belgium, Finland, France, Germany, Ireland, Italy, Luxembourg, the Netherlands, Portugal and Spain. Since 1 January 1999, the currencies of these countries have been fixed against the euro at an irrevocable conversion rate (see Table 7.1.1) and they have thus become non-decimal subdivisions of the euro. On that date the euro also replaced the ecu at a rate of 1 to 1. Rounding rules apply for the conversion of currencies (see box).

Rounding rules (summary)

Conversion from national currency to euro

The official euro conversion rates are always to six figures. In order to ensure accuracy, these rates must not be shortened or rounded off during conversion. To convert a national currency amount into euro, the amount must be multiplied by the appropriate conversion rate. An amount in euro can be converted to national currency by dividing by the conversion rate.

Conversion of two euro-zone currencies

Conversion must always be via the euro, using the conversion rates.

Conversion of euro-zone currency and third currency

Conversion must also be via the euro, but using the third currency's current exchange rate against the euro.

Milestones in EMU

1 January 1999

- Introduction of the euro and its use in non-cash form

- Entry into force of the legislation (principle of 'neither obligation nor prohibition', the rounding rules)

- Definition and implementation of monetary policy by the ECB and the ESCB

- Exchange transactions in euro

- Public debt issuance in euro

- Introduction of Target settlement system

---

1 January 2002

- Introduction of euro notes and coins

- All accounting in euro

- Gradual withdrawal of national currency notes and coins

28 February 2002 (D: 31/12/2001, NL: 28/01/2002, IRL: 09/02/2002, F: 17/02/2002)

- National currencies no longer legal tender

In June 2000, the European Council agreed that Greece would join the list of euro-zone countries with effect from 1 January 2001. Euro notes and coins will be introduced in cash form throughout the 12 countries of the euro-zone in January 2002, and national currency denominations will lose legal tender at 28 February 2002 or sooner depending on the national changeover scenario.

ERM and ERM II

Between March 1979 and the end of 1998 the exchange rate mechanism (ERM) linked the currencies that were part of the European Monetary System (EMS). From August 1993 their exchange rates were obliged to remain within fluctuation bands of 15 % around the bilateral central rates. In March 1998, when the Greek drachma joined the ERM, the central rates were adjusted for the last time, with the Irish pound being revalued by 3 %. For the last 10 months of its existence the ERM included 13 Member State currencies: only the pound sterling and the Swedish krona (a "notional" central rate applied to the former) were not part of the system.

ERM II came into existence on 1 January 1999, linking to the euro the Greek drachma and the Danish krone, the currencies of two Member States that did not join the euro-zone from the outset. (The other two currencies, the pound sterling and the Swedish krona, did not join ERM II). The aim of ERM II is to prepare the second-wave countries for eventual participation in the euro-zone, while helping to ensure exchange rate stability within the EU. The two currencies had a central rate against the euro of 340.75 in the case of the Greek drachma and 7.46038 for the Danish krone. Their fluctuation bands were ± 15 % for the Greek drachma and ± 2.25 % for the Danish krone. The fluctuation band is supported at the margins by unlimited intervention, with short-term financing available. However, the European Central Bank (ECB), as well as the national central banks not participating in the euro-zone, can suspend intervention if the main purpose — maintaining price stability — can no longer be guaranteed.

Greece entered the euro-zone in January 2001 at a conversion rate against the euro identical to its central rate in ERM II. From 1 January 2001 only the Danish krone remains a member of ERM II.

Exchange rates

The official exchange rates for the ecu, as it existed until 31 December 1998, against its constituent currencies and other currencies were calculated every day by the European Commission on the basis of the composition of the ecu basket.

Since 1 January 1999 (1 January 2001 for Greece), the exchange rates of the countries which formed the euro-zone have been fixed to the euro. Every day the ECB provides the official reference rates for the main international currencies against the euro.

Table 7.1.1 shows the exchange rates of the ecu (until 1998) and euro (from 1999) against the national currencies of the EU Member States, the US dollar and the Japanese yen since 1990. The figures indicate the value of an ecu or euro in national currency. For the countries belonging to the euro-zone from 1 January 1999, the exchange rates shown in 1999 and 2000 are the fixed conversion rates to the euro.

Table 7.1.1. Ecu/euro exchange rates annual average

		1990	1991	1992	1993	1994	1995
B/L	BEF/LUF	42.4257	42.2233	41.5932	40.4713	39.6565	38.5519
DK	DKK	7.85652	7.90859	7.80925	7.59359	7.54328	7.32804
D	DEM	2.05209	2.05076	2.02031	1.93639	1.92453	1.87375
EL	GRD	201.412	225.216	247.026	268.568	288.026	302.989
E	ESP	129.411	128.469	132.526	149.124	158.918	163.000
F	FRF	6.91412	6.97332	6.84839	6.63368	6.58262	6.52506
IRL	IEP	0.767768	0.767809	0.760718	0.799952	0.793618	0.815525
I	ITL	1521.98	1533.24	1595.52	1841.23	1915.06	2130.14
NL	NLG	2.31212	2.31098	2.27482	2.17521	2.15827	2.09891
A	ATS	14.4399	14.4309	14.2169	13.6238	13.5396	13.1824
P	PTE	181.109	178.614	174.714	188.370	196.896	196.105
FIN	FIM	4.85496	5.00211	5.80703	6.69628	6.19077	5.70855
S	SEK	7.5205	7.4793	7.5330	9.1215	9.1631	9.3319
UK	GBP	0.7139	0.7010	0.7377	0.7800	0.7759	0.8288
US	USD	1.2734	1.2392	1.2981	1.1710	1.1895	1.3080
JP	JPY	183.66	166.49	164.22	130.15	121.32	123.01
		1996	**1997**	**1998**	**1999** [1]	**2000**	**2001** [2]
B/L	BEF/LUF	39.2986	40.5332	40.6207	40.3399	40.3399	40.3399
DK	DKK	7.35934	7.48361	7.49930	7.43556	7.45381	7.46321
D	DEM	1.90954	1.96438	1.96913	1.95583	1.95583	1.95583
EL	GRD	305.546	309.355	330.731	325.763	336.630	340.750
E	ESP	160.748	165.887	167.184	166.386	166.386	166.386
F	FRF	6.49300	6.61260	6.60141	6.55957	6.55957	6.55957
IRL	IEP	0.793448	0.747516	0.786245	0.787564	0.787564	0.787564
I	ITL	1958.96	1929.30	1943.65	1936.27	1936.27	1936.27
NL	NLG	2.13973	2.21081	2.21967	2.20371	2.20371	2.20371
A	ATS	13.4345	13.8240	13.8545	13.7603	13.7603	13.7603
P	PTE	195.761	198.589	201.695	200.482	200.482	200.482
FIN	FIM	5.82817	5.88064	5.98251	5.94573	5.94573	5.94573
S	SEK	8.5147	8.6512	8.9159	8.8075	8.4452	9.0346
UK	GBP	0.8138	0.6923	0.6764	0.6587	0.6095	0.6265
US	USD	1.2698	1.1340	1.1211	1.0658	0.9219	0.9071
JP	JPY	138.08	137.08	146.42	121.32	99.4748	108.76

[1] The following currencies are fixed against the euro at the rates shown: BEF, LUF, DEM, ESP, FRF, IEP, ITL, NLG, ATS, PTE, FIM.

[2] January to May.

Source: Eurostat.

Table 7.1.2 shows the exchange rates of EU currencies, the US dollar and the Japanese yen against the ecu (until 1998) and euro (from 1999) in index terms. It shows the value in ecu/euro of one unit of national currency, the base year being 1996.

In 2000, between 1 January and 31 December, the following fluctuations against the euro took place:

- the ERM II member currencies: the Danish krone (DKK) depreciated by 0.3 % and the Greek drachma (GRD) by 3.2 %;

- the pound sterling (GBP) gained 0.1 % and the Swedish krona (SEK) lost 3.2 %;

- the US dollar (USD) appreciated by 10.5 % and the Japanese yen (JPY) depreciated by 3.9 %.

In the first five months of 2001 these currencies fluctuated against the euro as follows:

- the Danish krone (DKK), which is for the moment the only member of ERM II, appreciated by 0.1 %. The Greek drachma (GRD), formerly part of ERM II, now has a fixed conversion rate against the euro;

- the pound sterling (GBP) appreciated by 5.7 % and the Swedish krona (SEK) depreciated by 2.6 %;

- the US dollar (USD) and the Japanese yen (JYP) gained 11.1 % and 7.2 % respectively.

Table 7.1.2. Ecu/euro exchange rate indices, annual averages (base 1996 = 100)

		1990	1991	1992	1993	1994	1995
B/L	BEF/LUF	92.6	93.1	94.5	97.1	99.1	101.9
DK	DKK	93.7	93.1	94.3	96.9	97.6	100.4
D	DEM	93.1	93.1	94.5	98.6	99.2	101.9
EL	GRD	151.8	135.7	123.8	113.8	106.1	100.9
E	ESP	124.2	125.1	121.4	108.1	101.1	98.6
F	FRF	93.9	93.1	94.8	97.9	98.6	99.5
IRL	IEP	103.3	103.3	104.3	99.2	99.9	97.3
I	ITL	128.7	127.7	123.0	106.4	102.3	92.1
NL	NLG	92.5	92.6	94.1	98.4	99.1	101.9
A	ATS	93.0	93.1	94.5	98.6	99.2	101.9
P	PTE	108.1	109.6	112.1	104.1	99.4	99.8
FIN	FIM	120.0	116.7	100.7	87.1	94.2	102.1
S	SEK	113.2	113.8	113.2	93.4	92.9	91.4
UK	GBP	113.9	116.0	110.5	104.3	104.8	98.1
US	USD	100.0	102.8	98.0	108.5	106.9	97.1
JP	JPY	75.2	83.1	84.2	106.6	113.8	112.7

		1996	1997	1998	1999 (1)	2000	2001 (2)
B/L	BEF/LUF	100.0	97.0	96.7	97.4	97.4	97.4
DK	DKK	100.0	98.3	98.1	99.0	98.7	100.0
D	DEM	100.0	97.2	97.0	97.6	97.6	97.6
EL	GRD	100.0	98.8	92.4	93.8	90.8	91.0
E	ESP	100.0	96.9	96.1	96.6	96.6	96.6
F	FRF	100.0	98.2	98.4	99.0	99.0	99.0
IRL	IEP	100.0	106.1	100.9	100.7	100.7	100.7
I	ITL	100.0	101.5	100.8	101.2	101.2	101.2
NL	NLG	100.0	96.8	96.4	97.1	97.1	97.1
A	ATS	100.0	97.2	97.0	97.6	97.6	97.6
P	PTE	100.0	98.6	97.1	97.6	97.6	97.6
FIN	FIM	100.0	99.1	97.4	98.0	98.0	98.0
S	SEK	100.0	98.4	95.5	96.7	100.8	94.7
UK	GBP	100.0	117.5	120.3	123.5	133.5	131.6
US	USD	100.0	112.0	113.3	119.1	137.7	142.0
JP	JPY	100.0	100.7	94.3	113.8	138.8	128.6

(1) Euro from 1999.
(2) January to May.
Source: Eurostat.

7.2. Interest rates

Government bond yields are a good indicator of long-term interest rates, since the government securities market normally attracts a large part of available capital. They also provide a fairly good reflection of a country's financial situation and of expectations in terms of economic policy.

The significance of government bond yields as a measure of economic and monetary union is recognised in the Treaty on European Union, where it appears as one of the criteria for moving to stage three of monetary union, which got under way on 1 January 1999.

Table 7.2.1 shows the yields of 10-year government bonds, as defined in the Treaty of Maastricht.

From 1996 to the end of 1998, the situation was marked by two interesting features: a general fall in long-term yields — reaching record lows — in every Member State and a degree of convergence that had never been attained before.

At the start of 1999, when the third phase of monetary union became effective, the interest differential on 10-year bonds among the various countries involved in monetary union (EMU) had practically disappeared. At the end of 1995, the rate differential had been as much as 510 basis points in the case of Germany and Italy, and 388 between Germany and Spain.

It is also interesting to note that at the start of 1999 the interest differential on 10-year bonds between the 11 countries in the euro-zone (apart from Greece) and the countries not involved in EMU was only 40 basis points.

There was a slight rise in long-term interest rates in the EU Member States in 1999 until the end of October, when there was a slight drop. This lasted only a short time, however. Yields then increased significantly, peaking in January 2000. Subsequently there was a considerable downward trend during 2000, which has continued over the first three months of 2001.

The trend in bond yields in countries that are not part of EMU, with the exception of Greece, has followed a similar pattern to that in the countries that are. In Greece, long-term yields have dropped considerably since 1995. At the end of 1998, the rate differential with Germany was still 331 basis points, but, by the end of 2000, when Greece joined EMU, it had narrowed to only 65 basis points.

In 2000, the trend for long-term yields was also downwards in the United States, following an upward trend in 1999. With regard to Japan, in early 1999 the trend was towards an increase in yields. However, this was short-lived. By the end of the first quarter of that year, the yield on Japanese government bonds decreased, to become more stable over 2000.

Table 7.2.1. Long-term interest rates (10-year government bond yields, period average, as a %)

	1993	1994	1995	1996	1997	1998	1999	2000	Jan. 2001	Feb. 2001	March 2001	April 2001
EU-15	8.3	8.4	8.8	7.5	6.3	4.9	4.7	5.4	5.0	5.0	4.9	5.1
Euro-zone	8.1	8.2	8.7	7.2	6.0	4.7	4.7	5.4	5.0	5.0	4.9	5.1
B	7.2	7.8	7.5	6.5	5.8	4.8	4.8	5.6	5.2	5.2	5.1	5.2
DK	7.3	7.8	8.3	7.2	6.3	4.9	4.9	5.6	5.1	5.1	5.0	5.1
D	6.5	6.9	6.9	6.2	5.6	4.6	4.5	5.3	4.8	4.8	4.7	4.8
EL	23.3	20.8	17.3	14.4	9.9	8.5	6.3	6.1	5.4	5.4	5.3	5.4
E	10.2	10.0	11.3	8.7	6.4	4.8	4.7	5.5	5.1	5.1	5.0	5.2
F	6.8	7.2	7.5	6.3	5.6	4.6	4.6	5.4	4.9	4.9	4.8	5.0
IRL	7.7	7.9	8.3	7.3	6.3	4.8	4.7	5.5	5.0	5.0	4.9	5.1
I	11.2	10.5	12.2	9.4	6.9	4.9	4.7	5.6	5.2	5.2	5.1	5.3
L	6.9	7.2	7.2	6.3	5.6	4.7	4.7	5.5	5.1	5.1	4.9	5.1
NL	6.4	6.9	6.9	6.2	5.6	4.6	4.6	5.4	4.9	4.9	4.8	5.0
A	6.7	7.0	7.1	6.3	5.7	4.7	4.7	5.6	5.1	5.1	5.0	5.2
P	11.2	10.5	11.5	8.6	6.4	4.9	4.8	5.6	5.2	5.1	5.2	:
FIN	8.8	9.1	8.8	7.1	6.0	4.8	4.7	5.5	5.0	5.0	4.9	5.1
S	8.5	9.7	10.2	8.0	6.6	5.0	5.0	5.4	4.9	4.9	4.8	4.9
UK	7.6	8.2	8.3	7.9	7.1	5.6	5.0	5.3	4.9	5.0	4.8	5.0
US [1]	6.0	7.2	6.7	6.5	6.5	5.3	5.6	6.0	5.1	5.1	4.9	5.1
JP	4.1	4.3	3.3	3.0	2.2	1.3	1.8	1.8	1.5	1.4	1.2	1.4

[1] At least 10 years.
Source: Eurostat.

Short-term interest rates have also tended to show remarkable convergence in recent years (see Table 7.2.2). One of the major factors in this convergence was of course the third phase of monetary union that began on 1 January 1999. In this regard, it is obvious the official rates in the countries planning to take part in EMU needed to be the same on 31 December 1998.

For the 11 countries making up the euro-zone, the pattern of convergence was as follows:

On the one hand, there was a group of countries — Belgium, Germany, France, Luxembourg, the Netherlands, Austria and Finland — where official interest rates had been fairly low for some years and were more or less identical.

There was a second group of countries — Spain, Italy and Portugal — where official rates had recently been higher and where efforts had been made to lower them steadily to bring them into line with the rates in the other countries.

Lastly, Ireland had put up its official rates, which peaked at 6.75 % in May 1997 before cutting them several times in the last two months of 1998.

Since all 11 countries had identical rates on 31 December 1998, it was possible to launch EMU with the main key rate — the repo rate — at 3 %.

During 1999, the European Central Bank (ECB) cut the repo rate to 2.5 % in April, before raising it to 3 % in November. This upward trend was confirmed in 2000 by four hikes of the repo rate, which stood at 4.75 % at the end of the year. In May 2001, the ECB lowered the repo rate by 25 basis points to 4.5 %.

In the other EU countries, the situation is somewhat different. Denmark and Sweden lowered their official rates several times in 1999, before their central banks raised them again in November. In 2000, both countries continued to raise their rates, although this was more pronounced in Denmark than in Sweden. Rates in Denmark dropped slightly in the last quarter of 2000. At the end of 2000, the repo rate was 5.3 % in Denmark and 4.0 % in Sweden. In May 2001, the Bank of Denmark lowered the repo rate from 5.3 to 5.0 %.

For its part, the Bank of England raised its official rate twice at the beginning of 2000 (from 5.5 to 6.0 %), then left it unchanged for the rest of the year. By the end of May 2001, the rate sat at 5.25 %.

Greece cut its official rates a number of times during 2000, with the repo rate falling from 10.75 to 4.75 %. By the end of December 2000, the rate had been brought down to the official rate in effect in EMU member countries. Greece then became the 12th member.

In the United States, the Federal Reserve raised the rate for federal funds from 5.5 to 6.0 % in the first quarter of 2000, then left it unchanged for the rest of the year. Over the first five months of 2001, the rate for federal funds was cut from 6.5 to 4 %. In Japan, the discount rate, which had been set at 0.5 % since September 1995, was cut twice during the first quarter of 2001. It now stands at a record low of 0.25 %.

Table 7.2.2. Short-term interest rates (day-to-day money rates, period average, as a %)

	1993	1994	1995	1996	1997	1998	1999	2000	Jan. 2001	Feb. 2001	March 2001	April 2001
EU-15	8.7	6.3	6.5	5.1	4.7	4.5	3.3	4.5	4.9	5.1	4.9	5.1
Euro-zone	:	:	:	:	::	:	2.7	4.1	4.8	5.0	4.8	5.1
B	8.7	5.5	4.6	3.2	3.4	3.5	:	:	:	:	:	:
DK	12.1	5.8	6.0	3.9	3.5	4.1	3.1	4.4	5.2	5.2	5.2	5.2
D	7.5	5.4	4.5	3.3	3.2	3.4	:	:	:	:	:	:
EL	23.5	23.7	15.8	13.3	12.9	12.6	10.4	8.2	:	:	:	:
E	12.3	7.8	9.0	7.7	5.5	4.3	:	:	:	:	:	:
F	8.8	5.7	6.4	3.7	3.2	3.4	:	:	:	:	:	:
IRL	14.9	5.3	5.6	5.2	6.1	5.8	:	:	:	:	:	:
I	10.3	8.2	10.1	9.1	7.0	5.2	:	:	:	:	:	:
NL	7.1	5.1	4.2	2.9	3.1	3.2	:	:	:	:	:	:
A	7.2	5.0	4.4	3.2	3.3	3.4	:	:	:	:	:	:
P	13.3	10.9	8.9	7.4	5.8	4.3	:	:	:	:	:	:
FIN	7.7	4.4	5.3	3.6	2.9	3.3	:	:	:	:	:	:
S	9.1	7.4	8.5	6.3	4.2	4.2	3.1	3.8	4.1	4.1	4.1	4.1
UK	5.9	5.0	6.3	5.9	6.5	7.2	5.3	5.9	5.6	5.5	5.3	5.2
US	3.0	4.2	5.8	5.3	5.5	5.4	5.0	6.2	6.0	5.5	5.3	4.8
JP	3.1	2.2	1.2	0.5	0.5	0.4	0.1	0.1	0.3	0.3	0.1	0.0

Source: Eurostat.

7.3. Consumer prices

Consumer price inflation is best compared at international level by the 'harmonised indices of consumer prices' (HICPs). They are calculated in each Member State of the European Union, Iceland and Norway. HICPs form the basis of the monetary union index of consumer prices (MUICP), the EICP and the EEAICP. HICPs are not intended to replace national consumer price indices (CPIs). Member States have continued so far to produce their national CPIs for domestic purposes.

HICPs and the MUICP are used by, among others, the European Central Bank for monitoring inflation in the economic and monetary union and the assessment of inflation convergence. As required by the Treaty the maintenance of price stability is the primary objective of the European Central Bank (ECB) which defined price stability 'as a year-on-year increase in the harmonised index of consumer prices for the euro-zone of below 2 %, to be maintained over the medium term'. Strictly speaking this definition applies to the MUICP.

The MUICP was published for the first time for the 11 countries going to participate in the third stage of EMU with the release of the index for April 1998. At the beginning of 2001 Greece joined the euro-zone, so the MUICP covers the 12 Member States since then, since the euro-zone is treated as an entity regardless of its composition. The MUICP is chain-linked in December 2000 to include Greece starting with the January 2001 index.

Trends in consumer price inflation 1998-2001

The annual rate of change (m/(m-12)) is commonly used for analysing inflation trends. This measure is appropriate for short-term analysis, although it suffers from variability due to one-off effects (such as tax changes). Table 7.3.1 and Figure 7.3.1 show the annual rates of change in the HICPs, the MUICP and the EICP for every third month between January 1998 and April 2001.

The annual rates of change of the EICP illustrate an overall falling trend from 1.6 % in April 1998 to as low as 0.9 % in January 1999. This trend reversed from June 1999 and led to an annual rate of change of 2.6 % in April 2001. Since June 2000 the annual rates of change of the MUICP have passed significantly beyond the 2.0 % stability threshold defined by the ECB. It should also be noted that since October 1999 the annual rates of change of the MUICP have been generally higher than those of the EICP.

Table 7.3.1. Harmonised indices of consumer prices (1998–2001), annual rates of change as a % (m/m-12)

	1998				1999				2000				2001	
	Jan.	Apr.	Jul.	Oct.	Jan.	Apr.	Jul.	Oct.	Jan.	Apr.	Jul.	Oct.	Jan.	Apr.
B	0.5	1.3	1.2	0.7	1.0	1.1	0.7	1.4	0.3	2.3	1.7	3.7	2.7	2.9
D	0.7	0.9	0.8	0.4	0.2	0.8	0.6	0.9	1.9	1.6	2.0	2.4	2.2	2.9
EL	4.3	5.1	4.8	4.5	3.3	2.6	1.6	1.7	2.4	2.1	2.6	3.8	3.2	3.7
E	1.9	1.9	2.3	1.6	1.5	2.3	2.1	2.4	2.9	3.0	3.7	4.0	3.8	4.0
F	0.6	1.0	0.8	0.5	0.3	0.5	0.4	0.8	1.7	1.4	2.0	2.1	1.4	2.0
IRL	1.2	2.0	2.5	2.6	2.1	2.0	1.9	2.8	4.4	5.0	5.9	6.0	3.9	4.3
I	1.9	2.2	2.1	1.9	1.5	1.3	1.7	1.9	2.2	2.4	2.6	2.7	2.7	3.0
L	1.5	1.1	1.2	0.5	− 1.4	1.3	− 0.3	1.9	3.5	3.2	4.7	4.3	2.9	2.7
NL	1.6	2.5	1.8	1.5	2.1	1.9	1.8	1.8	1.6	1.7	2.8	3.2	4.5	5.3
A	1.2	1.2	0.8	0.7	0.3	0.1	0.3	0.8	1.4	1.8	2.0	2.2	2.2	2.5
P	1.6	2.2	2.8	2.5	2.5	2.7	1.9	1.8	1.9	1.9	3.3	3.7	4.4	4.6
FIN	1.8	1.7	1.1	1.1	0.5	1.3	1.4	1.6	2.3	2.5	2.9	3.4	2.9	2.8
MUICP	**1.1**	**1.4**	**1.3**	**0.9**	**0.8**	**1.1**	**1.1**	**1.4**	**1.9**	1.9	2.3	2.7	2.4	2.9
DK	1.7	1.6	1.4	1.1	1.2	1.7	2.0	2.6	2.8	2.9	2.8	2.8	2.3	2.6
S	2.1	1.4	1.3	0.1	0.0	0.3	0.2	1.0	1.0	1.0	1.3	1.3	1.6	3.0
UK	1.5	1.9	1.5	1.4	1.6	1.5	1.3	1.2	0.8	0.6	1.0	1.0	0.9	1.1
EICP	**1.3**	**1.6**	**1.4**	**1.1**	**0.9**	**1.2**	**1.1**	**1.3**	**1.8**	**1.7**	**2.1**	**2.4**	**2.2**	**2.6**
US	1.6	1.4	1.7	1.5	1.7	2.3	2.1	2.6	2.8	3.1	3.7	3.4	3.7	3.3
JP	1.8	0.4	− 0.1	0.2	0.2	− 0.1	− 0.1	− 0.7	− 0.9	− 0.8	− 0.5	− 0.9	0.1	− 0.4

NB: m/m-12 is the price change between the current month and the same month in the previous year.
Please note that for the United States and Japan the national CPIs are given which are not strictly comparable with the HICPs.
Source: Eurostat.

A more stable measure — the 12-month average change — is the average index for the latest 12 months compared with the average index for the previous 12 months. It is less sensitive to transient changes in prices but it requires a longer time series of indices. Nevertheless, similar trends to those described above may be noted, as shown in Table 7.3.2. In April 2001, however, the 12-month average rate of change is at 2.5 % for the MUICP and 2.3 % for the EICP. Both rates are indeed higher than 2.0 %, seen as a medium-term price stability threshold.

The protocol on convergence criteria relating to Article 109(j)(1) of the Treaty requires that a Member State's rate of inflation "does not exceed by more than 1fi percentage points that of, at most, the three best performing Member States". Table 7.3.2 shows some summary data based on 12-month average changes. Reference values have been calculated using a simple arithmetic mean of "the three best performing Member States" and "the three best performing Member States of the euro-zone".

Since the launch of the euro in January 1999, Austria, France, Germany and in the beginning also Luxembourg have been, as shown in Table 7.3.2, among the three best performing Member States in the euro-zone. Austria, France, Germany, Luxembourg and Sweden were among the three best performing

Member States in the EU in 1999. From May 2000 to April 2001, the United Kingdom, Sweden and France have then been permanently among the three best performing EU Member States.

Table 7.3.2 also shows which Member States were above or below the reference values in each month. Ireland, Portugal and Greece were above both reference values during nearly all of 1999. Ireland continued up to April 2001, while Greece and Portugal have been below both reference values during most of 2000. Since October 1999, Spain joined Ireland and lies nearly constantly above at least one of the two reference values. In the last months of 1999, the Netherlands were around the two reference values, but they had lower rates in 2000 to continue between the two reference values from February 2001 onwards. Denmark too was between the (present) lower EU reference value and the euro-zone reference value nearly the whole of the year 2000, before moving below both reference values again from December 2000 on. Since July 2000, Luxembourg has been above the EU reference value; some months later it also moved above the euro-zone reference value. A similar pattern can be seen for Finland from October 2000 on, though Finland stayed below the euro-zone reference value. Finally, Belgium was between the two reference values from January to March 2001 and met exactly the EU reference value in April 2001.

Figure 7.3.1. Consumer price indices (1998–2001), annual rates of change as a % (m/m-12)

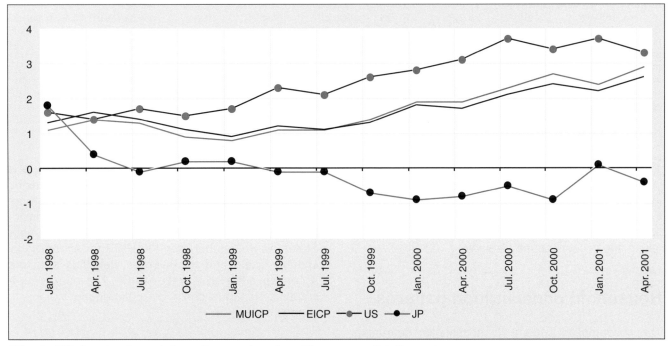

NB: m/m-12 is the price change between the current month and the same month in the previous year.
Please note that for the United States and Japan the national CPIs are given which are not strictly comparable with the HICPs.
Source: Eurostat.

Table 7.3.2. Harmonised indices of consumer prices (1998–2001), 12-month average rate ([1])

1999						2000			
Jan.	**Mar.**	**May**	**Jul.**	**Sep.**	**Nov.**	**Jan.**	**Mar.**	**May**	**Jun.**
D 0.6	D 0.5	S 0.4	S 0.2	A 0.3	A 0.4	S 0.6	S 0.8	S 0.9	S 1.0
F 0.6	F 0.6	D 0.5	D 0.4	D 0.4	D 0.5	F 0.6	UK 0.9	UK 1.0	UK 1.0
L 0.7	L 0.6	F 0.5	F 0.4	F 0.4	F 0.5	A 0.7	F 0.9	F 1.1	F 1.2
A 0.7	A 0.6	A 0.5	A 0.4	S 0.4	S 0.5	D 0.8	A 0.9	A 1.1	A 1.3
S 0.8	S 0.6	L 0.6	L 0.5	L 0.6	L 0.6	L 0.9	D 1.1	D 1.2	D 1.4
B 1.0	B 1.0	B 0.9	B 0.8	B 0.8	B 0.9	B 1.0	**MUICP** 1.3	B 1.5	**EICP** 1.6
MUICP 1.1	**MUICP** 1.0	**MUICP** 1.0	**MUICP** 0.9	**MUICP** 0.9	**MUICP** 1.0	**MUICP** 1.0	B 1.3	**EICP** 1.5	B 1.7
FIN 1.2	FIN 1.1	FIN 1.1	FIN 1.1	FIN 1.1	FIN 1.1	UK 1.0	**EICP** 1.4	**MUICP** 1.6	**MUICP** 1.7
DK 1.3	**EICP** 1.2	**EICP** 1.1	**EICP** 1.1	**EICP** 1.1	**EICP** 1.1	**EICP** 1.1	FIN 1.5	NL 1.9	NL 1.9
EICP 1.3	DK 1.2	DK 1.3	UK 1.4	UK 1.4	UK 1.4	FIN 1.1	I 1.7	P 1.9	P 1.9
UK 1.6	UK 1.6	UK 1.5	I 1.6	DK 1.6	I 1.6	I 1.6	NL 1.9	EL 2.0	EL 2.1
E 1.7	I 1.8	I 1.7	DK 1.6	I 1.6	DK 1.9	NL 2.0	P 1.9	FIN 2.0	I 2.2
NL 1.8	E 1.8	E 1.8	E 1.8	RV (EU) 1.8	RV (EU) 1.9	EL 2.1	EL 2.0	I 2.1	FIN 2.2
I 1.9	NL 1.8	NL 1.8	NL 1.8	NL 1.9	RV (EMU) 1.9	P 2.1	L 2.1	L 2.1	L 2.4
RV (EU) 2.1	RV (EU) 2.1	RV (EU) 2.0	RV (EU) 1.8	RV (EMU) 1.9	NL 1.9	RV (EU) 2.1	RV (EU) 2.4	RV (EU) 2.5	RV (EU) 2.6
RV (EMU) 2.1	RV (EMU) 2.1	RV (EMU) 2.0	RV (EMU) 1.9	E 1.9	E 2.1	DK 2.2	DK 2.4	DK 2.6	DK 2.7
IRL 2.2	IRL 2.4	IRL 2.4	IRL 2.3	IRL 2.2	IRL 2.2	RV (EMU) 2.2	RV (EMU) 2.5	RV (EMU) 2.6	E 2.8
P 2.3	P 2.5	P 2.6	P 2.4	P 2.4	EL 2.3	E 2.3	E 2.5	E 2.7	RV (EMU) 2.8
EL 4.4	EL 4.2	EL 3.8	EL 3.2	EL 2.6	P 2.3	IRL 2.3	IRL 3.1	IRL 3.6	IRL 3.9

2000						2001			
Jul.	**Aug.**	**Sep.**	**Oct.**	**Nov.**	**Dec.**	**Jan.**	**Feb.**	**Mar.**	**Apr.**
UK 0.9	UK 0.9	UK 0.9	UK 0.8	UK 0.8	UK 0.8	UK 0.8	UK 0.8	UK 0.8	UK 0.9
S 1.1	S 1.2	S 1.2	S 1.2	S 1.3	S 1.3	S 1.4	S 1.4	S 1.4	S 1.6
F 1.3	F 1.4	F 1.6	F 1.7	F 1.8	F 1.8	F 1.8	F 1.8	F 1.8	F 1.8
D 1.5	D 1.6	A 1.7	A 1.8	A 1.9	A 2.0	A 2.0	A 2.0	A 2.0	A 2.1
A 1.5	A 1.6	D 1.7	D 1.9	D 2.0	D 2.1	D 2.1	D 2.1	D 2.2	D 2.3
EICP 1.7	**EICP** 1.7	**EICP** 1.8	**EICP** 1.9	**EICP** 2.0	**EICP** 2.1	**EICP** 2.1	**EICP** 2.1	**EICP** 2.2	**EICP** 2.3
B 1.8	**MUICP** 1.9	**MUICP** 2.0	**MUICP** 2.1	**MUICP** 2.3	**MUICP** 2.3	**MUICP** 2.3	**MUICP** 2.4	**MUICP** 2.4	**MUICP** 2.5
MUICP 1.8	B 1.9	NL 2.1	NL 2.2	NL 2.4	I 2.5	I 2.6	DK 2.6	DK 2.6	DK 2.6
NL 2.0	NL 2.0	B 2.2	I 2.4	I 2.5	NL 2.5	NL 2.6	I 2.7	I 2.7	I 2.7
P 2.0	P 2.2	P 2.3	P 2.5	B 2.6	B 2.6	DK 2.7	RV (EU) 2.8	B 2.9	B 2.9
EL 2.2	EL 2.3	EL 2.4	B 2.5	EL 2.6	DK 2.7	RV (EU) 2.8	B 2.9	RV (EU) 2.9	RV (EU) 2.9
I 2.2	I 2.3	I 2.4	EL 2.6	P 2.6	P 2.8	B 2.8	NL 2.9	FIN 2.9	FIN 3.0
FIN 2.3	FIN 2.4	FIN 2.6	RV (EU) 2.7	DK 2.8	RV (EU) 2.8	EL 2.8	FIN 3.0	EL 3.1	EL 3.2
RV (EU) 2.6	RV (EU) 2.7	RV (EU) 2.7	DK 2.8	RV (EU) 2.8	EL 2.8	P 3.0	EL 3.0	NL 3.1	NL 3.4
L 2.8	DK 2.7	DK 2.8	FIN 2.8	FIN 2.9	FIN 2.9	FIN 3.0	RV (EMU) 3.5	RV (EMU) 3.5	RV (EMU) 3.6
DK 2.8	E 3.0	E 3.1	E 3.3	E 3.4	E 3.4	E 3.5	P 3.5	L 3.6	L 3.7
E 2.9	RV (EMU) 3.0	L 3.2	RV (EMU) 3.3	RV (EMU) 3.4	RV (EMU) 3.4	RV (EMU) 3.5	E 3.6	E 3.7	E 3.8
RV (EMU) 2.9	L 3.0	RV (EMU) 3.2	L 3.4	L 3.6	L 3.6	L 3.7	L 3.8	P 3.8	P 3.8
IRL 4.2	IRL 4.5	IRL 4.7	IRL 5.0	IRL 5.2	IRL 5.3	IRL 5.2	IRL 5.2	IRL 5.1	IRL 5.0

([1]) Average of the latest 12 months compared to the average of the previous 12 months.
NB: RV (EU) = reference value defined as unweighted arithmetic mean of the three best-performing countries in the EU/+1.5.
RV (EMU) = reference value defined as unweighted arithmetic mean of the three best-performing countries in the EMU/+1.5.
Source: Eurostat.

The average spread of inflation rates, which is shown in Figure 7.3.2, provides a useful tool for illustrating inflation convergence since the early stages of the EMU. The spread is calculated as the standard deviation of annual inflation rates of HICPs from the EICP taking into account country weights.

Household consumption patterns

The consumption patterns of households determine the relative importance ("weight") of household monetary expenditure that is attached to each of the categories of goods and services covered by the HICP. The impact on the all-items index of any price change is proportional to the size of the corresponding weight. There is no uniform basket applying to all Member States. The structure of the weights may vary considerably between the HICPs for individual Member States as well as between the HICP for an individual Member State and the average weighting structure according to the EICP or the MUICP. The index is computed as an annual chain-index allowing for weights to change each year.

Table 7.3.3 gives an overview about the weights used in the 15 Member States, the euro-zone (MUICP) and for the EU (EICP) in 2001.

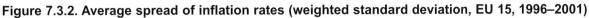

Figure 7.3.2. Average spread of inflation rates (weighted standard deviation, EU 15, 1996–2001)

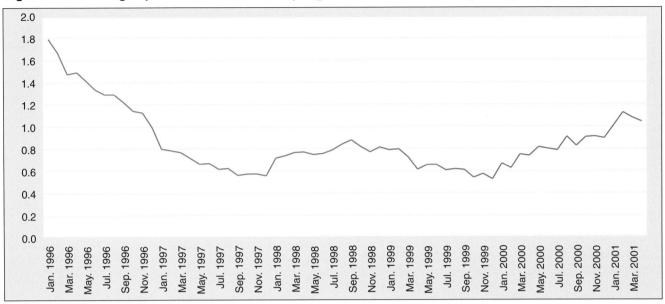

Source: Eurostat.

Table 7.3.3. Consumption weights in the EU, the EMU and the 15 MSs, as used in 2001 (‰)

	EICP	MUICP		B	DK	D	EL	E	F
Food and non-alcoholic beverages	154	163		167	159	136	206	211	167
Alcoholic beverages, tobacco and narcotics	42	40		31	60	46	51	32	40
Clothing and footwear	76	78		68	60	72	121	99	57
Housing, water, electricity, gas and other fuels	149	156		164	188	211	103	112	146
Furnishings, household equipment and routine maintenance of the house	78	79		77	69	74	79	62	68
Health	36	39		39	30	39	57	29	41
Transport	156	156		138	164	153	129	153	180
Communications	24	24		24	17	19	23	25	27
Recreation and culture	106	94		136	119	111	42	66	93
Education	10	9		5	9	7	22	16	5
Restaurants and hotels	97	88		83	55	50	112	150	85
Miscellaneous goods and services	72	74		68	70	81	54	46	91

	IRL	I	L	NL	P	A	FIN	S	UK
Food and non-alcoholic beverages	190	170	115	153	132	217	172	154	114
Alcoholic beverages, tobacco and narcotics	88	28	118	49	31	32	72	53	48
Clothing and footwear	48	105	71	63	70	68	52	74	67
Housing, water, electricity, gas and other fuels	85	106	107	196	144	94	159	181	112
Furnishings, household equipment and routine maintenance of the house	45	109	104	89	83	77	50	62	78
Health	22	37	14	42	42	58	48	31	25
Transport	119	147	193	132	149	207	162	157	152
Communications	14	31	12	18	29	19	24	34	25
Recreation and culture	113	77	110	112	113	39	114	117	159
Education	20	11	1	15	7	18	2	4	12
Restaurants and hotels	198	103	92	70	133	130	94	66	144
Miscellaneous goods and services	57	76	64	60	66	41	50	67	64

Source: Eurostat.

For 2001, according to the weighting patterns for the MUICP and the EICP, the divisions food, housing and transport are the three categories with the largest weights when calculated as averages for the country groupings concerned. A weight of approximately one sixth of the MUICP and slightly over 15 % of the EICP is attached to food, a slightly higher weight for both indices is attached to transport, about the same as for housing. A weight of around one tenth for both indices is attached to recreation and culture, though it is a little bit more important for the EICP than for the MUICP. Closely below are the weights for restaurants and hotels, again slightly higher for the EICP.

Within the national HICPs the weight for food varies between 11–14 % (the United Kingdom, Luxembourg, Austria and Germany) and 19–22 % (Ireland, Greece, Spain and Portugal). For transport the weight varies between 12–14 % (Ireland, Greece, the Netherlands and Belgium) and 18–21 % (France, Luxembourg and Portugal). In contrast, the weight for recreation and culture ranges between 4 % (Greece, Portugal) and 13–16 % (Belgium and the United Kingdom), and the weight for housing varies between 8–11 % (Ireland, Portugal, Greece, Italy and Luxembourg) and 18–21 % (Sweden, Denmark, the Netherlands and Germany). It should, however, be noted that HICPs capture only monetary expenditure and unlike national accounts or household budget surveys do not impute costs for the shelter service provided by owner occupied dwellings. This means that countries in which a larger proportion of the population live in rented dwellings tend to have a larger weight for housing than countries in which a larger proportion of households live in their own dwellings.

The weight of a Member State in the EMU or in the EU is its share of household final monetary consumption expenditure in the EMU or in the EU totals. The coun-

try weights used in 2001 are based on national accounts data for 1999 updated to December 2000 prices. For the EMU, weights in national currencies are converted into euro using the irrevocably locked exchange rates. For the EU, weights in national currencies are converted into purchasing power standards (PPS). The euro-zone country weight reflects its share in the EU total.

Table 7.3.4. Country weights (as a ‰) for 2001, price updated to December 2000 prices

	MUICP	EICP	EEAICP
B	33.50		
D	309.08		
EL	24.28		
E	104.44		
F	205.46		
IRL	11.72		
I	187.00		
L	2.46		
NL	52.52		
A	32.70		
P	20.94		
FIN	15.90		
MUICP	1 000.00		
DK		790.56	781.31
S		14.05	13.88
UK		18.62	18.41
EICP		176.77	174.70
IS		1 000.00	
NO			0.80
EEAIC			10.89
P			1 000.00

NB: Due to rounding effects, the weights may not add up exactly to 1 000.
Source: Eurostat.

7.4. Purchasing power parities

As noted in Chapter 1, in order to compare the size of different economies, it is useful to consider purchasing power parities (PPP) instead of exchange rates for the conversion. The reason for the euro ([1]) not being used as a conversion rate is that official exchange rates are mainly determined on the one hand by the supply of and demand for currencies necessary to effect commercial flows and on the other hand by a series of factors like capital flows, speculation and others such as a country's perceived political and economic situation.

In other words they do not necessarily reflect price level differences. Consequently, their use for conversion of economic aggregates expressed in nominal values does not allow real comparison of the volume of goods and services produced and consumed. The disadvantages of conversion using exchange rates may be eliminated by using purchasing power parities as conversion rates.

How are PPPs calculated?

The parities represent the relationship between the amounts of national currency needed to purchase a comparable, representative basket of goods in the countries concerned. The ratio between the prices of the individual products is aggregated in accordance with well-defined criteria, so as to obtain a parity for the main aggregates and the global parity of GDP itself. These parities are expressed relative to the value for the Union as a whole, and the unit in which the values are expressed is known as the purchasing power standard (PPS), which is, in fact, the euro in real terms.

Exchange rates and purchasing power parities

Table 7.4.1 gives the PPS figures established every year by Eurostat ([2]). The comparison of these figures with the exchange rates of the euro shown in Table 7.4.2 provides an interesting information. For example, on the basis of the official exchange rate fixed at the beginning of 1999, a euro was worth PTE 200.482, whereas on the basis of purchasing power parities, PTE 137.7 was sufficient to purchase the volume of goods and services corresponding to one PPS. In

Table 7.4.1. The purchasing power parities of GDP
1 PPS = ... national currency unit(s)

	1995	1996	1997	1998	1999	2000
EU-15	1.0	1.0	1.0	1.0	1.0	1.0
EUR-12	1.0	1.0	1.0	1.0	1.0	1.0
B	40.5	40.1	39.8	39.7	39.5	38.9
DK	9.3	9.2	9.1	9.1	9.1	9.1
D	2.2	2.2	2.1	2.1	2.1	2.0
EL	223.8	231.6	246.8	252.6	253.5	254.2
E	134.5	134.1	134.7	138.6	139.2	140.1
F	7.1	7.1	7.1	7.1	7.0	6.9
IRL	0.7	0.7	0.7	0.8	0.8	0.8
I	1 708.6	1 735.7	1 745.2	1 719.3	1 707.0	1 707.9
L	42.8	43.0	43.8	44.1	43.8	43.6
NL	2.2	2.3	2.2	2.1	2.1	2.1
A	15.1	14.7	14.4	14.6	14.4	14.1
P	131.2	133.7	129.8	136.5	136.9	137.7
FIN	6.5	6.5	6.4	6.5	6.5	6.5
S	10.7	10.6	10.4	10.5	10.4	10.2
UK	0.7	0.7	0.7	0.7	0.7	0.7
US	1.1	1.1	1.1	1.0	1.0	1.0
JP	189.3	181.9	178.2	175.2	169.1	161.1

NB: The year 2000 is an estimate by the Commission Services.
Source: Eurostat.

2000, therefore, the real purchasing power of the Portuguese escudo was much higher (+ 45 %) than a comparison based on the official exchange rate would suggest.

In Section 1.2, particularly, PPS have been used for inter-country comparison of GDP per head and component expenditure.

Table 7.4.2 shows the values of GDP per capita in euro and PPS, expressed as the ratio between GDP per head of population in each country and average per capita GDP in the Union (EU-15 = 100). It is interesting to note how each country's figure varies depending on whether it is calculated in euro or PPS.

Considering the four biggest EU countries in 2000, Germany's GDP per head in euro was higher than the EU average by 9.9 %, but the distance is reduced to 4.9 % when figures are expressed in PPS. A symmetrical situation is recorded in Italy: the euro figure is lower than the average by 10.2 %, but when considering PPS data is 1.7 % above the average. In the United Kingdom, both in euro and PPS, GDP per head is above the EU figure, but in euro by 14.1 % and in PPS by only 3.7 %.

([1]) As a convention, when referring to euro, we consider that in reality the euro only exists for 1999; for the previous years we refer to ecu (EUR 1= ECU 1).

([2]) 2000 year figures have been estimated by the services of the Commission.

As a general rule, the higher the nominal index figure (in euro) is, the lower the volume index figure (in PPS) is relative to it. Luxembourg is an exception, and the two index figures are very high. In Denmark, Portugal and Greece the differences between figures expressed in euro and in PPS are the widest, but opposite: this gives for Denmark a per capita index figure in euro above the Union's average by 46.4 %; compared with only + 20.2 % in PPS terms. In the table opposite, Portugal GDP per head in euro is below the EU average by nearly 50 % and when considered in PPS the gap is reduced to about 26 %. For Greece, the gap with the EU figure is 48.8 % when GDP per head is calculated in euro, but the gap is reduced to about 32 % when in PPS. Although figures are very similar, it is interesting to note that, in euro, the lowest GDP per capita among the 15 EU countries is recorded for Portugal, but when referring to PPS the lowest figure is for Greece.

Table 7.4.2. GDP per head in 2000 (EU-15 = 100)

	☐ EUR	■ PPS	
EUR-12	95.7	98.9	
B	106.5	110.6	
DK	146.4	120.2	
D	109.9	104.9	
EL	51.2	67.8	
E	68.2	81.0	
F	103.2	98.8	
IRL	121.0	118.3	
I	89.8	101.7	
L	205.9	190.3	
NL	111.8	116.6	
A	112.9	109.8	
P	50.7	74.1	
FIN	113.3	103.1	
S	123.5	102.0	
UK	114.1	103.7	
US	174.1	156.5	
JP	180.3	111.4	

Source: Eurostat.

Figure 7.4.1. Price level index of GDP, (EU-15 = 100)

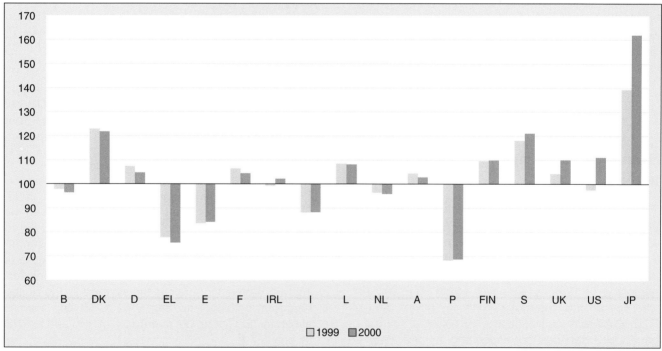

Source: Eurostat.

Price level index

The ratio between the value of a PPS and that of the euro allows us to calculate the price level index, which measures the difference between the general price level in a given country and the Union average (EU-15 = 100). It also permits direct comparisons between one country and another.

Table 7.4.3 shows that in 2000 Portugal had the lowest prices in the Union (31.3 percentage points below the Union average) and Denmark the highest (21.8 percentage points above this average). The United States comes out at 11.1 percentage points below the EU average, while Japan exceeds it by 61.9 percentage points.

Another way of interpreting Table 7.4.3 is to say that in 2000 a given basket of goods and services could be purchased for EUR 68.7 in Portugal and EUR 121.8, nearly twice as much, in Denmark.

Table 7.4.3. Price level index of GDP, (EU-15 = 100)

	1995	1996	1997	1998	1999	2000
B	105.0	102.0	98.2	97.7	97.8	96.4
DK	126.6	124.4	121.2	121.4	123.0	121.8
D	118.6	113.1	108.5	108.5	107.5	104.7
EL	73.9	75.8	79.8	76.4	77.8	75.5
E	82.5	83.4	81.2	82.9	83.7	84.2
F	109.1	109.1	107.9	107.8	106.5	104.5
IRL	85.8	91.4	95.9	97.2	99.3	102.2
I	80.2	88.6	90.5	88.5	88.2	88.2
L	111.1	109.3	108.0	108.5	108.6	108.2
NL	106.5	105.8	97.7	95.8	96.4	95.8
A	114.8	109.7	104.4	105.1	104.4	102.8
P	66.9	68.3	65.4	67.7	68.3	68.7
FIN	113.2	111.2	109.1	109.0	109.7	109.9
S	114.9	124.4	120.1	117.3	118.1	121.1
UK	87.0	86.9	99.8	102.3	104.3	110.1
US	82.2	83.8	92.8	93.4	97.5	111.1
JP	153.8	131.7	130.0	119.7	139.4	161.9

Source: Eurostat.

Symbols and abbreviations

EU   European Union

EUR-11   euro-zone before 1 January 2001 (Belgium, Germany, Spain, France, Ireland, Italy, Luxembourg, Netherlands, Austria, Portugal and Finland)

EUR-12   euro-zone after 1 January 2001 (EUR-11 and Greece)

EU-15   European Union of 15 Member States (EU-12 and Denmark, Sweden and the United Kingdom)

B   Belgium
DK   Denmark
D   Germany
EL   Greece
E   Spain
F   France
IRL   Ireland
I   Italy
L   Luxembourg
NL   Netherlands
A   Austria
P   Portugal
FIN   Finland
S   Sweden
UK   United Kingdom

CC   Candidate countries
BG   Bulgaria
CY   Cyprus
CZ   Czech Republic
EE   Estonia
HU   Hungary
LV   Latvia
LT   Lithuania
MT   Malta
PL   Poland
RO   Romania
SK   Slovak Republic
SI   Slovenia
TR   Turkey

US   United States of America
JP   Japan

EUR   euro
BEF   Belgian franc
DKK   Danish crown
DEM   German mark
GRD   Greek drachma
ESP   Spanish peseta
FRF   French franc
IEP   Irish pound
ITL   Italian lira
LUF   Luxembourgish franc
NLG   Dutch guilder
ATS   Austrian schilling
PTE   Portuguese escudo
FIM   Finnish mark
SEK   Swedish crown
GBP   Pound sterling

BGN   Bulgarian lev
CYP   Cyprus pound
CZK   Czech koruna
EEK   Estonian kroon
HUF   Hungarian forint
LVL   Latvian lat
LTL   Lithuanian litas

MTL   Maltese lira

PLN   Polish zloty
ROL   Romanian leu
SKK   Slovak koruna
SIT   Slovenian tolar
TRL   Turkish lira
USD   United States dollar
YEN   Japanese yen

billion   billion (thousand million)
:   data not available

European Commission

Economic portrait of the European Union — 2001

Luxembourg: Office for Official Publications of the European Communities

2001 — 161 pp. — 21 x 29.7 cm

Theme 2: Economy and finance
Collection: Panorama of the European Union

ISSN 1680-1687
ISBN 92-894-1207-0

Price (excluding VAT) in Luxembourg: EUR 30

This publication is designed to set out in a single volume wide-ranging macroeconomic data on the European Union and its Member States and to provide an analysis of those data. Along with business cycle effects, studies of structural differences between Member States and their developments are made. Although the analysis makes reference to specific national situations, its purpose is to draw a profile of the Union (EU-15) and the euro-zone (EUR-12) comparing it, where possible, with their main trading partners.

.... Eurostat Data Shops

BELGIQUE/BELGIË

Eurostat Data Shop
Bruxelles/Brussel
Planistat Belgique
Rue du Commerce 124
Handelsstraat 124
B-1000 Bruxelles/Brussel
Tél. (32-2) 234 67 50
Fax (32-2) 234 67 51
E-mail: datashop@planistat.be
URL: http://www.datashop.org/

DANMARK

DANMARKS STATISTIK
Bibliotek og Information
Eurostat Data Shop
Sejrøgade 11
DK-2100 København Ø
Tlf. (45) 39 17 30 30
Fax (45) 39 17 30 03
E-mail: bib@dst.dk
Internet:
http://www.dst.dk/bibliotek

DEUTSCHLAND

Statistisches Bundesamt
Eurostat Data Shop Berlin
Otto-Braun-Straße 70-72
(Eingang: Karl-Marx-Allee)
D-10178 Berlin
Tel. (49) 1888-644 94 27/28
Fax (49) 1888-644 94 30
E-Mail: datashop@destatis.de
URL:
http://www.eu-datashop.de/

ESPAÑA

INE
Eurostat Data Shop
Paseo de la Castellana, 183
Oficina 009
Entrada por Estébanez
Calderón
E-28046 Madrid
Tel. (34) 91 583 91 67
Fax (34) 91 579 71 20
E-mail:
datashop.eurostat@ine.es
URL: http://www.datashop.org/
Member of the MIDAS Net

FRANCE

INSEE Info service
Eurostat Data Shop
195, rue de Bercy
Tour Gamma A
F-75582 Paris Cedex 12
Tél. (33) 1 53 17 88 44
Fax (33) 1 53 17 88 22
E-mail: datashop@insee.fr
Member of the MIDAS Net

ITALIA - ROMA

ISTAT
Centro di informazione
statistica — Sede di Roma
Eurostat Data Shop
Via Cesare Balbo, 11a
I-00184 Roma
Tel. (39) 06 46 73 31 02/06
Fax (39) 06 46 73 31 01/07
E-mail: dipdiff@istat.it
Member of the MIDAS Net

ITALIA - MILANO

ISTAT
Ufficio regionale per la
Lombardia
Eurostat Data Shop
Via Fieno, 3
I-20123 Milano
Tel. (39) 02 80 61 32 460
Fax (39) 02 80 61 32 304
E-mail: mileuro@tin.it
Member of the MIDAS Net

LUXEMBOURG

Eurostat Data Shop
Luxembourg
BP 453
L-2014 Luxembourg
4, rue Alphonse Weicker
L-2721 Luxembourg
Tél. (352) 43 35-2251
Fax (352) 43 35-22221
E-mail:
dslux@eurostat.datashop.lu
URL: http://www.datashop.org/
Member of the MIDAS Net

NEDERLAND

STATISTICS NETHERLANDS
Eurostat Data Shop —
Voorburg
Postbus 4000
2270 JM Voorburg
Nederland
Tel. (31-70) 337 49 00
Fax (31-70) 337 59 84
E-mail: datashop@cbs.nl

PORTUGAL

Eurostat Data Shop Lisboa
INE/Serviço de Difusão
Av. António José de Almeida, 2
P-1000-043 Lisboa
Tel. (351) 21 842 61 00
Fax (351) 21 842 63 64
E-mail: data.shop@ine.pt

SUOMI/FINLAND

STATISTICS FINLAND
Eurostat DataShop Helsinki
Tilastokirjasto
PL 2B
FIN-00022 Tilastokeskus
Työpajakatu 13 B, 2. Kerros,
Helsinki
P. (358-9) 17 34 22 21
F. (358-9) 17 34 22 79
Sähköposti: datashop@stat.fi
URL:
http://tilastokeskus.fi/tk/kk/
datashop/

SVERIGE

STATISTICS SWEDEN
Information service
Eurostat Data Shop
Karlavägen 100
Box 24 300
S-104 51 Stockholm
Tfn (46-8) 50 69 48 01
Fax (46-8) 50 69 48 99
E-post: infoservice@scb.se
Internet:
http://www.scb.se/info/
datashop/eudatashop.asp

UNITED KINGDOM

Eurostat Data Shop
Enquiries & advice and
publications
Office for National Statistics
Customers & Electronic
Services Unit B1/05
1 Drummond Gate
London SW1V 2QQ
United Kingdom
Tel. (44-20) 75 33 56 76
Fax (44-1633) 81 27 62
E-mail:
eurostat.datashop@ons.gov.uk
Member of the MIDAS Net

Eurostat Data Shop
Electronic Data Extractions,
enquiries & advice r.cade
1L Mountjoy Research Centre
University of Durham
Durham DH1 3SW
United Kingdom
Tel. (44-191) 374 73 50
Fax (44-191) 384 49 71
E-mail: r-cade@dur.ac.uk
Internet:
http://www-rcade.dur.ac.uk

NORWAY

Statistics Norway
Library and Information Centre
Eurostat Data Shop
Kongens gate 6
Boks 8131 Dep.
N-0033 Oslo
Tel. (47) 21 09 46 42/43
Fax (47) 21 09 45 04
E-mail: Datashop@ssb.no

SCHWEIZ/SUISSE/SVIZZERA

Statistisches Amt des Kantons
Zürich
Eurostat Data Shop
Bleicherweg 5
CH-8090 Zürich
Tel. (41-1) 225 12 12
Fax (41-1) 225 12 99
E-mail:
datashop@statistik.zh.ch
Internet:
http://www.zh.ch/statistik

USA

HAVER ANALYTICS
Eurostat Data Shop
60 East 42nd Street
Suite 3310
New York, NY 10165
Tel. (1-212) 986 93 00
Fax (1-212) 986 69 81
E-mail: eurodata@haver.com

EUROSTAT HOME PAGE
www.europa.eu.int/comm/eurostat/

MEDIA SUPPORT
EUROSTAT
(only for professional journalists)
Postal address:
Jean Monnet building
L-2920 Luxembourg
Office: BECH A3/48 —
5, rue Alphonse Weicker
L-2721 Luxembourg
Tel. (352) 43 01-33408
Fax (352) 43 01-32649
E-mail:
Eurostat-mediasupport@cec.eu.int